WORKERS' CULTURE IN IMPERIAL GERMANY

WORKERS' CULTURE IN IMPERIAL GERMANY

*Leisure and Recreation in the
Rhineland and Westphalia*

Lynn Abrams

London and New York

First published in 1992
by Routledge
11 New Fetter Lane, London EC4P 4EE

Simultaneously published in the USA and Canada
by Routldege
a division of Routledge, Chapman and Hall, Inc.
29 West 35th Street, New York, NY 10001

© 1992 Lynn Abrams

Set in 10/12pt Bembo by
CentraCet, Cambridge
Printed and bound in Great Britain by
Biddles Ltd, Guildford and King's Lynn

British Library Cataloguing in Publication Data
Abrams, Lynn
Workers' Culture in Imperial Germany: Leisure and
recreation in the Rhineland and Westphalia.
I. Title
943.08

Library of Congress Cataloguing in Publication Data
Abrams, Lynn
Workers' culture in imperial Germany : leisure and recreation in
the Rhineland and Westphalia / Lynn Abrams.
p.   cm.
Includes bibliographical references and index.
1. Working class – Germany – Recreation – History.   2. Popular
culture – Germany – History.   I. title
HD7395.R4A37   1992
3063'6'0943 – dc20   91-12748

ISBN 0–415–076635–8

FOR MY MOTHER
AND IN MEMORY OF MY FATHER

Contents

Abbreviations   page ix

Preface   1

Introduction   3

1   A Time and Place for Leisure   13
    The industrial environment   13
    Time and inclination   22
    The ability to pay   27

2   The Industrialization of Popular Culture   34
    The traditional festival   34
    The working–class parish fair   37
    Conflicts and resolutions   43
    The segregation of festival culture   48
    Socialist festival culture   53
    Blueprint for the future   56

3   The Lubricant of Leisure   63
    Patterns of consumption   63
    Workplace drinking   69
    Drink and the family   76
    Drink and the labour movement   81
    Cultural aid to social stimulant   85

4   From the Street to the Stage   92
    Street entertainment   92
    The taming of popular entertainment   94
    Tingel-Tangels and music halls   99
    The dance craze   103
    Real entertainment   108

5   The Organization of Leisure   114
    Preconditions of organization   114
    The beginnings of associational life   117

Contents

An 'alternative' associational movement   121
Club life   129
Spontaneity to organization   132

6 The Struggle for Control   139
The social question and 'rational recreation'   139
Useful pursuits   145
Lungs of the city   154
Social reform or social control?   160

7 From Control to Commercialization   169
Entertaining the masses   169
The rise of the cinema   172
Commercial culture versus working-class culture   178
The triumph of commercial culture?   183

8 Conclusions: a Working-Class Leisure Culture?   189

Bibliography   196

Index   211

Abbreviations

AL	Amt Langendreer
AL-D	Amt Linden-Dahlhausen
AW	Amt Werne
B	Amt Bochum Stadt
DH	Düsseldorf Handelskammer
HStAD	Hauptstaatsarchiv Düsseldorf
KPD	Kommunistische Partei Deutschlands
KrA	Kreisausschuß
LA	Landratsamt
MS	*Märkischer Sprecher*
RA	Aachen Regierung
RD	Düsseldorf Regierung
RPA	Regierungspräsident Arnsberg
RPD	Regierungspräsident Düsseldorf
SPD	Sozialdemokratische Partei Deutschlands
StAB	Stadtarchiv Bochum
StAD	Stadtarchiv Düsseldorf
StJDR	Statistisches Jahrbuch für das Deutsche Reich

Preface

Leisure is taken for granted in contemporary society. Some would argue that leisure has now supplanted work as the more meaningful social activity for most people living in the modern western world. In little over a century leisure has become a right; the length of the working week continues to decline; the provision of leisure facilities has become big business, with considerable numbers relying on the leisure industry for their employment; and recreational provision is addressed by government, often through designated ministers and departments. On the other hand, it could be said that little has changed since the nineteenth century. Our ability to participate in leisure activities is still dependent upon having sufficient disposable income; time for leisure is still restricted by commitments to work, the family and the community. Leisure is still a commodity with a price. Moreover, the activities we choose to undertake in our leisure time have hardly changed. Pubs still attract crowds on Saturday nights, dancing remains one of the favoured leisure pursuits of the young and sporting events continue to attract thousands of spectators. In Germany traditional fairs like the *Kirmes*, carnival and the shooting festivals continue to be celebrated by millions across the country, while around 40 per cent of the population of what used to be the Federal Republic belong to one or more voluntary associations.

If people today regard their leisure activities to be of such vital importance to their personal fulfilment and satisfaction, surely in the past, when recreation was severely limited, it assumed an even greater significance. And yet we know little of what the majority of Germans, the working class, did in their leisure time. It is my contention that we should know, not merely to complete a part of the jigsaw depicting the everyday life of the German working class, but in order to gain an insight into the social relations governing German society in the age of industrialization, urbanization, Bismarck and Wilhelm II. Workers' actions in the workplace were governed by a regulated system of discipline and incentives. Leisure activity was comparatively free from such constraints and as such it offers a window through which one may gain an appreciation of the values and attitudes – culture – of the working class in Germany in the period between unification and the First World War.

1

Historians of leisure and recreation in Britain have already exploited this window of opportunity and my debt to them is great. A diverse body of literature exploring and analysing the leisure experiences of British workers in the modern, industrial period has provided a stimulus to social historians with its incisive insights into the social relations of Victorian and Edwardian Britain. The methodological approach adopted by historians like Gareth Stedman Jones, Peter Bailey and Stephen Yeo has been an inspiration to those of us who always believed an alternative to the history of the German working class 'from above' was possible. This study then, is history from below: a branch of *Alltagsgeschichte* which aims to reconstruct the politics of everyday life via the cultural strategies and practices of workers in their leisure time.

Researching this book was an enjoyable experience, sustained by recourse to the empathetic approach to history in the form of visits to the festivals, parks and pubs of Bochum and Düsseldorf. The bulk of the research was conducted between 1985 and 1986 in the Stadtarchiv Bochum, the Nordrhein–Westfälischen Hauptstaatsarchiv and Stadtarchiv in Düsseldorf, the Universitäts Bibliothek Düsseldorf, the Institut zur Erforschung der europäischen Arbeiterbewegung at the Ruhr–Universität Bochum and the Institut für deutsche und ausländischer Arbeiterliteratur in Dortmund. I am grateful to the staff of all these institutions for their invaluable help and advice. Funding for the initial research was provided by the University of East Anglia, supplemented by the German Historical Institute.

I am particularly indebted to Richard J. Evans who guided me through the initial research and who has been a constant source of encouragement, support and friendly advice ever since. Dick Geary and Stephen Wilson read an earlier version of the work and their comments benefited me greatly. I am especially grateful to Dick for having the time and patience to read the manuscript a second time and to Jim Retallack for his careful reading of the final draft. Many people at the universities of Bristol, East Anglia, Lancaster, Sussex and York, listened to early research papers and showed their interest by volunteering information, criticism and enthusiasm. John Biggart, Andrew Davies, Barry Doyle, Graham Ford, Peter Friedemann, Stephen Hickey, friends and colleagues in the school of Modern Languages and European History at the University of East Anglia and the School of History at the University of Bristol, all offered invaluable suggestions and provided intellectual stimulation and moral support when it was most needed.

Finally, my gratitude goes out to all friends and family who have sacrificed some of their leisure time to listen to tales of the exploits of German workers in theirs.

Lynn Abrams
Lancaster 1991

Introduction

The social history of leisure has been slow to attract the interest of historians of Germany. Outside the bourgeois cultural arena on the one hand and the recreational activities guided and led by the socialist labour movement on the other, the amusements of the German people have been confined largely to the pages of antiquarian publications and folklore studies of the pre-industrial period. In Germany leisure as a subject of legitimate historical research has been marginalized along with other aspects of working-class life not directly connected to work and politics. Working-class culture, a set of values, beliefs and attitudes held by this distinct socio-economic group, has been regarded as 'trivial . . . when it has not been openly and explicitly political', as one American historian wrote recently.[1] This can be attributed largely to the strong traditions of German historical scholarship which endorsed the primacy of politics and history from above, and the narrow perspective adopted by historians of the labour movement which, until recently, continued to build a solid but one-dimensional picture of socialist personalities, policies and organizational structures. Yet, as Jürgen Kocka has intimated, the study of workers' culture is not necessarily an antiquarian pursuit. It has the potential to capture patterns of thought and action that may fill the gaps between everyday life and collective action.[2] As leisure historians of Britain have made perfectly clear, leisure activities do not take place in a vacuum; they are part of a wider culture with its roots in the socio-economic structures of modern industrial society.[3]

German sociologists have treated leisure with greater respect. Following the publication of Thorsten Veblen's *The Theory of the Leisure Class* in 1912 and, later, a number of serious leisure studies, German sociological research began to address the role of leisure in modern societies.[4] Early studies tended to concentrate on the relationship of leisure to work, or contemplated the future role of leisure in society as working hours declined. The first socio-historical research was published in the 1970s, the most notable probably being the work of Wolfgang Nahrstedt whose explanations of the origins of leisure, from the pre-industrial *Feiertag* through to the early nineteenth-century experience of leisure as freedom from obligation, have provided important references for historians interested in the roots of modern leisure time.[5] Jürgen Reulecke, in a comprehensive and stimulating account of the emergence of leisure and holidays in industrial society, has provided further essential background material for the historian.[6] More recently, the leisure pursuits of the industrial working class have commanded attention, most notably in Siegfried Reck's *Arbeiter nach der Arbeit*, an analysis of the relationship between the worker, the family and the public house, and Dieter Langewiesche's *Zur Freizeit des Arbeiters*, a study of workers' education and self-improvement in Austria which treads a fine line between organized Social Democratic leisure activities and those undertaken by workers on their own initiative.[7] With these publications and the recent collection of articles edited by Gerhard Huck, *Sozialgeschichte der Freizeit*, leisure studies have begun to bridge the gap between the disciplines of sociology and history.[8]

The major reason behind the paucity of serious research into this area of everyday life has been the domination of labour movement studies by an organizational, top-down approach which has extended to the study of labour movement culture at the expense of the mass constituency of German labour, the workers themselves. The celebrated cradle-to-grave network of social and cultural associations affiliated to the Social Democratic Party (SPD) – youth clubs, gymnastic associations, music and choral societies, reading circles, sickness and burial insurance associations and many more – provided an organizational framework for the implementation of socialist cultural policy, but research into the *Arbeitervereine* has been embedded in traditional methods of historical inquiry; the organizational standpoint has predominated at the expense of the perspective of the workers' experience. 'A history of the workers' associational movement is, in itself, not a social history', argued Detlev Peukert. 'The organizational perspective must be overcome and one must question the everyday role of the associations in the leisure of the workers, the requirements which they expressed and the forms in which such needs were realized or channelled.'[9] It is only recently, then, that this field has opened up to embrace concepts and methodology pioneered by sociologists, anthropologists and labour historians in Britain, France and the United States. Consequently, workers' leisure, which at one time was only studied seriously as a branch of labour movement activity, is now the focus of a reaction from social historians who are keen to tell the whole story in the tradition of *Alltagsgeschichte*.

Following the publication of two collections of articles on the subject of workers' culture, edited by Jürgen Kocka and Gerhard Ritter, research into this area has been given a new lease of life and a set of new points of departure.[10] The conclusions of both collections can be neatly summed up by Ritter's proposal that:

> the general identification of workers' culture with the culture of the socialist workers' movement must be abandoned . . . It is also inapplicable to many features of workers' lives – like material culture and the

4

social history of day to day existence – which cannot be understood by investigating workers' associations alone.[11]

These comments provided an initial stimulus for a new generation of historians to go ahead and investigate the alternative, non-socialist, rough, so-called unrespectable side of workers' lives in Wilhelmine and Weimar Germany. Recent studies of prostitution, crime, illegitimacy and drinking behaviour (to cite just a few examples,) have already highlighted the discrepancy between a labour movement culture with its emphasis on education, cultural improvement and, above all, respectability, and a workers' culture which formulated its own response to modern capitalist society.[12] Dick Geary has pointed out that the socialist cultural initiative failed to reach the majority of the working class. Before 1914 only around 25 per cent of the German working class belonged to the SPD or a trade union and the majority of these were skilled workers. The unskilled, unemployed and casual labourers were not only unorganized but disregarded by the party, which labelled them with the pejorative term 'lumpenproletariat'. 'For broad strata of the German working class', writes Geary, 'the formulation of a future oriented way of life did not make sense.'[13] Certainly, for many, the 'culture of improvement' had little relevance to their daily lives, which were characterized by short-term need and immediate gratification. Michael Grüttner, whose work on Hamburg dockworkers has highlighted the apparant failure of the labour movement to address the real needs of the working class, writes of a considerable section of the working class 'who appeared to be aimless, without stable employment, wandering from firm to firm, doing many different jobs', consisting mostly of young, single, unskilled men who cultivated a 'culture of poverty' more relevant to their needs.[14]

In order to attempt to overcome the seemingly intractable dichotomy between workers' culture and the culture of the labour movement, Dieter Langewiesche's conciliatory point of view should be heeded. He has maintained that everyday life and labour movement studies are not really doomed to conflict. Research into the labour movement should also consider the experiences of the workers, while those who seek to discover the worker's 'subjective experience' should not forget that this was influenced by political decision making and socio-economic structures.[15] An alliance between the methodology of social history and the history of political structures is called for in order to place the history of workers' leisure in the context of social relations and the dynamics of political change.

The following chapters examine six areas of leisure, recreation and entertainment enjoyed by urban inhabitants in Germany from the early decades of industrial development, the 1860s and 1870s, until the outbreak of war in 1914. Popular festivals and fairs are the starting point. Their roots were grounded in the recreational patterns of pre-industrial society yet they survived well into the nineteenth century, undergoing transitions and adaptations on the way. By the First World War a multi-faceted festival culture had been created in Germany and had no parallel elsewhere in industrial Europe. The consumption of alcohol, a traditional festival enjoyment, is the subject of Chapter 3. Drinking too had a prominent role in pre-industrial society, a role that was to change somewhat in relation to the new working and living conditions in which the industrial working class found itself. Alcohol was the lubricant of urban life and so it is discussed here not only in its role as a popular leisure activity but also in relation to the home, the workplace and political organization.

The public entertainments and amusements that form the focus of Chapter 4 – street performances, music halls, circuses and dancing – mark the beginning of urban leisure in the real sense of time regularly spent in recreation away from the home in tandem with the emergence of a commercial leisure sector meeting the demands for amusement from those with time and some money to spare. The associational activities discussed in Chapter 5 mark a watershed in the development of workers' leisure in the period. A distinctly urban phenomenon, they represent a clear move away from the more spontaneous activities of the early industrial years and a step towards organized leisure for specific interest groups. Middle-class criticism of all forms of lower-class amusement was always forcefully articulated and in Chapter 6 the efforts of the bourgeois liberal reformers of the turn of the century are discussed in relation to increasing attempts to control and direct workers' leisure. Finally, the commercialization of leisure, illustrated by the emergence of mass amusements and spectator sports, is discussed in Chapter 7. This signals the entrance of leisure and recreation into the modern age.

Thus the sequence is roughly chronological, beginning in the first half of the nineteenth century with the customary religious festivals, and concluding with the mass commercial leisure culture which made a brief appearance before war put a stop to frivolous amusements but reached its apotheosis in the early Weimar years. It would be a mistake, however, to assume that the development of leisure followed a single, chronological, linear process. The appearance of what we now regard as the precursor of a modern leisure industry was never inevitable. Rather, changes in the evolution of leisure were a response to broader social, economic and political impulses. If one were to take a snapshot of any individual leisure pursuit at any one time it would be found to be a microcosm of society as a whole, reflecting the social relations and structural complexities of that society. The cinema, for example, reached its zenith in the 1920s owing to a combination of factors soundly based in the political and economic circumstances of the postwar years: shorter working hours, greater demand for amusement, technological improvements and so on. One could not have predicted the popularity of this form of entertainment in the 1890s when it was little more than another side-show at the annual fair. No form of recreational activity ever outlived its compatibility with the society of which it was born. Incongruous activities were either reformed or disappeared. One cannot emphasize this point too strongly.

This book addresses four major themes or debating points. Firstly, it is contended that leisure should not be studied in isolation but in terms of its relationship to other social configurations, namely work and the family. Sociologists have a long tradition of defining leisure in terms of its relationship to work, frequently in a rather negative sense. 'The meaning of leisure in a given civilization depends upon the meaning given to work . . . what the individual demands of leisure depends on what he has and has not found in his work', wrote Raymond Aron in 1962.[16] Contemporary sociological models are undoubtedly useful in establishing a conceptual framework for the structured analysis of leisure in society, but problems are encountered in applying such general models to the circumstances of early industrial society.[17] We are also apt to forget the role of the family in determining leisure activities, yet the structure, size and function of the household had variable consequences, acting both as a constraint on the recreations of individual family members and also as a focus for collective leisure pursuits.

The second theme concerns the changing nature of the activities undertaken during leisure time throughout the period. Germany under Bismarck and Wilhelm II was a country in an intense state of flux, a new nation state in the throes of industrialization, demographic change and accompanying political immaturity and social tensions. Leisure was both a victim and a beneficiary of the changes. Recreations and amusements were created, sustained and abandoned as a result of complex socio-economic relations and thus there was no inevitable progression from, say, pre-industrial festivals, via the music hall and the library, to the cinema. Certainly the heyday of the popular festival was before the turn of the century, while the movies became the major form of amusement of the 1920s, but the history of popular recreations does not allow for neat chronological slots and the reader should be aware of the capactiy of so-called traditional amusements for flexibility.

Whether popular leisure activities were a form of collective class expression or a manifestation of social control is the third theme running through this book. The framework of this debate has been constructed by British historians of the working class using concepts initially developed by American sociologists; nevertheless the dichotomy is as relevant to Germany in the late nineteenth century as it is to Britain in the Victorian era, notwithstanding its manifestation in a rather different guise.[18] Class expression was traditionally regarded as the prerogative of the Social Democratic cultural and educational movement, while the mass of the unorganized working class was susceptible to the imposition of bourgeois values by outside agencies of the state and church. The implicit assumption that social control succeeded when it was practised has particular resonance in the study of German society if allied with the common perception of the all-pervading authority of the state and its apparatus. Certainly workers' leisure activities were subject to repression and more subtle ideological manipulation, but the overriding impression is of a working class with a mind of its own, with the capacity to resist attempts to impose middle-class values on working-class everyday life. However, in an ironic twist to the argument, it has been suggested that a form of internal social control was affected by the SPD over its members through the emphasis on improvement and respectability.

Finally, the distinction between labour movement culture and workers' culture is at the very heart of this study. Implicit is the assertion that labour movement culture, expressed primarily through the socialist association network, was not representative of the working class as a whole and, moreover, could not lay claim to be the sole agency of class cultural expression. Although the SPD leadership dismissed the unorganized workers as rough and unrespectable this is no reason for historians to do the same. Indeed, outside the workplace the leisure sphere was a prime location for the conscious expression of working-class interests and collective action. It has been persuasively argued that over time the SPD cultural network cushioned the blows of state repression and discrimination by providing workers with a source of identity with the dominant culture. In Gunther Roth's words:

> The sub-culture was 'negatively' integrated into the dominant system because by its very existence it provided an important means for the controlled expression and dissipation of conflict and thus contributed, for decades of peacetime, to the stability of the Empire.[19]

Indigenous or grassroots workers' culture, on the other hand, was dynamic, ingenious, innovative and flexible. It expressed the basic needs of workers and paid little heed to bourgeois protestations or methods of state control. This is not to say that the role of the labour movement was derisory or insignificant. Indeed, the degree of conflict between Social Democratic culture and the culture of the workers may well have been overstated. As the author of the most recent work on the subject suggests, the two may have influenced each other more than academic historical intransigence has allowed itself to admit.[20]

A number of historians have regretted the fact that source problems have, until now, bedevilled the reconstruction of the day-to-day lives of working people in the prewar era. Yet we need not rely upon the institutional, top-down approach, via the comprehensive documentation of political parties and social and cultural organizations. By reading between

the lines of official reports, interpreting official statistics and adding flesh to
these bones in the form of autobiographical information and social survey
reports, it is possible to recreate the recreational world of the German
working class before the period when oral history becomes feasible. The
material informing the bulk of this study (Chapters 2 to 6 inclusive) is
drawn from the reports filed by the Prussian police and their correspondence with government officials in Düsseldorf, Arnsberg, Aachen, Cologne
and Koblenz. The remit of the police was extensive and the policing of the
amusements of the poor occupied a considerable proportion of their
manpower and time.[21] Although this source is undoubtedly problematical
in terms of the prejudices of the forces of law and order, any misgivings
are counterbalanced by the comprehensive nature of their investigations.
Local newspapers were scoured for reports, reviews and advertisements
but were often more notable for what they left out than for the information
gleaned. Supplementing these archival sources are the contemporary social
surveys such as those carried out by the *Schriften des Vereins für Sozialpolitik*
around the turn of the century, and autobiographies written by workers.
In order to convey some of the major changes in recreational provision
during the early years of the Weimar Republic, the material in Chapter 7 is
supplemented by a greater reliance on secondary sources than that concerning the pre–1914 period.

This book does not profess to be a comprehensive study of working-
class leisure in Germany. Many areas require further analysis. Women,
although not entirely invisible, feature much more infrequently than their
actual presence demands. It is surely naive to consign women's leisure
activities solely to the church and the home yet, in the absence of detailed
research, these are the places where women were most visible. Informal
and private forms of leisure activity remain in the shadow of more
exciting public events, but evidence from working–class autobiographies
and oral history suggests walking, reading and spending time at home
with the family were the most frequent leisure 'activities' of the working
class. Moreover, this is a regional study, based on the industrial nerve
centre of Germany in the nineteenth century, the Ruhr Valley and the
towns along the lower Rhine, in particular the towns of Bochum and
Düsseldorf. The recreational pursuits enjoyed by the inhabitants of this
area were to a large extent determined by the circumstances of the
region's economic and social history. Only further regional studies will
tell if workers' experience of leisure here was replicated in other areas of
Germany. Suffice it to say, this book is not just another rejoinder to the
workers' culture debate but a point of departure in the history of leisure
and society in Germany, providing the missing link between the pre-
industrial amusements of the lower classes beloved of historians of popular
culture and the commercial culture of the Weimar Republic which is
belatedly receiving deserved attention.

Notes

1 D. F. Crew, 'The Constitution of "Working-Class Culture" as a Historical Object, Britain and Germany 1870–1914', unpublished paper (1983), p. 4.

2 J. Kocka, 'Arbeiterkultur als Forschungsthema', in special issue of *Geschichte und Gesellschaft*, vol. 5 (1979), pp. 5–11.

3 There are too many British leisure studies to mention here but among the most important are: H. Cunningham, *Leisure in the Industrial Revolution* (London: Croom Helm, 1980), R. Malcolmson, *Popular Recreations in English Society 1700–1850* (Cambridge: Cambridge University Press, 1973); J. Walvin, *Leisure and Society 1830–1950* (London: Longman, 1978); J. Walton and J. Walvin (eds), *Leisure in Britain* (Manchester: Manchester University Press, 1983); S. G. Jones, *Workers at Play: A Social and Economic History of Leisure, 1918–1939* (London: Routledge, 1986). See also S. Clarke, C. Critcher and R. Johnson (eds), *Working Class Culture: Studies in History and Theory* (London: Hutchinson, 1979).

4 T. Veblen, *The Theory of the Leisure Class* (New York: Macmillan, 1912); S. De Grazia, *Of Time, Work and Leisure*, (New York: Anchor Books, 1962); J. Dumazedier, *Towards a Society of Leisure*, (Paris: The Free Press, 1967). Some of the most useful sociological studies of leisure by German authors include H. Giegler, *Dimensionen und Determinanten der Freizeit* (Opladen: Westdeutscher Verlag, 1982); H. W. Opaschowski, *Pädagogik der Freizeit* (Bad Heilbrunn: Klinkhardt, 1976); H-W. Prahl, *Freizeit Soziologie* (Munich: Kösch, 1977); E. Scheuch, 'Soziologie der Freizeit', in R. König (ed.), *Handbuch der Empirischen Sozialforschung 2* (Stuttgart: Enke, 1977); D. Kramer, *Freizeit und Reproduktion der Arbeitskraft* (Giessen: Pahl–Rugenstein, 1975); K. Hammerich, 'Skizzen zur Genese der Freizeit als eines Sozialen Problem', *Kölner Zeitschrift für Soziologie und Sozialpsychologie*, vol. 26 (1974), pp. 267–81.

5 W. Nahrstedt, 'Die Entstehung des Freiheitsbegriffs der Freizeit. Zur Genese einer grundlegenden Kategorie der modernen Industriegesellschaften (1755–1826)', in *Vierteljahrschrift für Sozial-und Wirtschaftsgeschichte*, vol. 60 (1973), pp. 311–42; Nahrstedt, 'Freizeit und Aufklärung: Zum Funktionswandel der Feiertage seit dem 18. Jahrhundert in Hamburg (1743–1860)', in *Vierteljahrschrift für Sozial-und Wirtschaftsgeschichte*, vol. 57 (1970), pp. 46–92.

6 J. Reulecke, 'Vom Blauen Montag zum Arbeiterurlaub. Vorgeschichte und Entstehung des Erholungsurlaubs für Arbeiter vor dem Ersten Weltkrieg', in *Archiv für Sozialgeschichte*, vol. 16 (1976), pp. 205–48.

7 S. Reck, *Arbeiter nach der Arbeit: Sozialhistorische Studien zu den Wandlungen des Arbeiteralltags* (Giessen: Focus, 1977); D. Langewiesche, *Zur Freizeit des Arbeiters: Bildungsbestrebungen und Freizeitgestaltung österreichischer Arbeiter im Kaiserreich und in der Ersten Republik* (Stuttgart: Klett Cotta, 1980).

8 G. Huck (ed.), *Sozialgeschichte der Freizeit* (Wuppertal: Hammer, 1960). See also E. Kosok, 'Arbeiterfreizeit und Arbeiterkultur im Ruhrgebiet. Eine Untersuchung ihrer Erscheinungsformen und Wandlungsprozesse, 1850–1914' (doctoral dissertation, Ruhr–Universität Bochum, 1989).

9 D. Peukert, 'Arbeiteralltag: Mode oder Methode?' in H. Haumann (ed.), *Arbeiteralltag in Stadt und Land: Neue Wege der Geschichtsschreibung* (Berlin: Argument, 1982), p. 20.

10 J. Kocka (ed.), *Geschichte und Gesellschaft*, vol. 5 (1979), special issue on 'Arbeiterkultur im 19. Jahrhundert'; G. A. Ritter (ed.), *Journal of Contemporary History*, vol. 13 (1978), special issue on 'Workers' Culture'.

11 G. A. Ritter, 'Workers' Culture in Imperial Germany: Problems and Points of Departure for Research', in special issue of *Journal of Contemporary History*, vol.

13 (1978), pp. 165–89. See also R. J. Evans, 'The Sociological Interpretation of German Labour History', in R. J. Evans (ed.), *The German Working Class* (London: Croom Helm, 1982), pp. 15–53.

12 See, for example, D. F. Crew, 'Steel, Sabotage and Socialism: the Strike at the Dortmund Union Steelworks in 1911', in R. J. Evans (ed.), *The German Working Class* (London: Croom Helm, 1982), pp. 108–14; M. Grüttner, 'Working-Class Crime and the Labour Movement – Pilfering in the Hamburg Docks 1888–1923', in Evans, *German Working Class*, pp. 54–79; S. Bajohr, 'Illegitimacy and the Working Class: Illegitimate Mothers in Brunswick, 1900–1933', in Evans, *German Working Class*, pp. 142–73; R. J. Evans, 'Prostitution, State and Society in Imperial Germany', *Past and Present*, vol. 70 (1976), pp. 106–29; L. Abrams, 'Prostitutes in Imperial Germany 1870–1918: Working Girls or Social Outcasts?', in R. J. Evans (ed.), *The German Underworld* (London: Routledge, 1988), pp. 189–209.

13 D. Geary, 'Arbeiterkultur in Deutschland und Großbritannien im Vergleich', in D. Petzina (ed.), *Fahne, Fäuste, Körper: Symbolik und Kultur der Arbeiterbewegung* (Essen: Klartext, 1986), pp. 91–100.

14 M. Grüttner, 'Die Kultur der Armut', in H. G. Haupt *et. al.* (eds), *Soziale Bewegungen: Geschichte und Theorie* (Frankfurt am Main: Campus, 1987), pp. 12–32.

15 D. Langewiesche, 'Politik–Gesellschaft–Kultur. Zur Problematik von Arbeiterkultur und kulturellen Arbeiterorganisationen in Deutschland nach dem 1. Weltkrieg', in *Archiv für Sozialgeschichte*, vol. 22 (1982), p. 367. Cf. G. Eley, 'Joining Two Histories: the SPD and the German Working Class, 1860–1914', in G. Eley (ed.), *From Unification to Nazism: Reinterpreting the German Past* (London: Allen & Unwin, 1986), pp. 171–99.

16 R. Aron, 'On Leisure in Industrial Societies', in J. Brooks (ed.), *The One and the Many: the Individual in the Modern World* (New York: Harper & Row, 1962).

17 Examples of this approach include: S. Parker, *The Future of Work and Leisure* (London: MacGibbon & Kee, 1971); Parker, *Sociology of Leisure* (London: Allen & Unwin, 1976); Parker, *Leisure and Work* (London: Allen & Unwin, 1983); A. W. Bacon, 'Leisure and the Alienated Worker: A Critical Reassessment of Three Radical Theories of Work and Leisure', in *Journal of Leisure Research*, vol. 7 (1975), pp. 179–90; H. Wilensky, 'Work, Careers and Social Integration', in *International Social Science Journal*, vol. 12 (1960), pp. 543–60.

18 See G. Stedman Jones, 'Class Expression versus Social Control: A Critique of Recent Trends in the Social History of Leisure', in *History Workshop*, vol. 4 (1977), pp. 162–70; Stedman Jones, 'Working-Class Culture and Working-Class Politics in London 1870–1900', in *Journal of Social History*, vol. 7 (1973–4), pp. 460–501; P. Bailey, *Leisure and Class in Victorian England. Rational Recreation and the Contest for Control* (London: Routledge, 1978); Society for the Study of Labour History, 'The Working Class and Leisure: Class Expression and/or Social Control' (unpublished conference papers, University of Sussex, 1975).

19 G. Roth, *The Social Democrats in Imperial Germany. A Study in Isolation and Negative Integration* (Totowa: Bedminster Press, 1963), p. 315.

20 W. L. Guttsman, *Workers' Culture in Weimar Germany: Between Tradition and Commitment* (Oxford: Berg, 1990), pp. 11–12.

21 E. G. Spencer, 'Policing Popular Amusements in German Cities. The Case of Prussia's Rhine Province 1815–1914', in *Journal of Urban History*, vol. 16 (1990), pp. 366–85.

1

A time and place for leisure

The industrial environment

Leisure is a creation of industrial society, the result of the introduction of measured and disciplined work time. Before industrialization the proportion of time spent on work and 'leisure' was determined by the agricultural and religious calendar, not bv the clock. Weeks and years were punctuated by the Sabbath, holidays and festivals. With the coming of the factory system, however, sirens signalled the beginning and end of the working day. This is not to say that the working day did not have its official and impromptu breaks, but to speak of leisure in the modern sense is to talk of significant periods of time sufficient to spend in doing something.

This chapter will examine the context in which leisure for the working man and woman emerged in the period between 1871 and 1918. The geographical contours of the region will be described, sketching its transformation from a predominantly rural and handicraft economy to the industrial heart of Germany. The social, economic and political developments that shaped the region and the lives of its inhabitants and formed the backdrop to the recreations and amusements enjoyed by the working class will be discussed, and an attempt will be made to establish just how much time and money was available to the industrial working class to pursue active leisure.

The area now incorporated within the federal state of North–Rhine Westphalia was the most densely populated region of Germany in the mid-nineteenth century, with the most mobile industrial workforce and the most diverse economic infrastructure. Consequently it is probably the most researched area of Germany. Politically it belonged to Prussia. Administratively the region was divided between the governments of Arnsberg and Düsseldorf. It was confessionally mixed and remained populated by Catholics and Protestants throughout the period. It contained nationalities other than Germans: Poles, Masurians and other Europeans formed distinct communities within the towns. Economically, established commercial centres nestled against the new towns of the industrial revolution, surrounded by a rural hinterland populated by small-scale farmers and artisans. Coal and steel were king, but heavy and light industry cohabited happily.

13

Only the region's politics were more predictable; National Liberals and the Catholic Centre Party dominated until the turn of the century, when the Social Democrats made tentative headway.

Neither Bochum nor Düsseldorf was typical of the region, which itself was characterized more by diversity than homogeneity; however, both display characteristics of certain kinds of urban centre that emerged during the last third of the nineteenth century. Bochum, a 'child of the industrial revolution', situated in the Ruhr valley between Essen and Dortmund, was created by the discovery of rich coal seams and the development of the complementary steel industry. Just 50 kilometres to the southeast as the crow flies lay Düsseldorf, already a thriving commercial and industrial centre for the region by the 1860s. Resplendent on the Rhine, Düsseldorf went on to develop a diverse industrial base while continuing to flourish as a financial and service centre. The two towns could not have been more different. Bochum was part of the continuous industrial landscape of the Ruhr, dominated by 'winding towers . . . and waste tips, chimneys and smoking furnaces', all 'enveloped and covered by a misty, gassy, dusty, dirty veil . . .'[1] Düsseldorf, on the other hand, promoted itself as a garden town where, it was said, one was hardly conscious of the industrial activity located on its outskirts.

Bochum and Düsseldorf had very different histories. While neighbouring towns in the Ruhr had earlier begun to industrialize on a small scale so that by the 1870s they already possessed a basic industrial infrastructure, Bochum remained a provincial market town, populated by livestock farmers, artisans and shopkeepers, until the middle of the century. Only 4,000 people lived there in 1842. Despite the opening of a number of mines in nearby Hamme during the 1840s and 1850s, it was not until the construction of a railway line connecting Bochum to Witten in 1860, and to Essen and Dortmund two years later, that Bochum's geographical location ceased to be a disadvantage. The steelworks of the Bochumer Verein became the most important employer in the town, with a workforce of over 4,000 by 1873, the population doubled and by the 1870s the rural county town had been transformed into one of Germany's major centres of heavy industry. In 1882 around 80 per cent of the economically active population were engaged in industry and two thirds of those were employed in mines and foundries. The rapid transformation of the town can be summed up by two contrasting descriptions. In the 1840s it was said Bochum had narrow, irregular streets and small houses and huts, and that the majority of the population were engaged in agriculture and rearing livestock. By the 1860s the local government report noted that in the past 'one could count hardly any very large buildings. Since then only such buildings have been constructed and a far greater proportion of the present buildings are massive.[2]

Düsseldorf was a town of some 40,000 inhabitants in 1850, increasing to around 70,000 by 1871. It had been a charming, grand town with its old centre and cultural institutions, but metal and machine working altered the complexion of the town dramatically. Undoubtedly these complementary industries dominated Düsseldorf's economy. However, located favourably on the river and connected to other towns by good roads, Düsseldorf attracted a variety of industries including a vigorous construction sector, textiles, woodworking and glass making. In this respect Düsseldorf resembled its important neighbour Cologne rather than the smaller towns in the region which tended to specialize in one type of industry. Barmen, Elberfeld, Krefeld and Mönchengladbach, for example, were all textile centres, Solingen was famous for its cutlery and Essen became dependent on Krupp steel. Düsseldorf also became the administrative centre for the region and industrial interest groups made the city their headquarters.

The demographic growth that transformed the entire region was fuelled not by natural population increase, although this was a factor, but by a massive influx of migrants attracted by employment opportunities in the mines and other rapidly expanding industries like construction, metal and woodworking. By 1871, two thirds of Bochum's inhabitants were recent immigrants, a proportion that was not unique but typical of industrializing towns at the same stage of development. The majority of immigrants hailed from the surrounding Westphalian and Rhineland hinterland. Fifty-two per cent of the inhabitants of Bochum in 1871 were classified as immigrants from nearby districts. Migration from more distant parts of the German Empire, especially the backward east, increased during the 1880s and 1890s when the demand for labour (especially unskilled labour) could no longer be satisfied by the local supply. The percentage of non-local immigrants in the population of Bochum rose from 14.8 in 1871 to 23.7 in 1907.[3] Düsseldorf too owed its remarkable economic growth to this army of immigrants. They were recruited primarily from other towns in the Rhineland and Westphalia, less so from the more distant regions of the empire, partly owing to the nature of the employment opportunities on offer. More skilled, semi-skilled and white-collar jobs were to be had in the economically diverse Düsseldorf than in the Ruhr towns which recruited in the east for unskilled workers to man the mines. By 1907 no less than 58.4 per cent of Düsseldorf inhabitants were not natives of the town.[4] The majority of these immigrants did not settle in the first town to which they moved or the first job which they took. As long as work opportunities were numerous they remained geographically mobile. In any year between 1880 and 1900 up to 20 per cent of Bochum's inhabitants had arrived in the previous twelve months and as much as 25 per cent of the city's population left every year.[5] Similarly, every year in the mid-1890s up to 25,000 of the 29,000 arrivals in Düsseldorf left the town within twelve months.[6] Labour turnover was at its highest in most towns among young, unskilled, male workers during periods of economic growth.

Owing to the availability and nature of the work on offer, the majority of immigrants were young, male and single. Three fifths of the entire working class in Düsseldorf was under the age of 30 in 1895, including 60 per cent of male employees in the major industries of mining, metalworking and construction.[7] David Crew certifies that 'between 1880 and 1900, unmarried immigrants, meaning for the most part men under the age of twenty-five, accounted for no less than 87 and sometimes as much as 93 per cent of the transient population' of Bochum.[8] There were very few work opportunities for women in towns like Bochum that were dominated by heavy industry; young women were limited to domestic service or the retail trade. Women accounted for only 12 per cent of the economically active population of the town in 1907.[9] In Düsseldorf, with its established bourgeoisie, service positions were fairly numerous, and young, unskilled women were also able to find employment in the declining textile industry and smaller industrial enterprises, although this work was poorly paid. In 1907, women supplied almost 50 per cent of Düsseldorf's textile workers and made up 63 per cent of those employed in the clothing trade, the only branch of industry where women outnumbered men. Even so, of the 16 per cent of women in the labour force ascribed to trades associated with the working class, 85 per cent were employed as domestics; over 3,000 women were employed in this way in 1907.[10] The acute housing shortage in all industrializing towns also discriminated against women. Single men could be accommodated in specially erected lodging houses (the lodging house erected by the Bochumer Verein in 1874 housed 1,200 of its workers) or found lodgings with a resident family. Such inequality in employment and housing reflected the different demand for male and female labour, and inevitably resulted in an imbalance in favour of men in the urban population. Hickey notes that until 1905 women were in a minority in Bochum, representing only 46–8 per cent of the population.[11] The limited work opportunities for women in these towns meant that a sharp distinction between the roles of men and women developed. Men were forced to assume the role of breadwinner, while women played a no less important role in the management of the household budget, particularly by taking in lodgers and supplementary domestic work to boost income.

The influx of immigrants was also the primary reason for shifts in confessional allegiances in the two towns. Düsseldorf was formerly a predominantly Catholic town: just over 80 per cent of the population declared themselves members of the Catholic church in 1861. By 1890, however, the dominance of Catholics had been slightly eroded (to 72.8 per cent) by the significant Protestant proportion of the new inhabitants. In 1910 Catholics numbered just over 67 per cent in Düsseldorf.[12] Bochum had been fairly evenly balanced in confessional terms before industrialization: in 1858 the Catholic-Protestant split was 59 per cent to 39 per cent. By 1895 this had changed only slightly, to 54 per cent Catholic and 43 per cent Protestant.[13] But confessional shifts were more dramatic in some individual parishes, especially in those to which large numbers of Catholic workers from the east had migrated. Moreover, there were structural differences within the two confessions. Catholic migrants were more likely to be unskilled workers and the large employers in both towns were disproportionately Protestant.

Included among the Catholics in the region was a significant number of Poles. As members of the Catholic faith they were classified along with German Catholics, but the two branches of the religion were quite separate. Almost 5 per cent of Bochum's inhabitants were Polish-speaking in 1910, compared with only 0.6 per cent in Düsseldorf.[14] The main wave of Polish migrants arrived in the 1880s and 1890s, encouraged by the recruitment policies of mine owners when demand for unskilled labour outstripped local supply; indeed, 81 per cent of Bochum's Poles were employed in mining, construction and other heavy industries in 1882. Distinct Polish communities grew up around mines and factories, sometimes encouraged by employers keen to establish settled communities of reliable workers. In Gerthe, a typical mining community near Bochum, the 1,555 Poles accounted for almost 20 per cent of the population in 1910.[15] Masurians similarly strived to maintain a separate identity, largely by means of a strong allegiance to their form of Protestantism.

In its social profile, the working class that was 'created' in the industrial towns of the Rhineland and Westphalia during the final third of the nineteenth century was extremely heterogeneous. 'There was no typical Düsseldorf worker', writes Mary Nolan:

> Metal was the largest industry, but its workforce ranged from artisanal smiths through unskilled helpers and semi-skilled machine operators to skilled factory turners and boilermakers. Migrant Protestant carpenters and joiners, native Düsseldorf painters, and unskilled, staunchly Catholic migrants all worked in the booming construction business. Woodworkers and printers were highly skilled, well paid, and had strong traditions, stable family lives and firm roots in Düsseldorf; whereas textile, chemical and paper workers were transient, semi-skilled and badly paid . . . Although most workers were migrants that fact did not overcome differences in occupation, religion, place of birth and length of stay. Neither culture nor community nor economic condition united Düsseldorf's proletariat.[16]

By the 1890s, 28 per cent of Düsseldorf's labour force were employed in the metal industry. The construction industry was the next largest employer, providing jobs for around 15 per cent of the working class in 1895, followed by the textile sector. Despite the greater dominance of heavy industry in Bochum – mining and the metal industry employed two thirds of the workforce in 1882 – the working class in Bochum was similarly 'socially fragmented without any broad historical or cultural experience in common', according to Hickey. 'The working-class [in the Ruhr] . . . was not an established, settled cohesive community; instead we see a class numerically strong but socially disoriented, geographically unsettled, and culturally diffuse.'[17] Even at the turn of the century this was a class still in the process of its own making.

Nor was the urban middle class homogeneous. Until the mid-nineteenth century towns like Bochum and Düsseldorf had been run, economically and politically, by members of the old *Mittelstand*, primarily shopkeepers, small merchants and artisans. The influx of the new industrialists and manufacturers in the 1860s, the majority of whom originated from Protestant *Mittelstand* families in other German (or, in the case of Düsseldorf, Belgian) towns meant a realignment of local economic and political structures and balances of power. The Düsseldorf industrialists, including Lueg, Poensgen, Haniel and the Irishman William Mulvany, soon formed themselves into a distinct new urban elite wielding considerable influence over the economic and political affairs of the city through their own powerful interest groups like the Westdeutschen Maschinenbauverband and the Stahlwerksverband. They also dominated the chamber of commerce and the city council. From the 1860s onwards many of Düsseldorf's new industrialists were elected onto the council where they dominated the first and second classes (under the Prussian three-class electoral system). From here they succeeded in influencing local planning decisions in their favour and managed to improve the city's infrastructure, particularly railway and river communications, to service their industries.[18]

In Bochum only Louis Baare, director of the Bochumer Verein, and some of the mine directors rose to the status of their Düsseldorf counterparts. Baare took his seat on the town council in 1863 and proceeded to dominate municipal politics in Bochum for thirty years. 'From the mid-1870s on', writes Bochum's historian Helmuth Croon, 'the economic, social and political leadership of the town lay in the hands of the Bochumer Verein and the mines.[19] The influence of this group of industrialists over local affairs and their general outlook distinguished them from the traditional town elites. 'Their primary identifications and concerns could never be the town itself', concludes Crew, 'nor even the rôle of their industry in the town, but rather the way in which the town and its inhabitants responded to the imperatives of the German and world economy.[20] This ideology inevitably caused conflict, not only between industrialists and their employees but with other political and economic interests in the town as well. Tensions arose over traditional labour issues and also in areas encompassing what Herbert Gutman has called 'traditional community norms', including popular amusements, festivals and so forth.[21]

The *Mittelstand* in both towns closely associated themselves with these

18

'traditional community norms'. While many artisans and shopkeepers had prospered in the early stages of the industrial and urban development of their towns, benefiting from the rise in the number of consumers (the industrial working class), their economic fortunes were dependent on those of heavy industry – a position they found threatening – and they were resentful at having to share local political power with this new industrial elite. Crew has shown that an opportunistic alliance between the *Mittelstand* (of the Centre Party) and industrialists (National Liberal) in municipal elections, primarily in order to head off the threat emanating from the Social Democrats, was always based on shaky ground and mutual trust was never established between them. In Düsseldorf even this limited form of cooperation was absent and small businessmen and shopkeepers there were eventually forced to set up their own economic interest group, the Handwerkskammer (artisans' chamber), owing to their gradual exclusion from the heavy-industry-dominated chamber of commerce. (Handelskammer). Culturally they were a more homogeneous group than the newcomers, with local roots and common economic concerns. They revived what Gottfried Korff has called a 'forced traditionalism' (the expression of 'traditional' forms of communal solidarity), as a means of showing collective strength in the face of collective weakness.[22] In Düsseldorf the revival of organized Catholicism was one way of coping with their decline in power and status. *Mittelstand* social life centred upon associations representing their trades and skills, and the ritual celebrations organized by the local small-town elite (in Bochum the *Maifest* and in Düsseldorf the carnival) served to reinforce their collective identification with a traditional community that was fast disappearing.

Tensions and differences, between and within socio-economic groups in this period, influenced the course of political, economic and social developments in Bochum and Düsseldorf to a degree not yet acknowledged. In Bochum the working class was fundamentally divided and highly stratified along religious and ethnic lines and further delineated according to levels of skill. Düsseldorf's workers 'were divided by occupation and skill, culture and religion, age and sex, birthplace and commitment to urban life and industrial work', writes Mary Nolan.[23] And it was precisely these divisions, exacerbated by the high degree of geographical mobility and job-changing in the region, that hampered the efforts of the Social Democratic Party (SPD) to unite the working class behind a single cause. Social Democratic organizations were only just taking their first steps in both towns when the anti-socialist laws of 1878 nipped them in the bud. The Bochum Workers' Electoral Association had only 21 members in 1876 and even the police appeared untroubled by their presence. Indeed, so weak was Social Democracy in Bochum that no activists were known to the police, no Social Democratic leaflets were distributed and 'associations with Social Democratic tendencies' were believed not to exist.[24] Social

19

Democratic candidates in the Reichstag elections of the 1870s polled less than 5 per cent of the vote.[25] In the Bochum district, only branch associations of the Rheinisch-Westfälisch Bergarbeiter Verband, the miners' union, were considered remotely dangerous.[26] It was not until the lifting of the anti-socialist laws in 1890 that Social Democrats engaged in active associational involvement in Bochum. In the space of six months in 1904 they held 26 public meetings, 19 party meetings and 8 festive occasions in the Bochum electoral district and also organized a number of recreational and social clubs.[27]

Trade union membership was considerably stronger than membership of the party. The predominance of one industry – mining – facilitated comparatively strong union organization and in 1890, after the unsuccessful strike of the previous year, the Verband zur Wahrung und Förderung der Bergmännischen Interessen in Rheinland und Westfalen (Alter Verband) had 26 branches in Bochum and its surrounding villages, with around 5,000 members.[28] But the unions in Bochum and the Ruhr were victims both of the volatile economic situation and of the heterogeneity of the workers. By the early 1900s, in addition to the Alter Verband, miners' interests were also represented by a Christian trade union, the liberal Hirsch–Dunker unions and a separate union for Polish mineworkers. With around 41 per cent of Ruhr miners organized by 1910 it would appear, as Stephen Hickey points out, that workers had no objection to associational membership as such; rather, the failure of a unified trade union movement in the Ruhr was due to hostility to Social Democracy and the fragmentation of the work-force by political, ethnic and religious divisions.[29]

The Düsseldorf Social Democrats comprised nine constituent associa-tions, with 140 members, on the eve of the anti-socialist law and the two public meetings that took place in 1878 attracted a maximum of 80 persons. With the implementation of the anti-socialist legislation these organizations dissolved themselves voluntarily and very limited underground activity was spotted during the twelve years of the ban. 'The local Social Democrats conduct themselves very peaceably', remarked the Düsseldorf chief of police in 1883, 'and in no respect provoke intervention'.[30] With the era of the so-called *milde Praxis* in the late 1880s some covert Social Democratic associations which had lain low during the early years of the law began to gain in strength. These were chiefly trade and welfare organizations like the Düsseldorf branch of the German Printers' Association, and the stronger and more overtly political Metalworkers' Trade Association which was founded in 1884.[31] It was not until the fall of the anti-socialist laws, however, that working-class associational activity really took off in Düssel-dorf. By 1891 the central Social Democratic association, the Verein für volkstümliche Wahlen und Volksbildung, consisted of around 200 mem-bers, compared with only 18 in 1875, and was able to attract up to 1,000 people to its public meetings.[32] Initially the process of re-formation was a slow one in Düsseldorf. Membership of the SPD remained at a low level; in 1900 the party could count on hardly more than 300 members.[33] But associational membership of a more 'instrumental' kind was gaining in popularity from the 1890s. In 1892 membership of the 11 free trade unions in Düsseldorf ran into the hundreds. In 1896 there were 27 of these skilled trade associations, with over 2,000 members, the largest being the metalworkers and the Association of German Woodworkers, each with over 200 members.[34] By 1905 almost 9,500 were members of a union, rising to 14,536 in 1910.[35]

It has been argued by Nolan that in Düsseldorf the heterogeneity of the working class was overcome by the unifying force of the labour movement following the repeal of the anti-socialist legislation. 'The Social Democrats created a party and union movement, a workers' culture and most important, a cohesive working class.' The labour movement was the voice through which workers from all backgrounds could articulate their grievances, so that by the war 'both the workers' movement and the skilled who formed its core continued to dominate and unify the culture and politics of the working class.'[36] For Nolan the SPD is the key to understanding the working class in Düsseldorf – it played the leading role in its making – but in Bochum the reverse would appear to be true. Radical Social Democracy failed to gain a foothold here, largely as a consequence of the continued divisions within the working class that could not be overcome by socialist ideology.

Stephen Hickey brings us somewhat closer to the experience of industrial workers in this period by taking us away from the organized labour movement and leading us into their homes and workplaces. In shifting the emphasis Hickey succeeds in illuminating alternative centres of power and influence, most notably the churches. The social and cultural life of industrial towns in this period has been neglected, however, although it is a clear indicator of fundamental divisions and conflicts in that society as a whole. By examining the non-work activities of the working class a wider perspective can be gained on the balance of economic and political forces within communities. The Social Democrats were just one player on a very wide and crowded stage.

This thumbnail sketch of society, economics and politics in these two towns merely serves as a backdrop to the games played in the name of leisure and recreation, which acquired serious overtones and implications. In the fledgling bourgeois capitalist society a battle was being waged over the use and abuse of free time, a battle that witnessed unlikely alliances, often traversing class boundaries and setting women and men, employers and employees, tradesmen and municipal authorities, publicans and police, bourgeois reformers and working-class consumers, and Social Democrats and the lumpenproletariat, against one another in the pursuit of profit and pleasure.

Time and inclination

The quality of leisure activities enjoyed by workers was, to a large extent, determined by the amount of work-free time at their disposal, explained Rudolf Morf in 1898:

> A person who has to be at work from early morning until late in the evening, mostly badly or insufficiently nourished, is exhausted by the evening and stops in the next pub before going home for a beer, a glass of wine or schnapps to give him strength. As he sets down his tired limbs he feels even more tired and stays there . . . If the worker had a shorter working day . . . he would not always be exhausted and he would feel strong enough to forego the schnapps on the way home . . . perhaps he has a garden to tend, or some wood to chop, or he would go for a walk with the family, or read or study something or go to a club.[37]

This is an optimistic view, perhaps, of the benefits to be gained from the introduction of the eight-hour day. In fact these hours were not achieved until 1918. Working hours remained considerably higher in most industries throughout the second half of the nineteenth century. In the 1860s and 1870s a working day of 12 to 13 hours was not unusual, although by the end of the century 11 hours was regarded as the norm in many factories. Average working hours, however, disguise considerable variations from one industry to another. Throughout the period 1870–1900 workers in the building and machine trades worked significantly longer hours than their counterparts in woodworking and printing. Miners were in the somewhat unusual position of working eight-hour shifts – a practice dating back to the previous century – but these eight hours did not include the time taken to travel from the surface to the coal face, and back again – winding-time – which could amount to an hour or more each way in some of the older pits. The six-day week was common in most occupations but it was not until 1892 that Sunday was legally established as a day of rest. Very limited legislation was introduced to regulate working hours and employers were only required to limit the employment of women and children. They had a free hand as far as their male employees were concerned.

The annual work cycle was rather more erratic. A number of religious holidays were observed, as were some traditional local festivals in the first two or three decades of industrialization. There was nothing in Germany to compare with the 1871 Bank Holiday Act in England or the increasing acceptance of the Saturday half-holiday during the 1860s and 1870s. Apart from sporadic days off, workers were not officially entitled to any holiday either with or without pay. In 1900 between nine and ten thousand workers were given some sort of annual holiday, but this amounted to less than 1 per cent of the total wage-earning manual labour force.[38] In Bochum only the brewing industry operated a systematic holiday scheme by 1910.[39] Ruhr miners were allowed to take unpaid holidays but there was no statutory rights to these until after the war. It was not until 1919 that miners who had one year's continuous service in a Ruhr mine and six months' employment at the same pit were entitled to three days' paid holiday per annum for one year's employment, rising to a maximum of six days for four years or more. If the holiday was not taken holiday pay was not awarded in lieu.[40]

However, in the words of Dieter Langewiesche, 'pure work time offers no adequate criteria for actual available leisure time.'[41] Apart from sleeping and eating there were numerous additional demands on a worker's time. The time taken to travel to and from the place of work was often quite considerable; up to three hours a day was not unusual. The unique problem faced by miners has already been mentioned. The issue of what constituted actual work time was a controversial one in the mining industry, and was confused still further by the widespread practice of compulsory overtime after the normal shift had ended. This frequently amounted to an extra two hours and sometimes as much as another eight-hour stint underground.[42]

The number and length of breaks during the working day varied from one workplace to another. Most workers stopped for breakfast and lunch for between 30 minutes and an hour. These breaks were generally meant to replenish the workers' strength. Yet employers persistently tried to reduce the amount of time given over to non-work activities. Working on Sunday was another variable. One is accustomed to thinking that Sunday was a day of rest for workers; indeed a decree of 1875 stated: 'On Sundays as well as the major Christian festivals, New Year's Day, the general saints' days and Ascension Day, all public work including employment in private houses is forbidden.'[43] Only transport workers were exempt from this law which was based on the premise of the need to maintain Sunday as a day of religious worship. It is quite clear, however, that the law prescribing at least 24 hours 'guaranteed rest' was exploited by employers who sought to keep their factories running at optimum efficiency. A number of loopholes permitted Sunday employment in certain circumstances, such as the need to perform essential repairs; in the case of an accident; to prevent deterioration of raw materials, and the loading and unloading of ships.[44] And while specific regulations applied to every branch of industry (for example, steelworks were permitted to operate at full strength to carry out 'repair work and the firing of ovens' between 12 pm and 6 am on Sundays and holidays), employers still managed to evade them and openly abused the Sabbath, forcing their employees to do likewise.[45] The working day or week then was often longer than the official number of hours spent on the job.

It would be a mistake to assume that the reduction in the working day was the natural consequence of the modernization of industry. Only a few employers, primarily those in small-scale businesses, recognized the benefits to be accrued from shorter hours in terms of a stronger, more alert workforce. Most saw the introduction of mechanization and the division of labour as an opportunity to raise production targets. As a consequence, between 1860 and 1902, a period when the average working day decreased from 13 to 10 hours, the measure of work intensity is estimated to have almost doubled.[46]

Not only were employers determined to squeeze the last drop of energy from their employees, they were also afraid that an increase in work-free time would be detrimental to their businesses. In 1890 Wilhelm II echoed their sentiments when he said, 'the adult worker will spend his free time in pubs, will participate in agitation meetings more than before, and even though his wages will stay the same . . . he will still be dissatisfied.'[47] By refusing to give in to demands to reduce hours employers left themselves open to workers manipulating the time they were forced to spend at the workplace. Resistance to factory regulations and time schedules took the the form of starting late and finishing early, playing tricks and practical jokes on one another and generally wasting time. Even in the authoritarian environment of the Krupp steelworks it was noticed that 'many workers arrive erratically and . . . many leave their place of work before the bell'. A few years later, in 1871, Krupp complained that 'Hundreds of workers wash themselves 10 and 5 minutes before 12 o'clock [the beginning of the midday break] and hundreds are on the way home 5 minutes before 12.'[48] The opportunity to gain temporary relief from the monotony and burden of work cannot be underestimated. The greater the individual's control over his or her work, the more communication and cooperation was engaged in, the less likely it was that the actual work activity dominated the worker's life experience.

Did workers value the little free time grudgingly permitted them and where did their priorities lie? The relationship between free time and wages is complex. The question of hours did feature prominently in industrial disputes, but it would appear that the demand for shorter hours was never a serious consideration unless wage rates remained stable. Between 1900 and 1914 throughout the Reich a total of 344 strikes were called over hours alone, compared with almost 6,000 concerning hours and wages and just over 8,000 about wages alone. Hours therefore featured in over 40 per cent of strikes during this period.[49] The question of hours was almost always a source of conflict in the mining industry. By the 1880s the traditional eight-hour shift was regularly increased by compulsory supplementary two- and four-hour shifts. The demand for shorter hours took second place to higher wages in the 1889 Ruhr strike and six years later the reinstatement of the eight hours, minus winding-time, was at the top of the agenda.[50]

In 1895 a Protestant pastor, Paul Göhre, experienced for himself the working conditions in a Chemnitz machine-tool factory and wrote, 'It is no trifle to be with 120 men for eleven hours in one hot room which is filled with oily, greasy fumes, the workers' exhalation, and coal and metal dust . . . factory work is exhausting.'[51] Workers in these conditions were hardly capable of making the best use of their limited leisure time. In this sense leisure was intrinsically linked to work in a negative way: leisure was a form of escape but also simply time to rest and recuperate. However, to quote Dumazedier:

> just as labour is more than the negation of idleness, leisure is more than the negation of labour . . . Leisure is activity – apart from the obligation of work, family and society – to which the individual turns at will, for either relaxation, diversion, or broadening his knowledge and his spontaneous social participation, the free exercise of his creative capacity.[52]

Work was clearly the major limitation on the ability to pursue leisure activities, yet family and living conditions could also act as a constraint. It is impossible to generalize about the size and structure of working-class families in German towns in this period. In the early stages of industrialization much of the labour was seasonal; immigrant workers spent spring to autumn in the towns, returning to their homes in the winter. By the 1860s these workers began to settle in the towns in greater numbers, resulting in an imbalance in the population in favour of young, single men and a chronic housing shortage. The answer was to resort to temporary lodgings. In 1858 there was an average of 13 persons per household in Bochum, many of them lodgers or *Kostgänger*.[53] The 1860s saw a number of housing projects in the town initiated by the larger employers. The Bochumer Verein was a leader in this field; by 1874 it owned a total of 400 houses located in the Stahlhausen district of the town, in addition to the 1,200 places in its lodging house.[54] By 1912 about 35 per cent of their employees were housed by the company.[55] Some form of stable family and community life was fostered in the company housing colonies. The colony built by the Harpener Bergbau Gesellschaft for its employees in Werne was a classic example of the early company housing; each family had its own apartment, with sanitary arrangements behind the house and a stall for an animal. Often there was room in the attic for a lodger.[56] Shops, schools and pubs were also included in the plans for some colonies. Leisure activities were even provided on site for some lucky inhabitants. Many had access to allotments and in Dahlhausen the mining colony was equipped with a hall for 800 people, billiards, reading rooms, a bowling alley and meeting rooms.[57] Not surprisingly, employers did not go to the expense of housing their employees for purely altruistic reasons. 'The purpose of the colony culminates in the stability of the worker', wrote Carl Debus in

1890, 'and through this stability is promoted a sense of domesticity and family life, from that springs a greater desire and strength for work which in turn benefits the employer.'[58]

But these were atypical of the conditions endured by most workers and their families. Housing density remained high throughout the nineteenth century, with the problem aggravated by the continued use of residential rooms as workshops. The construction of new houses for working-class families in Bochum spectacularly failed to keep pace with the demand. Homelessness was a recurring problem, reaching a peak in 1891 when the authorities were forced to house over 300 people in barracks.[59] The majority of dwellings constructed during the 1870s were not suitable or affordable for working-class families. Between 1871 and 1885 some 1,090 new houses were built, in a period when the population increased by almost 20,000.[60] Private sector rents accounted for about a fifth of income in the 1880s and frequent job-changing and short-distance migration meant a high turnover of rented accommodation.[61]

Bochum's Mayor Lange was more aware than most of the potential effects of overcrowding in his town. He highlighted the problems engendered by the rising marriage rate – just over 300 a year between 1875 and 1879, but 368 annually between 1880 and 1885 – which contributed to the rising population and the demand for family accommodation.[62] But Lange, writing in 1886, was also afraid of the consequences of the rise in the number of lodgers in the town; by the 1890s around 20 per cent of miners were lodgers:

> It is often the case . . . that while the married man is working away from the house bathed in sweat to support himself and often a large family, an unmarried worker will be found in lodgings with the family. Here it appears that he takes advantage of the absence of the head of the family, receiving board and lodging from the wife, to seduce the unmarried daughter and bring unmentionable unhappiness to the family.[63]

Lange was almost undoubtedly exaggerating but he articulated a commonly held view and served to emphasise the overcrowding that bedevilled the existence of a stable family life in these towns.

In such conditions family life was therefore under some considerable strain. While the taking in of lodgers, especially when they were relatives or kin, may have alleviated economic problems and provided additional hands in the event of an emergency, the overcrowding and consequent poor sanitation endured by the majority of town dwellers were hardly conducive to happy family evenings by the fireside. More often than not family groups would spend their leisure time walking in the surrounding countryside to escape from their cramped living conditions and it was not unusual for men to 'escape' to the pub in the evening, not, as Brian Harrison has suggested, to escape a nagging wife, but to find some peace away from a crowded apartment.[64] The poor state of housing also encouraged young people to leave home as soon as they were economically independent, contributing to the pool of young, single people with more time and money at their disposal to be spent, it was said, on drink and dancing. Even those lucky enough to be housed in company dwellings were hard put to maintain a semblance of the type of family life it was hoped the housing arrangements would encourage. Some family activities were focused around the allotments and neighbours would sit together in the evenings in front of the houses and talk,[65] but everyday reality in towns like Bochum was somewhat less idyllic. Women were frequently employed outside the home and yet

> they still had to look after the house and the garden and care for the children. After a long working day – in 1900 around 9 to 10 hours – the men had to maintain the garden and look after the animals as well. 'Family life' just about looked after itself, there was no time left for visiting the pub and the politicization there which was so feared.[66]

At another level company housing isolated families and groups from community life and preserved distinctions between particular occupational and ethnic groups. Some colony regimes were even quite draconian; drinking and other 'anti-social' behaviour were not tolerated.

Work and the family could act as constraints on an individual's leisure time and the activities he or she chose to undertake. Later chapters are primarily concerned with leisure activities, in other words, 'positive' pursuits involving obligations to and relationships with other individuals and organizations. In order to enter into these relationships workers needed money.

The ability to pay

Few leisure pursuits could be enjoyed for free, although the popularity of walking among the working class tells us as much about their financial circumstances as their love of fresh air and exercise. In order to be able to afford the price of a pint, a ticket for a music-hall performance or a subscription to a club, workers had to have some measure of disposable income once the essentials like the rent, food and clothing had been paid for.

Average real weekly earnings increased by 35 per cent between 1871 and 1913. From 1879 on money earnings in Germany moved steadily upward with an especially high rate of increase from the mid–1890s to the outbreak of war in 1914. Actual wages are a poor guide to the standard of living, however; the economic reality for working-class families was determined by the retail price index. Increases in money wages were, more often than not, precipitated by increases in the cost of living; thus wage rises were offset by more expensive consumer items. A more realistic picture, therefore, shows real wages increasing in the *Gründerjahre* of 1871–5, decreasing markedly with the onset of the Great Depression and only picking up again in the mid-1880s from whence a gradual increase was experienced until 1913.[67] Stephen Hickey reports that miners' wages in Bochum did not rise above subsistence level until the 1890s.[68]

Our workers in the Ruhr and Rhineland industrial centres were likely to have received higher average wages then their comrades elsewhere in the Reich, partly the consequence of the favoured geographical position of the area, the relative ease of access to raw materials and a labour shortage in certain sectors. Wage differentials between industries were also quite considerable. Generally, skilled workers commanded higher wages than their semi- and unskilled colleagues, with printers and metalworkers, for example, earning more than workers in the building and mining trades. Miners do not fit easily into the equation. Certainly in the Ruhr, where labour was often scarce, the wages of hewers and hauliers compared favourably with the earnings of workers in the metal industry. The level of wages was said to be the only reason men worked underground. The accident rate and sickness levels among miners and others in dangerous occupations probably outweighed the advantages of higher daily wage rates.

Estimates of the financial position of workers vary tremendously. While Stephen Hickey notes that Bochum miners were experiencing real financial difficulties, sometimes living below subsistence levels despite the popular perception of miners being a well-paid group, more contemporary observers remark upon the sense of wellbeing of workers in the steelworks there in 1906. In 1905 the average daily earnings of a machinist employed by the Bochumer Verein was said to be 4.3 marks, while in Düsseldorf the equivalent worker in the Lueg factory received close to 4.8 marks.[69] The wages of Düsseldorf workers were, on average, probably higher than that of their counterparts in Bochum, owing to the predominance of skilled work in the former town. In reality, household income depended on more than just the wages brought home by the man at the end of the week. The age of the breadwinner, family circumstances, number of children, a wife in employment and even the ability to grow vegetables and balance the budget influenced a family's eventual standard of living. Work for women was more plentiful in industrially diverse Düsseldorf than it was in Bochum. Ruhr wives often resorted to taking in lodgers to swell the family income. For the majority of industrial workers earnings reached a peak relatively early in their working lives. In a period when late marriage was common and limiting the number of children became feasible, it was young, single men and those in the early years of marriage who had the most disposable income: 'there is some reason to believe', reported the Gainsborough Commission on a visit to Bochum in 1905, 'that rather too much money is put into the hands of young people, young men and girls, who are apt to yield to the temptation of spending too much on pleasures.'[70]

It is virtually impossible to calculate the amount of disposable income workers had to spend on non–necessities, bearing in mind the discrepancies between workers in different branches of industry and the variations in expenditure on essential items and family circumstances. A worker in Berlin on a weekly wage of just under 30 marks in 1905, supporting a wife and two children, estimated he had about 15 per cent of his income spare at the end of the week to spend on tobacco, clothes and amusements. This was at a time when deposits in company savings banks in Berlin were on the increase, suggesting a level of subsistence considerably healthier than that enjoyed by Ruhr miners, who even in a relatively good period for real wages found themselves living within tight budgets.[71] All that can be said with certainty is that skilled workers, and possibly the young in all occupations, were the first to demarcate for themselves a separate leisure sphere. It is also probably fair to say that men had more money to spend on amusements than their wives did. Although it was fairly common for men to hand over their pay packets for their wives to manage the household budget, any extra they may have earned over and above the standard wage was often retained as pocket money. Until the turn of the century the leisure patterns of women would tend to bear out this inference, the most popular 'leisure' activities enjoyed by married women being walking and talking with friends and going to church. Single women were the exception, particularly those who worked in factories who had more independence than most women of their generation.

Expenditure on leisure pursuits was sometimes budgeted for, especially in the case of annual festivals, for which families would often save months in advance, and alcohol consumption, with beer and spirits purchased with the weekly groceries. Many managed to pursue their favourite hobby of reading by purchasing weekly instalments of novels or by visiting the reading rooms of libraries. Few working–class families were able to afford books. The cost of enjoying some other amusements like a dance or a music-hall performance was often negligable; a few pfennigs were usually enough to gain entrance. A visit to a circus would be anticipated and money set aside specially. Moreover, it is impossible to determine the frequency of working-class participation in recreations and amusements. For some a visit to a dance hall was an infrequent treat, while others went regularly. Club membership was the only leisure pursuit requiring regular commitment and the payment of a subscription. The relative density of working–class leisure activities is impossible to measure, although from evidence gleaned from autobiographies and oral histories it seems unlikely that many working-class families were able to frequent commercial amusements on a regular basis. Of course a number of leisure activities could be enjoyed for free. Walking in the park and the countryside, street football and street entertainment required no expenditure.

It is probably fair to say that during the early decades of industrialization workers' enjoyment of leisure activities was limited by lack of time, money and choice.[72] The gradual erosion of the long working day and the increase in real wages after the end of the Great Depression stimulated demand for amusements to which various groups – publicans, the churches, the Social Democratic Party, reform-minded middle classes and municipal authorities – responded. Greater prosperity stimulated demand for more sophisticated amusements which people were prepared to pay for. The real break-through, however, was only achieved with the introduction of the eight-hour day in 1918 by the newly installed socialist government, but by then this was only able to act as a catalyst. The genesis of a leisure industry had already been established.

What follows is both an account of the development of the German leisure industry and, within this framework, a discussion of the nature of a workers' culture before the First World War. It is therefore a contribution to the social history of industrial society, but it is also a communication with historians of the labour movement and the working class regarding the culture of everyday life and the contributions of the socialist movement to the collective consciousness of the working class. Festivals and fairs open the debate, since they epitomize the transition from pre-industrial to modern forms of amusement and thus transported the workers with them from the traditional world of harvests and domestic production to the modern world of commercial production and regulation of time. Festivals were also all-encompassing; from drinking to primitive cinemas, the whole gamut of entertainment was there.

Notes

1 L. Pieper, *Die Lage der Bergarbeiter im Ruhrgebiet* (Stuttgart and Berlin: Studien, 1903), p. 214.
2 StAB, Bochum Verwaltungsbericht, 1860–2.
3 D. F. Crew, *Town in the Ruhr: A Social History of Bochum 1860–1914* (New York: Columbia University Press, 1979), pp. 60–1.
4 F-W. Henning, *Düsseldorf und seine Wirtschaft: Zur Geschichte einer Region*, 2 vols. (Düsseldorf: Droste, 1981), p. 385.
5 Crew, *Town in the Ruhr*, p. 61.
6 M. Nolan, *Social Democracy and Society: Working-Class Radicalism in Düsseldorf 1890–1920* (Cambridge: Cambridge University Press, 1981), p. 17.
7 Ibid., p. 22; StJDR, 108 (1895), p. 85.
8 Crew, *Town in the Ruhr*, p. 63.

9 S. H. F. Hickey, *Workers in Imperial Germany: The Miners of the Ruhr* (Oxford: Clarendon, 1985), p. 20.

10 Nolan, *Social Democracy and Society*, percentages calculated from Table A.6, pp. 312–13; StJDR,207 (1907), p. 476.

11 Hickey, *Workers in Imperial Germany*, p. 21

12 N. Schlossmacher, *Düsseldorf im Bismarckreich: Politik und Wahlen. Parteien und Vereine* (Düsseldorf: Schwann, 1985), pp. 20–1; G. Knopp, *Die Preussische Verwaltung des Regierungsbezirks Düsseldorf 1899–1919* (Cologne: Gröte, 1974), p. 24.

13 M. Seippel, *Bochum Einst und Jetzt. Ein Ruck und Rundblick bei der Wende des Jahrhundert 1901* (Bochum: Rheinisch-Westfälische Verlags-Anstalt, 1901).

14 K. Klessmann, *Polnische Bergarbeiter im Ruhrgebiet 1870–1914* (Göttingen: Vandenhoek & Ruprecht, 1978), pp. 261, 267; Knopp, *Die Preussische Verwaltung*, p. 23.

15 H. Croon, 'Studien zur Sozial-und Siedlungsgeschichte der Stadt Bochum', in P. Busch, H. Croon, C. Hahne (eds), *Bochum und das mittlere Ruhrgebiet* (Paderborn: Gesellschaft für Geographie und Geologie Bochum e. v., 1965), p. 99.

16 Nolan, *Social Democracy and Society*, pp. 21–2.

17 S. H. F. Hickey, 'The Shaping of the German Labour Movement: Miners in the Ruhr', in R. J. Evans (ed.), *Society and Politics in Wilhelmine Germany* (London: Croom Helm, 1987), p. 218; Hickey, *Workers in Imperial Germany*, p. 35.

18 Nolan, *Social Democracy and Society*, pp. 18–19; Crew, *Town in the Ruhr*, pp. 104–12; P. Hüttenberger, 'Die Entwicklung zur Großstadt bis zur Jahrhundertwende (1856–1900)', in H. Weidenhaupt (ed.), *Düsseldorf: Geschichte von den Ursprüngen bis ins 20. Jahrhundert*, vol. 2 (Düsseldorf: Schwann, 1988), pp. 563–8.

19 H. Croon, 'Bürgertum und Verwaltung in den Städten des Ruhrgebiets im 19. Jahrhundert', in *Tradition*, vol. 9 (1964), pp. 34–5. See also H. Croon, 'Die Stadtvertretungen in Krefeld und Bochum im 19. Jahrhundert', in R. Dietrich and G. Oestrich (eds), *Forschungen zu Staat und Verfassung–Festgabe für Fritz Hartung* (Berlin: Humboldt, 1958), pp. 289–306.

20 Crew, *Town in the Ruhr*, p. 110.

21 H. G. Gutman, *Work, Culture and Society in Industrialising America* (New York: Blackwell, 1977), cited in Crew, *Town in the Ruhr*, pp. 110–11.

22 G. Korff, '"Heraus zum 1 Mai": Maibrauch zwischen Volkskultur, bürgerlicher Folklore und Arbeiterbewegung', in R. van Dülman and N. Schindler (eds), *Volkskultur* (Frankfurt am Main: Fischer, 1984), p 264.

23 Nolan, *Social Democracy and Society*, p. 301.

24 StAB, LA 1299: Bochum Amt reply to circular of 12 June 1878: Sozialdemokratische Agitation, 24 June 1878.

25 Hickey, *Workers in Imperial Germany*, p. 249.

26 StAD, LA 1299: Arnsberg Verfügung re. vorhandenen Vereine und Verbindungen aller Art mit socialdemokratische, socialistische oder communistische Tendenz, 30 July 1878.

27 StAB, Nachlass Küppers, vol. 5, p. 329.

28 Hickey, *Workers in Imperial Germany*, p. 228.

29 Ibid., pp. 242–3.

30 StAD, III 6915: 6 August 1878; H. Tillmann, 'Das Sozialistengesetz in Düsseldorf bis 1887: Reaktionen der Oeffentlichkeit und Unterdrückung der Arbeiterbewegung', Dissertation Universität Düsseldorf, 1980), pp. 23–4; StAD, III 6918: Sozialdemokratie 1879–95, 9 September 1883.

31 Tillmann, 'Das Sozialistengesetz', p. 76.

32 StAD, III 6915: Verzeichnis sämmtlicher im Stadtkreise Düsseldorf bestehender politscher und nicht politischer Vereine, 18 March 1891.

33 Tillmann, 'Das Sozialistengesetz', p. 89.

34 StAD, III 5922: Nachweisung der Fachvereine zu Düsseldorf, October 1896.
35 P. Gerlach, 'Die Arbeiterbewegung', in H. A. Lux (ed.), *Düsseldorf* (Düsseldorf: Weidlich, 1925), p. 131.
36 Nolan, *Social Democracy and Society*, pp. 301–2.
37 R. Morf, *Die Verkürzung der täglichen Arbeitszeit* (Zurich: 1898), p. 17.
38 Reulecke, 'Vom Blauen Montag', p. 226.
39 Hickey, *Workers in Imperial Germany*, p. 136.
40 *Bochumer Volksblatt*, 17 September 1919, 'Urlaub für Ruhrbergleute'.
41 Langewiesche, *Zur Freizeit des Arbeiters*, p. 37.
42 Hickey, *Workers in Imperial Germany*, Ch. 4 (Work in the Mines), pp. 109–68, reference here from pp. 132–3. For more detailed information on miners' working conditions see K. Tenfelde, *Sozialgeschichte der Bergarbeiterschaft an der Ruhr im 19. Jahrhundert (1815–1899)* (Bonn/Bad Godesberg: Neue Gesellschaft, 1977) and F-J. Brüggemeier, *Leben vor Ort: Ruhrbergleute und Ruhrbergbau 1889–1919* (Munich: C. H. Beck, 1983).
43 StAB, LA 1174: Polizei Verordnung, December 1875; Reulecke, 'Vom Blauen Montag', p. 219.
44 StAB, LA 1174: Berlin Ministerium für Handel und Gewerbe, 23 July 1885.
45 StAB, LA 1174: Berlin Special-Verzeichniss der zulässigen Arbeiten an Sonn- und Feiertagen, 23 July 1895.
46 J. Kuczynski, *Die Geschichte der Lage der Arbeiter unter Kapitalismus*, vol. 4 (Berlin: Akademic, 1960–9).
47 K. A. Otto, 'Arbeitszeit: Erfahrungen und Erwartungen der Kampf um die Arbeitszeit im Kaiserreich', in *Geschichtsdidaktik*, vol. 10 (1985), p. 386.
48 Alfred Krupp, cited in A. Lüdtke, 'Arbeitsbeginn, Arbeitspausen, Arbeitsende. Bedürfnisfriedigung und Industriearbeit im 19. und frühen 20. Jahrhundert', in Huck (ed.), *Sozialgeschichte der Freizeit*, p. 99.
49 Otto, 'Arbeitszeit', p. 386.
50 Brüggemeier, *Leben vor Ort*, pp. 163–4.
51 P. Göhre, *Three Months in a Workshop*, trans. A. B. Curr (London: Swan sonnenschien & Co., 1895), p. 75.
52 Dumazedier, *Toward a Society of Leisure*, pp. 16–17.
53 Croon, 'Studien zur Sozial-und Siedlungsgeschichte', p. 92.
54 Ibid.
55 C. Debus, *Arbeiterwohnungswesen im Rheinisch–Westfälisch Industrie-Bezirk* (Zur Sozial und Gewerbepolitik der Gegenwart, 1890).
56 Croon, 'Studien zur Sozial-und Siedlungsgeschichte', p. 97.
57 S. H. F. Hickey, 'Class Conflict and Class Consciousness: Coal Miners in the Bochum Area of the Ruhr 1870–1914' (PhD thesis, University of Oxford, 1976), p. 84.
58 Debus, *Arbeiterwohnungswesen*, p. 12.
59 Hickey, *Workers in Imperial Germany*, p. 39.
60 C. Lange, 'Die Wohnungsverhältnisse der ärmeren Volksklassen in Bochum', in *Schriften des Vereins für Sozialpolitik*, vol. 30 (1886), p. 78.
61 Hickey, 'Class Conflict', p. 50.
62 Lange, 'Die Wohnungsverhältnisse', p. 76.
63 Ibid., p. 92.
64 B. Harrison, *Drink and the Victorians: the Temperance Question in England 1815–72* (London: Faber, 1971).
65 R. Günter u.a., 'Eisenheim: Die Erfahrung einer Arbeiterkolonie', in L. Niethammer (ed.), *Wohnen im Wandel: Beiträge zur Geschichte des Alltags in der Bürgerlichen Gesellschaft* (Wuppertal: Hammer, 1979), p. 200.

66 J. Haspel and K. H. Reuss, 'Alltagskultur in Ulmer Arbeiterquartieren während der Industrialisierung', in H. E. Specker (ed.), *Stadt und Kultur* (Sigmaringen: Thorbecke, 1983).
67 G. Bry, *Wages in Germany 1871–1945* (Princeton, NJ: Princeton University Press, 1960), pp. 71–3.
68 Hickey, *Workers in Imperial Germany*, p. 155.
69 *Life and Labour in Germany: Reports of the Gainsborough Commission* (London: Simpkin, Marshall, Hamilton, Kent & Co. Ltd., 1906), pp. 25, 52.
70 Ibid., p. 29.
71 Ibid., p. 200.
72 Cf. A. Davies, 'Leisure and Poverty in Salford', unpublished paper. Anglo-German Conference on Working-Class Culture, Lancaster University, 1988.

2

The industrialization of popular culture

The traditional festival

Since the Middle Ages festivals had been an intrinsic part of life throughout Germany. Simple parish fairs, elaborate carnival celebrations and national celebrations all offer a valuable insight into many aspects of community life. Indeed, festivals are born from the very day-to-day life from which they offer a temporary escape. Communal celebrations can be regarded as a microcosm of the culture of a community, albeit with its features somewhat exaggerated. Attitudes towards religion, the family, marriage, sexuality, work and the social hierarchy are all highlighted at festivals. These celebrations are thus not only excellent indicators of local and regional trends but also mirrors of broader social, economic and political changes. While festivals are unique experiences for the participants, they are nonetheless rooted in the culture of the community in which they are celebrated.

The rural calender that was still adhered to in many areas until the mid-nineteenth century was determined by a combination of seasonal work obligations and significant occasions in the religious year, that is to say Christmas, Easter, Whitsuntide and local holy days. The majority of festivals celebrated in Germany, therefore, were either of religious or of seasonal origin. The great Christian festivals took place between Lent and Whitsun and these were supplemented by regional and local commemorations of saints' days, church consecrations and pilgrimages. Harvest festivals took place everywhere, the precise date dependent upon the nature of local agricultural production. Indeed, festivals were innately local in character. Catholic towns and villages held *Kirchweih* festivals (commemorating the founding of a place of worship) and pilgrimages to holy relics. In both Catholic and Protestant areas festivals were held to bless horses, to protect them against disease and accidents, most frequently in the name of St Leonhard, the patron saint of horses. *Brunnenfeiern*, festivals to bless the local spring, were widespread. All communities were dependent upon the purity of the water supply and sacred and profane rituals were invoked to maintain it; salt was sometimes sprinkled into the source spring, or the young bachelors of the village bathed in the waters. In towns with a strong handicraft tradition festivals organized by the guilds were common: fish-mongers and sailors frequently enjoyed the festive amusement of *Fischer-stechen*, a kind of medieval jousting game, and *Gänsereissen*, which involved manoeuvring one's boat until it was under a rope hung with geese, then seizing a goose by its head and dunking it in the water.[1]

From the medieval through to the modern period festivals can be seen as unique occasions when the whole gamut of recreational, pleasurable activities were indulged in a short space of time. Eating and drinking, singing and dancing, games and sports, gambling, matchmaking, sexual impropriety, the purchase of luxuries and trinkets mingled with every form of entertainment imaginable; the festival really was the total recreational experience. But festivals played a more fundamental role in the community. 'The principle function of the fête', writes the French cultural historian Robert Muchembled, 'was to reduce the tensions that had accumulated, and to defuse and rechannel ambient aggression in order to keep the community from shattering.'[2] Festivals thus had a regulatory function, not only in rural areas but in the towns too, where the tensions and strains of urban life made the release of energy even more necessary.

The towns in the Rhine–Ruhr region celebrated a variety of festivals although, as the area was predominantly Catholic, most had some religious significance. More than 2,000 religious processions took place annually in the Düsseldorf district, many of them lasting for several days.[3] The most widespread and frequently celebrated festival throughout the nineteenth century was the parish fair or *Kirmes*. It had originated in medieval times, when a festival was held to commemorate the consecration of a newly erected place of worship. The date chosen was usually a Sunday or saint's day and more often than not would fall between the months of August and October, when the granaries were full of harvest produce and the stringencies of the winter months were some way ahead. Indeed, the importance of the time of year should not be underrated. Attempts by central authorities to alter traditional dates of fairs were invariably resisted by local communities. When the Uedesheim fair near Düsseldorf was arbitrarily moved from August to October the inhabitants made it plain to the Düsseldorf authorities that the new date was inconvenient because the festival had been timed to coincide with the harvest. October was not suitable as all hands would be required for sowing, and in any case friends would be reluctant to visit in the inclement weather.[4]

The *Kirmes* was probably the most important event in the religious, social and recreational lives of lower-class rural inhabitants. It was used to date occasions in the family and community and it functioned as a safety valve too, siphoning off tensions and uniting the community. With the natural break in the agricultural year came the opportunity to relax, enjoy oneself, renew acquaintances and patch up differences in a convivial atmosphere fuelled by copious quantities of food and drink. Over the course of several days inhabitants and visitors would typically join the church procession, attend a religious service, extend hospitality to friends and relations, and enjoy excursions into the countryside and dancing in the evenings. It was the most merry, lively festival of the year, when excess and generosity compensated for the worries and privations of the rest of the year. As one farmer explained in 1819, 'I expend hard work and effort throughout the year. The parish fair is the *only* time of the year when I can devote myself to my friends.'[5] Three days was the average duration of the parish fair, although one or two villages in the Düsseldorf district extended their celebrations for up to eight days. In some districts more than 100 days a year were officially designated *Festtage*, each village ensuring that its celebrations did not clash with those of a close neighbour.[6]

By the mid-nineteenth century, the *Kirmes* had become a feature of urban life too. As the towns grew and spawned working-class residential suburbs traditional fairs were incorporated into urban culture and new ones were invented. Thus the famous Crange *Kirmes* in Herne, a new town created by industrialization and by mining in particular, was revived in the mid-nineteenth century by the miner's welfare association primarily so that the inhabitants of Herne (who were predominantly immigrants from the east and Poland) could have their own festival.[7] Düsseldorf's fair was centuries old, held to commemorate the city's patron saint, St Apollinaris. By 1860 a total of 28 *Kirmes* days were celebrated within the city boundaries on prominent Catholic religious holidays. Many of these fairs took place in Düsseldorf's burgeoning working-class suburbs.

Around the 1880s many urban fairs experienced a dramatic transformation as they gradually became divorced from their religious origins. Of course commercial influences were present in the villages too, and always had been in a limited sense, but it was in the towns that commercial incentives emerged as the dominant feature, even the *raison d'être*. The celebration of church consecration was but a dim memory for many urban *Kirmes* revellers. As the role of the clergy diminished, publicans, trades-people and entertainers exerted greater influence. The focal point of the fair moved away from the church and towards the market place, which was usually well provided with taverns and dance halls. Dances proliferated. Over 130 separate dances took place in the Düsseldorf district on the occasion of the main fairs in 1895.[8] The towns were flooded with itinerant salespeople, showpeople and entertainers, with visitors from farther afield, as well as with beggars, prostitutes and crooks. In 1905 the Düsseldorf *Kirmes* had bands, orchestras, barrel-organs, wheels of fortune, numerous side-shows housed in 100 tents, as well as stalls selling gingerbread and hot saugages, beer and lemonade.[9] In Bochum too, the traditional Easter fair with its panoramas, menageries, theatres, carousels and shooting galleries was altogether a more commerical event in 1885, providing stallholders with receipts on a scale never seen before.[10]

The view of the clergy and local authorities was rather predictable. The urban *Kirmes* of the turn of the century had become an excuse for fun and commercial trade and, as such, did not deserve the religious connotations of its name. Consequently the active participants in the parish fair began to change. The clergy withdrew and the middle and upper classes, who had at one time tolerated and even encouraged the celebrations, became active opponents. Their arguments were based more on false perceptions than reality, as we shall see later. The traditional rural village fair, once described as 'a beautiful oasis in the eternal monotony of everyday life', was never the idyllic peasant festival portrayed by critics of the urban *Kirmes*.[11] The secularization of popular religious festivals had actually begun much earlier than the mid-nineteenth century. In the eighteenth century local festivals had been fairly ambiguous in meaning; the fertility rites, processions and symbolic acts had all had crypto-materialist overtones, and the sacred and secular had always been closely entwined.[12] Even in the most Catholic of towns, Aachen, the pilgrimage to worship the relics of the cathedral had been perverted as early as the 1840s by commercial enterprise.[13]

The characer of the *Kirmes* adapted to changing circumstances. It had to accommodate the shifting values of its participants if it was to survive, and its participants were predominantly members of the urban working class whose expectations had changed as a consequence of their experience of living in towns and cities with a greater variety of entertainment on offer. The antipathy directed towards the fairs in the second half of the nineteenth century was a direct result of the adaptation of the fairs to the new urban environment – and their subsequent success. In this chapter it will become clear that festivals were not the 'traditional' cultural throwbacks to an idyllic pre-industrial era so beloved by folklorists and contemporary critics, but dynamic, adaptable events that incorporated the needs of the communities or groups who sponsored and supported them. It is the flexibility of festival culture that lends itself so well to the study of workers' culture in a period spanning early industrialization, the consolidation of industrial work practices and the beginning of mass entertainment before and after the First World War. Festival culture is certainly a thematic study in its own right but, unlike some of the other leisure activities featured in this book, it does not fit neatly into a chronological slot. Through the medium of festivals the sequence of change from the domination of one mode of leisure to another can be accurately predicted, providing a blueprint for major trends in urban working-class culture and recreation between 1870 and 1920.

The working-class parish fair

By the 1880s the *Kirmes* had been embraced by the urban working class. Certainly in Düsseldorf and the suburbs where the majority of workers and their families lived, the fairs were enthusiastically celebrated by those who understood little of their religious origins and who cared even less. The festival season in Düsseldorf still extended from Whitsun to October. Workers who lived in the city were easily able to visit any number of the fairs that took place in heavy concentration within the city boundaries. The dense tramway network and the availability of cheap weekly tram tickets liberated workers from their homes and places of work, enabling them to travel all over the city. Thus a worker with the time, money and inclination could visit up to 16 fairs in a year without stepping outside the city boundaries:

> Take, for example, a worker from Derendorf who is perhaps employed in Oberbilk; on the third or fourth Sunday after Whitsun, the early Derendorf fair takes place and of course he is certain to stay at home on the Monday. The following Sunday is the day of the early fair in Oberbilk. Most of the factories will be closed on the Monday, so he must either stay at home or go to the *Kirmes* himself. After that, he does not work on the other days either, after spending half of the night awake. A couple of Sundays later the great Düsseldorf fair comes round. Hardly any factories are open on the Monday and Tuesday, and again the worker is forced to celebrate. Incidentally, I would also like to point out that on the Sunday after the Düsseldorf fair is the day of the fair in Rath. The Oberkassel fair is on the following Sunday, and then the fair in Neuss; and all of these are heavily visited by the people of Düsseldorf . . . Now we come back into the city district, and after one Sunday's rest there is the Oberbilk late *Kirmes*, and after this the Flingern and Derendorf late fairs, which represent the last of the fairs in town. On different interim Sundays in the future there are still the fairs of Hamm, Stoffeln, Vollmerswerth, Wersten, Eller as well as Grafenberg and Gerresheim to come.[14]

Once they arrived at the fairground the visitors were faced with a dazzling display of amusements and consumer items. Stalls selling food and drink, confectionery and haberdashery were the most numerous but in 1886 the diversions at the Linden *Kirmes* included balloons, monkeys, waffles, shooting galleries and carousels, among others. By 1903 the fair in Linden accommodated no fewer than 325 stalls and side-shows.[15]

It is clear that the urban *Kirmes* had quickly become part of the culture of the working class in the towns and cities of the region by the end of the century. Many of these workers hailed from the rural hinterland of the new industrial centres and were familiar with the *Kirmes* tradition even if their connection with their local fair was a tenuous one. It might be suggested that the workers' obvious attachment to the fair was an expression of some deep-rooted rural religious consciousness which was revived by the

38

memory of *Kirmes* celebrations of the past. Certainly migrant workers from strong Catholic rural areas, such as Cleve and Geldern in the Düsseldorf *Landkreis*, tended to maintain their links with rural Catholicism. Returning to their native villages at *Kirmes*-time and participating in urban fairs were just two ways of doing this. The majority of Catholic workers, however, particularly the skilled and semi-skilled among them, had a stronger commitment to urban life, making them less likely to cling to manifestations of rural Catholicism which, in any case, had less influence over rural inhabitants than the church itself wished to believe. In the towns the Catholic clergy refrained from participating in or even supporting the fairs, preferring to strike an unholy alliance with their Protestant counter-parts who were unhesitatingly hostile towards the fairs and popular amusements in general. A typical position was that of the Presbyterian Synod of Unterbarmen in 1905, when it presented a petition to the Düsseldorf district commissioner protesting against the Barmen fair with its 'amusements and stalls which have a harmful effect on young people; the irritating noise [which] is bad for the nerves of the old and infirm' and the 'moral and social danger' which the fair constituted.[16]

The sour grapes exhibited here only served to highlight the insecurity of the church in the face of a secularization rate among Protestant workers in working-class districts that was higher than that of Catholics in similar areas. This was happening by the 1880s, as was the encroachment of Catholics into what were historically Protestant towns like Dortmund and Duisburg.[17] Bearing in mind, too, the Catholic origins of the *Kirmes* it is hardly surprising that the Protestant church should distance itself so forcefully from the celebrations. As far as the Catholic church was concerned, despite a Catholic revival following the *Kulturkampf* and the formation of a Catholic subculture or milieu constituting the Centre Pary, Christian trade unions and a network of subsidiary social and educational organizations, its constituency in the new industrial towns of the region was not overly strong and the *Kirmes* was one fight the church could do without.

If the adoption of the fairs by the urban working class was not encouraged by the church, and the religious significance of the event seems to have been forgotten by the participants, what reason did workers and their families have for continuing to support the festivities? The desire to maintain links with the pre-industrial rural past was not manifestly the reason. While many workers clearly did make the trip back to their native villages and towns at festival time, other, less tangible actions represented conscious or unconscious continuity of behaviour. Absenteeism at *Kirmes*-time may well have stemmed from dislike of work and desire for more time off to enjoy oneself, particularly in view of the limited number of official holidays, but there is also a reminder here of the irregular work rhythms of rural and artisan society to which people developed a strong

39

attachment.[18] For some workers, absenting oneself from work on *Kirmes*-Monday can be seen as a throwback to the artisan tradition of Saint Monday (*Blauer Montag*), which some have argued represented individual control over the working week and over the distribution of the workload. In a number of industries, it was fairly common for workers to rest on Monday as late as the last third of the nineteenth century.[19]

Celebration of the parish fair went ahead through good times and bad. Erhard Lucas in his study of the Ruhr towns of Remscheid and Hamborn notes that working-class families would save up for the *Kirmes* weeks in advance.[20] Their enjoyment of the fairs does seem to have been affected by the prevailing condition of the economy – in hard times they would have had less to spend than in good – but the pleasures of the fair were rarely foregone altogether. The 'eat, drink and be merry' philosophy prevailed, even if the extent to which this could be followed varied with economic circumstances.[21] The fair in Harpen near Bochum in 1885 was 'extremely well attended by stallholders and the public' but 'early complaints about the small profits were ascribed not to a lack of desire to buy but rather to the generally slack times.'[22] Employers and other critics disapproved of this desire of the working class to enjoy itself at any cost; the Düsseldorf Chamber of Commerce spoke of the 'obvious search for entertainment, and the imprudence of the working class, who never let an occasion for celebration pass them by'. The spectre of the impending financial ruin of working-class families as a result of the man of the house's carefree and irresponsible squandering of the week's wages at the fair was conjured up to shame the working class into providence and thrift.[23] Nonetheless, disapproving comments on 'amusement-hungry workers' and their 'endless search for entertainment' had a good deal of truth in them. It was important for workers to be *seen* to be celebrating the customary fairs even if this involved financial hardship. 'It is certainly no exaggeration to say that many Cologne families live on potatoes, cabbage and coffee so that they can be seen to celebrate the festivals and spend money on all the shooting festivals, concerts, fairs, excursions etc', reported the *Rheinische Merkur* in 1888.[24]

The relationship between the health of the economy and popular festivities was always a close one. In agricultural communities, of course, a poor harvest would have tempered the celebrations somewhat, and in the 1880s the stagnant economy had a similar effect on the urban working class's ability to control the work-leisure relationship on its own terms. During the early 1880s workers rarely stayed away from work for recreational reasons; their incomes were already insufficient to maintain a basic standard of living so to risk unemployment for the sake of an extra day at the fair would have been foolhardy. On the other hand, from around 1894 onwards, a time of economic expansion and numerous employment opportunities, the bargaining position of workers was vastly improved and they were likely to take time off from work more readily. In Aachen in 1896, the District Metallurgy Association noted that 'The workers always want to celebrate; in fact they prefer to celebrate rather than earn more money.'[25] What the workers considered as a legitimate opportunity for a holiday posed a problem of considerable proportions for their employers, or so the employers persuasively argued. According to the Düsseldorf Chamber of Commerce, in 1897, during which 17 of the 29 *Kirmes* days in Düsseldorf were working days, 60 factories with a total workforce of over 12,000 had to cease working owing to the absenteeism of employees or drunkenness among those who did appear for work. The chamber of commerce calculated that in all 338,710 working hours were lost, or 26 hours per worker. Expressed in terms of wages, this was a loss of 6.24 marks per worker (a total of 80,000 marks). In the iron and steel industry alone it was found that 22 large factories had come to a standstill in 1905–6 for up to three and a half days each, owing to the shortfall of workers.[26]

The scale of the problem was undoubtedly exaggerated by the Düsseldorf employers. It was probably the smaller firms with greater overheads and lesser profits who suffered the most. Nevertheless, throughout the second half of the nineteenth century and beyond, the magnates of heavy industry took it upon themselves to seize the bull by the horns in the name of good management and employer–employee relations. The figures produced by economic pressure groups like the chambers of commerce only gave more ammunition to the growing army of critics of 'amusement-hungry workers' and prompted a propaganda campaign focusing on the plight of those 'willing to work' (*Arbeitswilliger* or blacklegs) whose livelihoods were being threatened because of the desertion of their irresponsible comrades. The *Kölnische Zeitung* raised the spectre of men arriving at the factory gates on Monday morning only to be told to return home,[27] and the Cologne Industrialists' Association recommended the restriction of the fairs in order that 'those willing to work are protected from involuntary holidays.'[28] Few employers were prepared to introduce the rational solution which had been practised by industry in England for years. The total shutdown of factories for the entire duration of the local festival was only adopted in Aachen, where the mayor regarded the three-day fair as a 'welcome opportunity for the workers and clerks of the factories to take pleasure trips', although in Remscheid factory owners did close down at midday and paid wages on the first *Kirmes* day.[29]

It was not only male workers who took to celebrating the urban fairs. Women were key figures at *Kirmes*-time. They cleaned and decorated the houses and prepared the food and drink. Their work began before the official start of the celebrations and extended beyond the Monday. Women who worked in the industrial towns did not abandon these traditional tasks; this was noted particularly in those industries like textiles where a large proportion of women was employed. 'When the nuisance of the fair is extended to the Monday or Tuesday', remarked the Düsseldorf Chamber of Commerce, 'they [women] are quite unfit for work for the entire week.'[30]

Measures by employers to stop the so-called exodus were largely ineffective. In the relatively lean years of the early 1880s workers had been punished with heavy fines, and a repetition of the offence had guaranteed dismissal, but in 1896 the Aachen employers admitted they were powerless. 'When a business is doing well', they added, 'the workers use this to their advantage, so that when they want to take a Monday off they obtain a sickness certificate on the Saturday, in order to avoid being fined.'[31] In the final year of the 1888–91 boom the Düsseldorf Chamber of Commerce noted that moving from job to job during the *Kirmes*-months had reached great proportions despite the penalties imposed.[32] Similarly, a spate of complaints by industrialists in the late 1890s about the difficulties encountered in preventing the workforce from taking time off to celebrate were issued during a period of economic recovery. And the Düsseldorf Chamber of Commerce's inquiry into worker absenteeism at *Kirmes*-time, published in 1908, followed a period characterized by strikes and worker unrest.

How should worker absenteeism for the purpose of attending the fairs be interpreted? Some workers had difficulty in adapting to industrial work rhythms and discipline; migrant workers were particularly prone to unpredictability. In the metallurgy sector, absenteeism and frequent job-changing have been interpreted as constituting a vehicle for protest in the absence of collective communication between employers and the workforce.[33] Alternatively, attendance at a festival may have functioned as a form of escape for workers, acting in a regulatory way, channelling the energy and aggression accumulated in everyday urban life. Certainly, absenteeism was a peculiarly individual form of protest, a strategy adopted by those workers who preferred shorter working hours to higher pay, especially during economic booms when working hours were frequently extended and there was pressure to work overtime in the evenings and at weekends.[34]

While acknowledging the carefree attitude of the urban working class for whom enjoyment of the fair came high on the list of priorities, the fact that the health of the economy affected the success of the fair also reflected the fact that the nature of the festivities themselves was changing in character. By the 1880s the *Kirmes* had become a secular festival, a *Volksfest*, dominated by commercial trade and amusement, an extension of a tendency evident in many of the rural fairs even before they were 'contaminated' by influences from the towns. However, the fact that so many workers continued to celebrate the *Kirmes*, in their new town of residence and in their native villages as well, and were willing to absent themselves from the workplace (sometimes under the threat of a fine or sacking, or at the very least losing a day or two's wages), indicates not merely an 'insatiable hunger for amusement' but also an attachment to traditional customs and celebrations which were increasingly threatened by the combined pressure of more powerful groups in society. The customary hospitality and the visiting of family or friends continued to be a prominent feature of the fairs, especially for the wives and children of workers whose opportunities for entertainment were few and far between.

The working class was a potent force in the adaptation of the *Kirmes* to modern, industrial society, aided by the increasing reliance on the fairs as a source of income by local tradespeople, shopkeepers and publicans. The fairs needed the participation and support of these groups if they were to survive the turn of the century. Indeed many urban fairs did not survive, in spite of working-class patronage. As the following section will show, the *Kirmes* became a minature battleground waged through the pages of the local press, in city council chambers and via the correspondence between the local police chiefs and city halls. The fairs stood for far more than a popular custom that inconvenienced factory owners. The *Kirmes* represented many things to many different groups. In the final analysis the fate of fairs in towns like Düsseldorf, Aachen, Bochum, Essen and Barmen depended upon a complex configuration of local politics, confessional allegiances and economic exigencies in which the working class had little direct influence.

Conflicts and resolutions

Throughout the region the *Kirmes* had become a convenient focus for the conflicts inherent in a society undergoing deep and irreversible change. Employers, mayors and local government officials had already found that isolated voices were not sufficient against the massive weight of opinion in favour of the continuation of the fairs. Although the chambers of commerce had consistently lobbied for comprehensive state legislation to limit the celebration of the *Kirmes*, none was forthcoming. Majority opinion in the Reichstag favoured local decisions made by those in a position to appreciate particular local circumstances. Pressure or interest-group politics was the name of the game the employers decided to play. As a result the battle was fought not along class lines, as the working class was not represented except by its actions, but between various alliances of economic interest groups, local government representatives and the forces of law and order. After 1895 the fate of the *Kirmes* was to be decided by constellations of local interests. The debate was admittedly conducted in a relatively low-key fashion. Supporters did not take to the streets or cause public disturbances; protagonists preferred to debate in the pages of local newspapers and in council chambers. Nevertheless, by examining the case of Düsseldorf in more detail it will become clear that what initially looked like a mere fit of pique by employers unhappy that their factories were not one hundred per cent productive every working day of the year, soon developed into a campaign with its roots firmly embedded in the city economy and politics.

In 1890, in response to a representation to the city government by a local welfare association proposing the reduction of *Kirmes* festivities, the city council arranged a meeting to debate the question. In an attempt to influence the decision of the deputies, particularly those who had already spoken in favour of the proposal who, it was suggested, were too far removed from popular festivals in terms of their social standing to make a valid judgement, a document setting out the arguments in favour of maintaining the Düsseldorf fairs was attached to a petition signed by hundreds of citizens of all social classes and areas of the city and sent to the mayor of Düsseldorf in December of that year. 'It may be', the statement read, 'that a reduction in the number of amusements for the working class is desirable and necessary . . . but it is more than doubtful whether by reducing the number of fairs one will succeed in protecting the working class from excessive amusement and expense.' Even if it was successful in this respect, it continued, the success

> would be far outweighed by the damage suffered by the other important class of the population, artisans, tradesmen and so on . . . Fairs, like those which are celebrated in the town and its suburbs, have existed for centuries and have become intimately bound up with the customs and feelings of the majority of the citizenry.

The main thrust of the petition, therefore, was to highlight the certain plight of the city's small traders, stallholders and artisans if the fairs were to be restricted in any way.[35]

Although it may be safely assumed that the instigators of the document were not altogether unbiased themselves, it is fair to say that life was not easy for Düsseldorf's small businesses. The rapid increase in the population of the city from the 1860s on had initially benefited these groups, but soon intense competition meant that many were struggling to keep their heads above water. Publicans were especially affected. Throughout the 1870s and 1880s the number of public houses in Düsseldorf multiplied at a rate commensurate with the increase in the population, encouraging entrepreneur publicans to risk expansion and take out loans. The ceiling was reached in the early 1890s, however, resulting in bankruptcy for those at the bottom of the pile, success for the few at the top and precarious survival for the rest. Income from day-to-day trade was often not enough to break even, leaving many publicans dependent on special occasions like the fairs for a significant proportion of their income. In Düsseldorf it was said that publicans earned half their annual income from trade conducted during *Kirmes*-time (not simply from the sale of beverages but also from hiring out their back rooms for dances and various forms of entertainment), so any restriction on the celebrations would have dealt them a severe blow.[36]

The local traders and shopkeepers were traditionally hostile to the itinerant stallholders and entertainers who flooded the city during the festivities. They were accused of taking away trade from local people and even of taking advantage of the working class who were allegedly tricked into buying overpriced 'trash'.[37] But native and itinerant traders were interdependent, even if this was not explicitly acknowledged. Publicans opened their rooms to travelling entertainers and the itinerant stallholders attracted custom, thus stimulating trade for local business. The relationship between this economic group and the working–class consumers or punters was a symbiotic one at all times, but particularly during the festival season. By putting forward carefully worded arguments to local authorities, playing on the connection between their own financial wellbeing and that of the wider economic community, and portraying small businesses as the key to economic prosperity. the shopkeepers, traders and publicans acted as proxies for the working class, who lacked an effective voice in the matter.

Although the native tradespeople and artisans were represented by their own interest group, the Central Association of Shopkeepers and Trades-people, their power and influence was limited in the face of the organized industrialists. The Düsseldorf Chamber of Commerce, the mouthpiece of heavy and manufacturing industry in the city, was essentially an elitist organization, especially so after 1900 when members representing smaller businesses broke away to form the Düsseldorf Artisans' Chamber. The real power of the chamber of commerce lay not in its promotion of economic interests but in its representation in the upper chamber of the city council. From the turn of the century onwards the magnates of heavy industry in Düsseldorf identified with the old Prussian elites. They were predominantly Protestant, even in a mainly Catholic town like Düsseldorf, and their religious convictions were readily translated into social and political affilia-tions. The majority of industrialists on the council were National Liberals. By the turn of the century the balance of economic and political power in the city had shifted as Protestant industrialists ousted native Catholic businessmen from positions of economic and political power.

One must assume that the Düsseldorf council meeting voted against implementing the welfare association's proposal since throughout the first decade of the twentieth century the Düsseldorf Chamber of Commerce persistently presented its case for the limitation and abolition of the fairs in the city and its suburbs. In 1908 it published a bulletin solely concerned with the *Kirmes*. Two years later, in December 1910, a decree of the Prussian trade minister placed responsibility for the future of fairs in the district firmly in the hands of local government. 'The Ministerial Decree fell on fertile ground', wrote the *Rheinisch-Westfälischen Wirte-Zeitung*, 'as the representatives of industry regard the abolition of the *Kirmes* as an advantage for their enterprises . . . the Düsseldorf Chamber of Commerce is proceeding in a particularly acute one-sided industrial way.'[38] The chamber of commerce certainly appears to have used the decree as an opportunity to rekindle its campaign against the fairs in the city. Throughout 1911 it intensified its pressure on the city council and the police department. On 11 March the chamber stated that it intended to do whatever was in its power to abolish or restrict the celebrations.[39] This prompted the Düsseldorf branch of the Association of Shopkeepers and Tradespeople to organize a protest meeting to demonstrate the strength of feeling on the matter, and a parallel meeting was held by the Düsseldorf butchers and market traders.[40] About a month later the chamber of commerce counterattacked by sending the Düsseldorf mayor a list identifying the ownership of fairgrounds around the city. A number of the fairgrounds were public property and therefore the police were entitled to rescind permission for a fair to take place.[41] In May the chamber announced it was working hand-in-hand with the police to stamp out the fairs and three months later it appeared that there was some truth in this claim when several fairs in the suburbs were amalgamated on the same three days in September. This must have placated the industrialists to some extent, although the main city *Kirmes* held over four days in July was not affected.[42]

Some of the industrialists' demands had been met but the restrictions placed on the dates of the fairs was as good as abolition to the publicans and traders, who could not be in two places at once. The Düsseldorf publicans continued to assemble strong arguments to present to the mayor and the police. A questionnaire sent to all the mayors in the district found they were more sympathetic to the people's needs. Even chambers of commerce in neighbouring towns adopted a more positive attitude than their Düsseldorf colleagues.[43] The pro-*Kirmes* campaign was given added impetus by the support of all the presidents of the local shooting associations. They were a considerable pressure group in Düsseldorf. Members were predominantly members of the old elites and the *Mittelstand* and their plea for the continuation of the fairs was not taken lightly, especially as they seemed to have Wilhelm II on their side. He was rumoured to have proclaimed, 'The Rhineland people shall not have their Rhineland festivals taken away'.[44]

By 1912 the heat seems to have abated somewhat. Although the chamber of commerce still petitioned the mayor from time to time, while their opponents, including the artisans' chamber, made sure their voices were heard too, the campaign withered away. In 1914 the industrialists finally achieved their aim, although in less than happy circumstances. All festivals were abolished for the duration of the war. As a postscript it is interesting to note that after the war the various combatants reverted to their previous positions. In December 1920 the chamber of commerce once more proposed the restriction of the festival in the interests of the economy and morality.[45]

The struggle over the Düsseldorf fairs was neither dramatic nor even decisive, but it is indicative of the shifting balance of interests in towns undergoing economic change. In Düsseldorf, a city with a more even balance of economic interest groups than most, efforts to restrict or abolish the fair were successfully thwarted even though the representatives of heavy industry and the police combined to try to stamp out the amusements of the masses. The old city elites were left to defend their corner, which they managed fairly successfully. An unlikely and temporary alliance was struck between the Düsseldorf *Mittelstand*, the shopkeepers and artisans, the old bourgeois members of the shooting associations, the small business interests in the artisans' chamber and, indirectly, the Catholic church whose representatives on the city council failed to capitulate to the strength of Protestantism and heavy industry.

Because of the diversity of its economy and its Catholic inheritance Düsseldorf was always likely to retain its festivals more or less intact. Fairs in the new industrial centres were more vulnerable. It is noticeable in Düsseldorf that the working class did not feature to any significant extent in the arguments, and was unable to participate in the campaign. In the Ruhr towns, on the other hand, other considerations such as the possibility of disturbances and crime at the fairs came to the fore. Complaints about pimps, prostitutes and other characters of the underworld who plied their trade at the fairs did not fall on deaf ears. In Essen, for instance, a town likely to succumb to anti-*Kirmes* pressures, dominated by the giant steel magnate Krupp, with a large proportion of migrant industrial workers and confessionally equally divided, the police provided the Düsseldorf authorities with a long diatribe against the fair and the working class. This culminated in the decisive assertion that 'the infringements of police orders and excesses and brutalities increase from year to year to such a degree that it is hardly possible for a freedom-loving and upright citizen to visit the fair for fear of endangering his life.[46] The fair was abolished in 1889. Similarly, the Hamborn fair was a victim of the 'imposition of capitalist work discipline', according to Erhard Lucas. The Hamborn industrialists emphasized the disruptive effect of the festivities on the smooth functioning of industry, as well as the alleged adverse effect they were having on the employer-employee relationship. In the decisive town council debate, however, the councillors were swung in favour of abolition by the police's failure to guarantee public order and safety.[47] Clearly, the dominance of a system run on industrial work discipline in the new industrial centres of the Ruhr meant that the fairs here were subjected to intense pressure from those groups in whose interests the system operated, while limited, if any, support was forthcoming from the groups who campaigned in favour of the *Kirmes* in Düsseldorf. The fairs were regarded as outmoded relics of the pre-industrial system, no longer valid in a society reliant on the profit motive.

The nature and level of popular support for and participation in the festivities certainly was a factor in their continuation or decline. In Düsseldorf it was repeatedly asserted that all classes of the population took part in the customary celebrations. The wider the social base and the greater the involvement of local elites, the more likely a fair was to survive. In the newer industrial towns the fairs quickly became working-class festivals, providing their enemies with plenty of ammunition for attack. In these instances the class dimension of the conflict is much clearer. The dominant class, that is the employers, subjected their employees to a form of exploitation that included the regulation of their non-work time and their public behaviour in the interests of industrial efficiency and moral and social control. In towns like Düsseldorf such a straightforward analysis is not credible; what was significant there was the more unstable balance of the economic and political interests of an older-established society under the impact of industrialization.

The segregation of festival culture

It is perhaps rather ironic in an era characterized by attempts to control the enjoyment of popular, public events that the number and variety of festivals celebrated from 1870 onwards was probably far greater than during any other period in Germany's past. The decline of the parish fair was countered, in the first instance, by the construction of a vibrant bourgeois festival culture and later by the creation of explicitly working-class labour festivals. Increasingly festivals were used to express the cultural values of specific socio-economic groups. On the one hand there were the shooting festivals and traditional small-town celebrations of the *Mittelstand*, bourgeois-orchestrated expressions of national unity like Sedan Day and imperial commemorative events. On the other hand were the working-class festivals organized by the Social Democratic Party and the trade unions: May Day, commemoration of the March Revolution of 1848, and the death of the founder of German Social Democracy, Ferdinand Lassalle. These modern festivals were not the harmonious, class-transcending occasions beloved of those in search of a Germanic folk idyll. They were socially divisive, a reflection of the diversification of economic, political and religious interests that was proving such a threat to the *Kirmes*.

At face value carnival, the three-day orgy of festivities held before the commencement of Lent in a number of Rhine towns, including Düsseldorf, was a real community occasion involving all sectors of the urban populace. Supporters of carnival frequently drew attention to the harmonious nature of the festivities, but a closer look reveals two carnivals: one organized by the bourgeois carnival associations behind closed doors; the other a more spontaneous street party for the urban masses. Carnival thus epitomizes the segregation of festival culture in Imperial Germany.

The official carnival celebrations, sanctioned and often partially financed by the city council, were organized months in advance by special carnival committees at carnival meetings. Members of the committees were recruited overwhelmingly from the bourgeoisie, professionals, artisans and the *Mittelstand*. It was the solid, middle stratum of society that gave carnival its respectability and ability to attract and maintain official approval.[48] In Aachen, Cologne and Düsseldorf the mayor extended his benevolence to the traditional antics of the carnival committees and in Düsseldorf a proportion of the 23,000 marks required to pay for the 1904 celebrations was met from city coffers.[49]

The respectable bourgeois carnival consisted of customary well rehearsed, respectable activities; the election of the carnival prince, his coronation, the accompanying balls and theatrical events and even the *Rosenmontagzug*, the procession through the streets, aroused little consternation among the upholders of law and order. Such was the perversion of carnival by the nineteenth century, however, that early traditions had been turned on their head. In the early modern period the carnival prince would have been the local fool, or at least a member of the lower classes, and he would have been paraded around the streets sitting back-to-front on a donkey, symbolizing the world turned upside down. This was a far cry from the elaborate forms of transportation arranged for the bourgeois carnival prince in nineteenth century Düsseldorf which only served to reinforce the status quo.[50]

The working-class carnival, on the other hand, was an entirely different affair. This carnival did bear more relation to that upside-down world which reigned during carnival in the sixteenth and seventeenth centuries. The working-class participants dressed up in costumes and masks, painted their faces, paraded and danced in the streets, consumed excessive quantities of food and drink and generally enjoyed themselves, notwithstanding the panoply of measures introduced to prevent them doing so. During the last three decades of the century masquerades were outlawed, as were the wearing of false beards, the blacking of faces and dressing in clothes of the opposite sex.[51] In 1880 the so-called *Gänsemarschlaufen* (the deliberate playing of out-of-tune instruments) was forbidden in Düsseldorf. So were music-making, singing and shouting on the streets: all activities intrinsic to the traditional enjoyment of carnival.[52] Needless to say the revellers defied the laws and continued to enjoy carnival in the customary fashion.

In Düsseldorf, Aachen and Cologne, as well as a number of smaller towns, carnival survived the turn of the century and continues to the present day. Almost certainly the key to understanding the reasons for its survival when other popular festivals were being suppressed was the continued participation of local elites. They used carnival to reaffirm the existing social and economic order and their place within it. As long as their security was assured the masses could be permitted to enjoy themselves in a limited period of time within the perameters laid down by the police. The majority of employers closed down their factories for the duration in an act of goodwill and self-interest. In short, carnival was used as a safety valve much as earlier festivals had channelled tensions and aggressions. The abolition of the carnival was never seriously considered. Complaints registered with the chief of police concerned the loss of the old traditions, the excessive commercial exploitation, the immorality and profanity, but such criticisms were tackled sensitively; reform, not abolition, was the answer.

It would be no exaggeration to say that instances of bourgeois festival culture in the imperial period represent a clear attempt by local notables and the petit bourgeoisie to hold on to their positions of power and associate themselves with authority at a time when the composition, structure and organization of industrial society were undergoing a transformation, bringing new groups to the fore in political and economic terms. The increasingly high profile of both the owners of industry and the industrial working class was particularly significant. In creating for themselves a distinct festival culture, professionals, artisans, traders and shopkeepers were attempting to maintain their footing and not give way to the industrialists who were beginning to make considerable headway in terms of representation in community power structures. Bochum did not celebrate carnival but here the local petit bourgeoisie appropriated the *Maiabendfest* for much the same purpose as their counterparts in Düsseldorf. The Bochum petit bourgeoisie's adoption of a festival dating from the mid-eighteenth century was clearly a reaction to feelings of displacement. The central participants, all members of Bochum shooting associations (incidentally not founded until 1829) dressed in uniform, elected a shooting king and marched around the town in military fashion. In fact, the claim by Bochum's old elite that it was invoking a 500-year-old tradition was a false one (since the tradition can only be traced back to 1768), but it served the purpose which, according to Gottfried Korff, was to establish the identity and document the claims of the bourgeoisie and so help to cope with the loss of familiarity caused by rapid urbanization.[53]

The Bochum May Festival eventually assumed all the trappings of a popular urban *Volksfest* with 'shooting galleries, instant photography and other market stalls', attracting more than just the disaffected Bochum *Mittelstand*.[54] In 1910 Bochum's mayor happily informed the Arnsberg authorities that 'Workers, petit bourgeoisie, artisans and academically educated people participate in harmony, so that from a social standpoint this festival is particularly good for the settlement of class differences.'[55] However, the festival remained in essence an expression of bourgeois civic pride and local patriotism. Moreover, it had nationalist overtones based on the 'love of Kaiser and Reich'. As such it bore a striking resemblance to every other shooting festival in the area. Shooting associations celebrated festivals that were characterized by pseudo-military ceremonial: uniforms, marching and cannon-fire. All these expressions of local and national bourgeois consciousness assumed a more legitimate and official character in 1871, with the institution of the commemoration of the victory over France by Prussia at the battle of Sedan in 1870.

The Sedan Festival was, in the first instance, designed to promote the unity of the new German Reich and national consensus, as well as to assist in the glorification of an emperor who wanted to be seen to represent the new nation state. A cultural consensus was envisaged: the national festivals would forge a social and cultural order soundly based on the unitary state, transcending regional and class differences. The basic principles of the festival, conceived by the disciplinarian Protestant minister Friedrich von Bodelschwingh, rested on the elevation of church and state. Yet these noble principles were soon undermined, firstly by bourgeois domination of the Sedan Festival (as they had come to dominate other so-called national celebrations, like the Kaiser's birthday), and then by the degeneration of the festival into just another excuse for dancing and amusement. What is more, the majority of working people, Catholics and other minority groups were excluded or excluded themselves from active participation.

More than any other of the bourgeois festivals, Sedan Day was organized by the local war veteran, militia and shooting clubs and celebrated with much flag-waving, military bands and parades, patriotic speeches and cannon-fire. Local dignitaries were invited to special concerts and banquets, while the lower classes were literally relegated to the side-lines, lining the streets (although some Protestant Workers' Associations did participate in the procession). The organizers of the national festivals did pay lip-service to the idea of a national popular festival: schoolchildren were recruited in their hundreds to cheer and wave on the streets, and central and local government attempted to include all groups in some part of the proceedings.[56] In Düsseldorf the festival committee expressed the wish that 'the poorest man should also be given the opportunity to take part in this great patriotic festival, particularly factory workers who are not usually able to', largely because their employers would not allow them the time off.[57] In fact a free concert was staged in the zoological garden but the festival committee only allocated a small proportion of its budget to this element; the main celebration took place in the city concert hall, accompanied by military music, beyond the means and the taste of the working man and woman.[58]

51

Working class participation in these 'national' festivals was fairly passive. Catholics of all classes, however, stayed away altogether.[59] The increasing isolation of the Catholic population from the Protestant-oriented state, combined with the reinforcement of this tendency by Bismarck's anti-Catholic legislation, rendered the Sedan Day celebrations an expression of Protestant domination even in predominantly Catholic towns like Düsseldorf, where, in 1876, the Centre Party newspaper reported that:

> In Düsseldorf like everywhere else the Catholics have been reproached for staying away from the so-called national celebrations and people have taken this as proof of a lack of patriotism. We want to point out that real patriotism is not the swinging of torches, feasting and cheering – we have seen often enough how the loudest of these torch-patriots who yesterday were shouting 'Hosannah' are raging 'crucify, crucify!' today. Anyone who has noticed this and who has observed the situation without predjudice can say that a large proportion of the population, particularly Catholics, stay away from these festivities because they do not want to take part in a celebration which bears the mark of religious and political discord and hatred.[60]

Similarly in Bochum, where confessional allegiance was less a confrontational issue but socio-economic divisions were more pronounced, the normally unprovocative bourgeois newspaper, the *Märkischer Sprecher*, observed on the dual occasion of the Kaiser's birthday celebrations and the *Bismarcktag* that it was no longer possible 'to hold a great popular festival to unite everyone loyal to the Chancellor without class segregation.'[61]

These festivals degenerated into an excuse for pomp and display on the part of the local notables and petit bourgeoisie and reduced the public to the status of mere spectators. After 1871 celebrations lacked any particular local significance and in the absence of a long history from which a myth could be constructed, their legitimation in the eyes of the masses never materialized. Where the organizers of the Bochum *Maiabendfest* succeeded in inventing tradition the supporters of the national festivals failed. 'The Wilhelmian festivities', concludes George Mosse:

> never broke through to become genuine rites with a liturgy that made room for popular participation. The dynamic that had assured the success of the festivals before German unification was missing, and Germany's glory was chiefly represented by marching soldiers.[62]

Festivals could no longer be called popular. By the 1890s they were more class-based than ever before. The emergence of a distinct and exclusive working-class festival culture nailed the lid on the coffin of the national *Volksfeste*.

Socialist festival culture

The Social Democrats consistently opposed the patriotic, bourgeois and religious festivals of the Second Empire. The *Kirmes* was portrayed as a degenerate version of the traditional rural fairs where the working class was exploited by those who treated the fair as a commercial opportunity. In open debate the SPD failed to represent the opinions of the rank and file working class and indeed on some occasions even undermined their actions, condemning workers who absented themselves from work to go to fairs for preventing 'respectable' workers from providing for their families.[63] But the party's criticism was subdued. Possibly its hostility was tempered by the recognition of the importance of these fairs to the industrial working class. More significant was the SPD's unwillingness to ally itself with the most outspoken critics of the festivities, namely the church and the employers' organizations. Futhermore, the party also feared alienating a group upon whom the whole socialist–cultural movement relied: the publicans. They had become indispensable during the period of the anti-socialist laws and now provided the only available meeting rooms.

The SPD reserved its venom for the new national festivals imposed upon the German people by a government seeking self-aggrandizement and vindication of its policies. The Bochum Social Democrats expressed a typical attitude of organized labour when they described the shooting festivals in the town as 'nothing more than a demonstration of stupidity, and the number of participants is a measure of the amount of stupidity which still exists in the big village of Bochum, and that is an enormous amount.'[64] These celebrations were regarded as a propaganda weapon of the dominant classes. The instigators were accused of fabricating a festival culture that served to affirm their own identity and position of power in society while alienating subordinate groups. In 1892 the labour movement in Dortmund criticized the military precision with which these festivals were 'celebrated'; the participants were commandeered and attendance considered a 'duty'. Barracks and schools were 'mobilized', highlighting the real intentions of the festival promoters.[65] Yet well articulated criticism of national festival culture in the Social Democratic press was not the prime force in discouraging working–class participation in these celebrations. Only a more positively formulated policy and the presentation of an alternative socialist festival culture as a counter to nationalist, bourgeois forms could begin to wean workers and their families away from state-sponsored festivities and more traditional celebrations.

Social Democratic festival policy was not conceived merely as an antidote to bourgeois festival culture. Like all other aspects of Social Democratic theory it was based on a critique of the organization of capitalist class society; festivals were to be part of a utopian socialist future. 'In a class state there can be no unanimous popular festival; there is only the class festival', sums up the official policy of the SPD.[66] As Liebknecht revealed, the new festivals were to be distinct from the 'traditional "pure entertainment" festivals of the prosperous, from the unthinking gaiety . . . of the trade festivals and particularly from the religious festivals.'[67] As such, festivals were regarded as part of a wider cultural policy, the final stage in a series of steps that included the education of the working class, the formation of working-class associations and the preparation of this class for a full contribution to and participation in public cultural life. Festivals brought attention to these developments, affirmed the values hitherto taught and, in Lidtke's words, 'gave a public presentation of the alternative culture in symbolic and recreational form.'[68] Clearly then, socialist festival policy was as much a confirmation of Social Democratic cultural values as it was a signal to the dominant groups in society. The propaganda of the socialist idea had an internal as well as an external purpose and in this respect was no different from the festival ideology of other groups.

Apart from the dissemination of the vision of a socialist utopia, festivals were also good recruiting grounds and often financially advantageous for the local party. The May Day celebrations, however, were also more overtly political. The whole concept of May Day was intrinsically bound up with an international working-class struggle that had social, economic and political demands, placing the *Maifest* on a different level to earlier, more ideological and compensatory socialist festivals like the commemoration of the Paris Commune. Indeed, it was originally conceived as a demonstration and only became a festival when attractions in addition to the marches and speeches were deemed necessary to encourage large numbers of workers to participate. The demand for the introduction of the eight-hour day, the extension of workers' insurance, the elimination of the worst abuses of female and child labour, and so on, made May Day appear more of a threat to political opponents and employers' groups than, for instance, the *Märzfeier* which had even been described by the *Märkischer Sprecher* as 'harmless'.[69]

The presence of an alternative socialist festival culture allows a more three-dimensional analysis of working-class intensions. From their enjoyment of the urban parish fairs and their willingness to defy their employers it has been possible to argue that workers were not just clinging to the customs of a pre-industrial past, but were adapting recreational forms to the urban environment and, furthermore, making a statement about their relationship to the work ethic and the owners of industry. Attendance at a festival organized by the SPD had, in theory at least, far greater implications for the political consciousness of the workers and the strength of the labour movement in a given area. In SPD strongholds the local party organizations were able to boast thousands at their May Day rallies. The number of similar events in Bochum and Düsseldorf were rather less impressive. Throughout the 1890s, only a few hundred Düsseldorf workers attended the meetings and speeches on May Day.[70] In 1897 around 600 Düsseldorf people, of whom 150 were women and children, heard a lecture on the significance of 1 May for the working class;[71] – a speech that seems to have been repeated almost every year, which may account for the ever-decreasing audience: in 1899 some 500 people assembled to listen, and by 1901 just over 300 were present.[72] Participation at the May Day celebrations in the Bochum area was even more desultory, bearing in mind the high percentage of workers in the population, although again SPD membership was fairly low.[73] Events in neighbouring Hamme and Weitmar managed to attract around 200 people in 1904, but in most other Bochum satellite towns the numbers present rarely rose above 30.[74] It was not for another decade that the celebration of May Day became more popular in numerical terms. Around 3,000 people attended a meeting at the Bochum shooting lodge in 1910, the same year that 20,000 people from the city and suburbs of Düsseldorf were said to have marched to the city woods for speeches and festivities.[75] In some years the low attendance figures were undoubtedly the result of May Day falling on a weekday.[76] May Day was not a public holiday and few employers allowed their workers to take time off. It was said that Krupp's workers 'stood at the factory windows and doors and greeted the demonstrators sympathetically' as the Essen marchers passed by the factory in 1900.[77]

Did the workers who attended May Day and other socialist festivals recognize the political implications of their participation? While the political leaders always stressed the ideological premise of the festivals, local party activists soon realized that working-class participation on any significant scale could only be achieved if the event was given a popular character. Mass participation was guaranteed if the organizers included a procession, music, an excursion, a picnic or popular amusement and arranged the festivities for a Sunday. As the police commented on the relatively small number of people at a public lecture on 1 May 1899, 'From this is to be inferred that people are less interested in a lecture than entertainment.'[78] The 1905 Düsseldorf May Day festival was described by the Social Democratic *Volkszeitung* as 'impressive and splendid', with the afternoon excursion attracting 'three thousand and more', demonstrating 'that the spirit of the May festival strikes deeper and deeper roots in the proletariat.'[79] Düsseldorf party and trade union leaders appear to have exploited the entertainment side of their festivals to the full. Trade union festivals held in the summer around the turn of the century attracted up to 30,000 people, including many from Social Democratic clubs and associations from the surrounding district. This 'vast carnival' offered all the amusements and entertainments usually present at the *Kirmes* including shooting competitions, bowling, sack and running races and a carnival-like procession.[80]

It has been argued that the socialist festivals soon departed from the form originally intended, degenerating into just another popular festival, mimicking the patriotic and national festivals they were supposed to replace.[81] Clearly the attendant amusements became just as, if not more, important that the political speechmaking and many of the features of religious and national celebrations found their way into the ritual and 'tradition' of May Day. But the rituals and symbolism on this occasion were associated with the values of the labour movement. The red paper rose became the May Day flower in Germany, and wearing it was an expression of solidarity.[82] Because such symbolism was only recognized within the labour movement it therefore denoted a distinct cultural milieu. In his convincing reassessment of socialist festival culture, Vernon Lidtke writes:

> The fact that more festival programs . . . were not officially recognized as statements of party or trade union policies in no way diminishes their meaningfulness as manifestations of the social-cultural milieu of the socialist labour movement . . . All labour movement festivals embodied political significance.'[83]

Unfortunately the picture is not so clearcut. Although the numbers attending the May Day and trade union festivals in Düsseldorf did steadily increase throughout the 1890s and 1900s, reaching thousands, there is no evidence to suggest any decline in the popularity of the *Kirmes* among the working class during the same period; in fact an increase in the numbers of those attending the traditional fair is apparent. Moreover, workers were still absenting themselves from the workplace without permission and ignoring threats of fines and dismissal in order to attend the parish fairs right up to the outbreak of war, whereas fewer workers were willing to risk their employers' wrath for the May Day festival. There is some evidence to suggest that the working-class was increasingly divided between the respectable artisan subculture which formed the backbone of the labour movement and whose members rejected the traditional festivals, and the rough, unorganized lumpenproletariat who continued to frequent and enjoy them. Certainly in mining areas by the 1880s, political as well as religious and ethnic differentiations were beginning to have an impact on festive culture, as Klaus Tenfelde points out.[84] Workers were not as undiscriminating as their political spokesmen feared. While not denying the attraction of the amusements on offer at the *Kirmes*, working-class support for national festivals was generally unenthusiastic.

Blueprint for the future

It is hardly surprising that one expression of popular culture has proved to be such a reliable guide to the conflict-riven society created in the towns of the Ruhr and Rhineland during the early stages of industrialization. As

Jonathan Sperber has pointed out, the region experienced unusually deep economic, political and social change in the context of a traditional Catholic area that had been subjected to Prussian Protestant rule. The festivals were such an intrinsic part of local life that it was inevitable they would feature in the struggle for supremacy when the old order began to break up. Peculiarly local balances of economic, political and religious power, products of the late eighteenth and early nineteenth centuries overlaid with the new interests of the industrial era, determined the fate of the parish fairs. Those in the new industrial towns fell victim to the powerful industrialist-local authority power blocs, while in the older cities like Düsseldorf and Aachen the *Kirmes* survived because of pressure from established interests. These factors also influenced the development of the more modern festival forms; the strength or weakness of Sedan Day or May Day in a particular town depended to a large extent on the respective power of those groups attempting to impose their festival culture on society. Festivals in Imperial Germany reflected the tensions and contradictions in an industrializing society. Conflicts over the fate of the parish fair were merely an echo of the deeper and more basic economic interests of particular groups, complicated by the confessional dimension.

By the 1880s and 1890s, festivals began to be assimilated into the industrial, capitalist, class-based society that characterized the towns in this area. The all-encompassing *Volksfeste*, symbols of a passing era, that had reflected collective values, beliefs and fears gradually gave way to events more synonymous with a class society; now the new festivals expressed the values and beliefs of class intersts. The concept of a community culture which was associated in the bourgeois press with the idyllic peasant festival was lost. The integration strived after by the state with its 'national' festivals was never attained. By the turn of the century, festival culture in Germany had become irrevocably segregated along class lines.

The absence of any effective working-class representation on official bodies, such as town councils or economic pressure groups, means that their position with regard to festivals, at least before 1914, must be interpreted from their actions rather than their words. But these tell us that their motives were no different to those of other groups. Workers used the various celebrations in ways that reflected their own economic and psychological needs and beliefs. Undoubtedly the fairs meant a release from the rigid industrial work discipline, and a break in the everyday monotony; workers' persistent abuse of factory regulations on these occasions indicated a rejection of the system and the industrial hierarchy, if only temporarily. For the early immigrant workers, the celebration of the parish fair may have maintained a link with their past. This in turn occasioned a temporary return to pre-industrial concepts of work and leisure. This traditionalism was an early response to industrialization, a reliance by workers on familiar practices and cultural forms in an attempt to survive in an environment beyond their control.[85] But workers were not mere passive elements in the process of the transformation of urban festival culture. Many of the parish fairs would have disappeared or been quickly abolished had it not been for the adaptation of these events by the working class. While the parish fairs retained many of their traditional elements, working–class participants incorporated these into urban recreational culture; hence the centrality of the tavern at the urban fair and the preponderance of side-shows, amusements and traders, all patronized by working–class punters. Even attempts to control and suppress the urban popular festivals were not entirely negative, as these measures provided the working–class with the impetus to take control of its own recreational activities. The socialist festivals are but one manifestation of a trend which is discernable across the entire urban leisure scene.

If the festivals of this period were a total recreational experience for the participants, then trends within the festival culture offered a blueprint for the pattern of more everyday recreational experience. Festivals began to lose their uniqueness as self-sufficient and extraordinary occasions; by the turn of the century they were well and truly integrated into the urban recreational culture. The class segregation evident at the carnival celebrations and national festivals was increasingly a feature of urban leisure in general. Workers withdrew to their taverns, the bourgeoisie to its cafés and clubs; the infiltration of the festivals by the associations and societies reflected the operation of the associational movement along class lines. The attempt by employers and local authorities to control working-class enjoyment of the festivals was to be repeated over and over again across the entire recreational spectrum; the principles underlying the imposition of the national, patriotic festivities had their equivalent in the bourgeois recreational policy that believed in intra-class activities of a rational and uplifting nature. Festivals succumbed early to the inevitable impact of commercialization which enabled them to be at the forefront of recreational provision, effectively competing with the vast array of amusements on offer to the urban masses by 1914.

Notes

1 See L. Petzoldt, *Volkstümliche Feste. Ein Führer zu Volksfesten, Märkten und Messen in Deutschland* (Munich: C. H. Beck, 1983).
2 R. Muchembled, *Popular Culture and Elite Culture in France, 1400–1750*, trans. L. Cochrane (Baton Rouge, La.: Louisiana University Press, 1985), p. 49.
3 HStAD, RD 30460: Zahl der althergebrachten Prozessionen in Düsseldorf Bezirk, 1874.
4 HStAD, RD 121: Uedesheim Bürgermeister to RDA, 29 August 1827.
5 Ibid.: Kirchweihfesten, Krefeld 7 December 1819. Cf. W. Blessing, 'Fest und Vergnügen der kleinen Leute: Wandlungen vom 18. bis 20. Jahrhundert', in R.

Notes

van Dülmen and N. Schindler (eds), *Volkskultur* (Frankfurt am Main: Fischer, 1984), pp. 352–79.

6 HStAD, RD 30475: Uebersicht der im Kreise bestehenden Haupt- und Früh-Kirmes 1860; Nachweisung über die im Landkreise Düsseldorf pro 1860 feiernden Kirmessen, 31 January 1860; Verzeichniss der in der Oberbürgermeisterei Düsseldorf bestehenden Kirmestage, 9 February 1860.

7 Petzoldt, *Volkstümliche Feste*, p. 385.

8 HStAD, RD 30477: Tanzlustbarkeiten in den Ortschaften des Regierungsbezirks Düsseldorf bei Gelegenheit der Kirmessfeier, 1895.

9 *Düsseldorf General Anzeiger*, 17 July 1905.

10 MS, 5 April 1885.

11 *Kölnische Zeitung*, 24 July 1903.

12 Muchembled, *Popular Culture and Elite Culture*, pp. 137–9. See also M. Scharfe, 'Distances between the Lower Classes and Official Religion: Examples from Eighteenth Century Württemberg Protestantism' in K. von Greyerz (ed.), *Religion and Society in Early Modern Europe 1500–1800* (London: Allen & Unwin, German Historical Institute, 1984), pp. 157–74; W. Blessing, *Staat und Kirche in der Gesellschaft. Institutionelle Autorität und Mentaler Wandel in Bayern während des 19. Jahrhunderts* (Göttingen: Vandenhoek & Ruprecht, 1982), and the discussion of work on this subject by C. Köhle-Hezinger, cited in R. J. Evans, 'Religion and Society in Modern Germany', in *European Studies Review*, vol. 12 (1982), pp. 249–88, especially pp. 265–7. On the combination of sacred and secular at the festivals see R. Scribner, 'Cosmic Order and Daily Life: Sacred and Secular in Pre-Industrial German Society', in von Greyerz (ed.), *Religion and Society*, pp. 17–32; P. Burke, *Popular Culture in Early Modern Europe* (London: Temple Smith, 1978) for a general European perspective; E. Weber, *Peasants into Frenchmen* (London: Chatto & Windus, 1977) for the situation in France.

13 J. Sperber, *Popular Catholicism in Nineteenth Century Germany* (Princeton, NJ: Princeton University Press, 1984) p. 69; cf. W. Schieder, 'Kirche und Revolution. Sozialgeschichtliche Aspekte der Trierer Wallfahrt von 1844', in *Archiv für Sozialgeschichte*, vol. 14 (1974), pp. 419–54, especially p. 447.

14 HStAD, RD 8950: Vorstandsmitglieder des Vereins christlicher Arbeiter und Handwerker, 1891.

15 StAB, AL-D 79: Verzeichniss über die am 22.–23. August 1886 auf der Kirmess zu Linden aufgestellten Buden und erhebenen Standgelde.

16 HStAD, RD 30476: Barmen, Antrag der Gemeinde Unterbarmen betreffend Kirmessunfug (Presbyterian Synod), 18 January 1905.

17 Sperber, *Popular Catholicism*, p. 45; for details of secularization in Düsseldorf see J. D. Hunley, 'The Working Classes, Religion and Social Democracy in the Düsseldorf Area,' in *Societas*, vol. 4 (1974), pp. 131–49, and for a more general discussion of secularization among the working class in Europe see H. McLeod, *Religion and the People of Western Europe 1789–1970* (Oxford: Oxford University Press, 1981), especially pp. 118–31. Also, H. McLeod, 'Protestantism and Workers in Imperial Germany', in *European Studies Review*, vol. 12 (1982), pp. 323–43; and V. Lidtke, 'Social Class and Secularisation in Imperial Germany. The Working Classes', in *Leo Baeck Institute Yearbook*, vol. 25 (1980), pp. 21–40.

18 E. P. Thompson, 'Time, Work Discipline and Industrial Capitalism', in *Past and Present*, vol. 38 (1967), pp. 58–97.

19 For a discussion of the *Blauer Montag* custom see Reulecke, 'Vom Blauen Montag', pp. 205–48. Cf. D. Reid, 'The Decline of Saint Monday. Working-class Leisure in Birmingham 1760–1875', unpublished paper, Society for the Study of Labour History Conference, (University of Sussex, 1975).

20 E. Lucas, *Arbeiterradikalismus: Zwei Formen von Radikalismus in der Deutschen Arbeiterbewegung* (Frankfurt am Main: Roter Stern, 1976), p. 10.
21 Cf. Lancashire wakes which were badly affected by economic depressions but never entirely given up, to be revived even more vigorously when the economy improved. See R. Poole, 'Lancashire Wakes Week', in *History Today*, vol. 34 (August 1984), p. 25. Also J. Walton and R. Poole. 'The Lancashire Wakes in the Nineteenth Century', in R. Storch (ed.), *Popular Culture and Custom in Nineteenth Century England* (London: Croom Helm, 1982), pp. 100–24, especially p. 117, on people's determination to celebrate at all costs throughout the slumps of the 1830s and 1840s.
22 MS, 20 August 1885.
23 HStAD, RD 8950: DH, 14 March 1891.
24 K. Jasper, *Der Urbanisierungsprozess, dargestellt am Beispiel der Stadt Köln* (Cologne: Rheinisch–Westfälischen Wirtschaftsarchiv zu Köln e.v., 1977), p. 240. *Rheinische Merkur*, 21 June 1888, cited in Jasper, *Der Urbanisierungsprozess*, p. 240.
25 HStAD, RA 22753: Verein für hüttenmännische Interessen, Protokoll der 220. Sitzung – Beschränkung der Kirmessfeiern, 22 July 1896.
26 HStAD, RD 30476: Monatsschrift der Handelskammer zu Düsseldorf, June 1908.
27 *Kölnische Zeitung*, 22 July 1897.
28 HStAD, RD 30476: Monatsschrift der Handelskammer zu Düsseldorf, June 1908.
29 HStAD, RA 22755: Aachen Bürgermeister, Beschränkung der Aachener Kirmes, 17 November 1908; Lucas, *Arbeiterradikalismus*.
30 HStAD, RD 8950: DH, 14 March 1891.
31 HStAD, RA 22753: Verein für hüttenmännische Interessen, Protokoll der 220. Sitzung – Beschränkung der Kirmessfeiern, 22 July 1896.
32 HStAD, RD 8950: DH, 14 March 1891.
33 P. Stearns, *Lives of Labour* (London: Croom Helm, 1975), pp. 241–2, 247.
34 S. H. F. Hickey, 'The Shaping of the German Labour Movement', pp. 223–8.
35 HStAD, RD 8950: Betrifft Beschränkung bezw. Verlegung der Kirmessen in der Bürgermeisterei Düsseldorf, 12 December 1890.
36 HStAD, RD 8951: Gesuch der Saalinhaber um Abänderung der Kirmesordnung to RPD, 20 August 1896.
37 HStAD, RD 9003: Essen publicans to RPD re: Kirmesse und Tanzlustbarkeiten, 1 September 1896.
38 StAD, III 5452: Beilage zur *Rheinisch-Westfälischen Wirte-Zeitung*, 18 October 1911.
39 StAD, III 5452: DH, 11 March 1911.
40 Ibid.: Zentral-Verband der Handelsleute und Berufsgenossen Deutschlands (Sektion Düsseldorf), 15 March 1911.
41 Ibid.: DH, 22 April 1911.
42 Ibid.: Table showing permitted fairs, 3 August 1911.
43 Ibid.: Beilage zur *Rheinisch-Westfälischen Wirte-Zeitung*, 18 October 1911.
44 Ibid.: Presidents of local shooting associations to Düsseldorf Bürgermeister, 17 November 1911.
45 Ibid.: DH, 11 December 1920.
46 Lucas, *Arbeiterradikalismus*, p. 104.
47 Ibid., pp. 105–6.
48 HStAD, RK 8074: Köln Polizei Präsident, 5 December 1905; StAD, II 1314: Carnevals Comité zur Holzmühle, 1844; StAD, III 5772: Carnevals-Verein

Narrische Auslese, January 1902; F-J. Grosshennrich, *Die Mainzer Fastnachtvereine. Geschichte, Funktion, Organisation und Mitgliedstruktur* (Wiesbaden: Franz Steiner, 1980), pp. 195–206.

49 StAD II 1314: Vereinigten evangelischen Vereine, 17 January 1904.

50 On the 'world upside-down' theory of carnival see M. Bakhtin, *Rabelais and his World* (1965, repr. Bloomington, Ind.: Indiana University Press, 1984); Burke, *Popular Culture in Early Modern Europe*; R. Scribner, 'Reformation, Karneval and the World Upside-down', in *Social History*, vol. 3 (1978), pp. 303–29; N. Schindler, 'Karneval, Kirche und die Verkehrte Welt. Zur Funktion der Lachkultur im 16. Jahrhundert', in *Jahrbuch für Volkskunde*, vol. 7 (1984), pp. 9–57.

51 StAD, III 5770: Polizeiverordnungen 1877.

52 Ibid.: Polizeiverordnungen 1880.

53 G. Korff, 'Heraus zum 1 Mai', pp. 204–81. Cf. M. Seippel, *Das Maiabendfest in Bochum* (Bochum: Rheinisch-Westfälische Verlags-Anstalt, 1881).

54 StAB, B 90: *Bochumer Zeitung*, 28 July 1900.

55 StAB, B 91: Oberbürgermeister Bochum to RPA re: Schützenfest, 25 July 1910.

56 StAD, III 1050: Berlin, Die Feier des 100 jr. Geburtstages Wilhelm des Großens, 1 January 1897.

57 HStAD, RD 8996: Die Feier des hundertjährigen Geburtstages seiner Majestät Kaiser Wilhelm des Großens, 17 March 1897.

58 StAD, III 1050: Comité für die Verbreitung des Festlichkeiten, 13 February 1897.

59 Tenfelde notes that the organized working class and Catholics absented themselves from the Kaiser's birthday celebrations; see K. Tenfelde, 'Mining Festivals in the Nineteenth Century', in *Journal of Contemporary History*, vol. 13 (1978), p. 393. Cf. W. Blessing, 'The Cult of the Monarchy. Political Loyalty and the Workers' Movement in Imperial Germany', in *Journal of Contemporary History*, vol. 13 (1978), pp. 357–75.

60 HStAD, RD 8955: *Düsseldorfer Volksblatt* no. 239, 1876 (no precise date available).

61 MS, 31 March 1885.

62 G. Mosse, *Nationalization of the Masses* (New York: Fertig, 1975), pp. 92–3.

63 *Düsseldorfer Volkszeitung*, 29 March 1905.

64 StAB, B 90: *Bochumer Volksblatt*, 3 August 1907.

65 *Dortmunder Mai Zeitung*, 1 May 1892.

66 Ibid.

67 Liebknecht cited by P. Friedemann, 'Anspruch und Wirklichkeit der Arbeiterkultur 1891–1933', in Petzina (ed.), *Fahne, Fäuste, Korper*, p. 101.

68 V. Lidtke, *The Alternative Culture: Socialist Labor in Imperial Germany* (New York: Oxford University Press, 1985), p. 76.

69 Friedemann, 'Anspruch und Wirklichkeit', p. 103.

70 Nolan, *Social Democracy and Society*, pp. 137–8.

71 StAD, III 6923: public meeting of Düsseldorf Sozialdemokratische Volksverein, 1 May 1897.

72 StAD, III 6924: Düsseldorf SPD public meeting on subject of 'Der 1 Mai und das arbeitende Volk', 3 May 1899; III 6925: 3 May 1901.

73 P. Friedemann, 'Feste und Feiern in Rheinisch-westfälischen Industriegebiet', in Huck (ed.), *Sozialgeschichte der Freizeit*, p. 172.

74 Ibid. p. 172. See B. Kehm, *der 1. Mai im Spiegel der Bochumer Presse 1927–55* (Bochum: D. G. B., 1986).

75 *Düsseldorfer Volkszeitung*, 2 May 1910.

76 Cited in Friedemann, 'Anspruch und Wirklichkeit', p. 105.

77 *Niederreinische Volkstribune*, 2 May 1900.
78 StAD, III 6924: Public meeting, 'Der 1. Mai und das arbeitende Volk', 3 May 1899.
79 *Düsseldorfer Volkszeitung*, 2 May 1905.
80 Friedemann, 'Anspruch und Wirklichkeit', p. 106.
81 See Friedemann, 'Anspruch und Wirklichkeit'; Tenfelde, 'Mining Festivals', and the contemporary documents featured in W. van der Will and R. Burns (eds), *Arbeiterkulturbewegung in der Weimarer Republik* Vol. 2, 'Texte-Dokumente-Bilde' (Frankfurt am Main: Ullstein, 1982).
82 See E. Hobsbawm, 'The Transformation of Labour Rituals' in his *Worlds of Labour: Further Studies in the History of Labour* (London: Weidenfeld & Nicolson, 1984), pp. 66–82.
83 Lidtke, *The Alternative Culture*, p. 81.
84 Tenfelde, 'Mining Festivals', pp. 400–1.
85 P. Stearns, 'The Effort of Continuity in Working-Class Culture', in *Journal of Modern History*, vol. 52 (1980), pp. 626–55.

3

The lubricant of leisure

Patterns of consumption

The consumption of alcoholic beverages was a prominent feature of festive occasions; workers and bourgeois alike often placed ritual drinking at the centre of the festivities. Yet alcohol was as much an imprisonment as a form of escape. Although it momentarily freed one from the suffering of everyday life it could also lead to poverty and despair. On the one hand it 'created for the poor man a counsel for his distress, solace for his lack of possessions, a place in which to be happy to compensate for his lack of a home, and it taught him to forget what depressed him',[1] but on the other it could deprive a man of respect and ruin his family. First-hand accounts of working-class drinking habits confirm the existence of this double-edged sword. A number of respondents to Adolf Levenstein's social survey carried out between 1907 and 1911 blamed their reliance on drink on their social and economic circumstances: 'With deadening work and a miserable dwelling amidst a horde of children, amusement is out of the question. Capitalism destroys family life and for that reason I go to the public house.'[2] Wives and children of habitual drinkers, however, tell a different story of poverty and violence and a large proportion of crimes committed were alcohol-related.

Concentration on these behavioural extremes by contemporary observers obscured the reality of working-class alcohol consumption. Nineteenth-century critics regarded drinking as a social problem. *Die Alkoholfrage* – the drink question – was born of a fear of the consequences of changes in popular drinking behaviour. What had been regarded as the 'proper man's pleasure' was now the 'poor man's vice', and temperance movements were formed to exert some kind of moral control over those too weak to refuse the evil spirit. But, as James Roberts points out:

> alcohol permeated working-class life more thoroughly than the conventional emphasis on these drunken sprees might imply. In fact the tavern was a crucial institution of popular life and drinking an essential part of working-class sociability. Drink and the drink place thus provided not only a means of escape for those who wanted it, they

also contributed to the formation and reinforcement of important social ties.[3]

Working-class drinking needs to be placed within the social and economic context of everyday life. As well as establishing the presence of alcohol at a variety of recreational occasions, this chapter will assess the social function of drinking, the relationship between drinking and work and leisure patterns, and the importance of drink and the tavern in the emergence of a working-class culture in this period. By examining the consumption of alcohol in a variety of scenarios it should be possible to determine the extent to which alcohol and the tavern were devices aiding an uprooted industrial proletariat to obliterate reality, and at what point alcohol became a lubricant of change.

It is to pre-industrial society that one must look to discover the origins of the drink question. Far from constituting a problem, alcohol in pre- and early industrial communities had a number of vital functions; in fact alcohol was an aid rather than a hindrance in the successful completion of a variety of tasks. Alcohol consumption marked important events in the agricultural year and in the family, and helped to dictate the rhythm of work. Alcohol was often imbibed to celebrate the completion of a task such as a harvest or a slaughter. It was present at sales and markets, weddings and funerals, rites of passage and community festivities like the parish fair. Among craftsmen, and particularly within the guilds, drinking assumed various ritualistic forms and an artisan could expect alcohol to accompany every important turning point in his career.[4] Alcohol complemented a pattern of rural life in which everything had its place.

In the first place alcoholic drinks, namely beer and potato schnapps, were thirst-quenchers. Until the late 1870s drinking water in urban areas was often unhygienic and unpalatable in the absence of properly filtered and centralized municipal water supplies. Pure, fresh milk was often difficult to obtain before the age of refrigeration and even mineral water could be unsafe to drink. Tea and coffee remained luxuries largely on account of their price. Moreover, the labouring poor believed beer to be an essential source of nourishment and energy, especially when diets were nutritionally inadequate and lacking variety. Beer was often regarded as food rather than refreshment and belief in its goodness was perpetuated by sayings and proverbs such as, 'if you drink a lot of beer you will have a long life'.[5] Alcohol was prominent in household expenditure, a greater proportion of wages being spent on this than on other non-necessities, in spite of the prevailing opinion among a number of social observers that deficiencies in the diet bore a close relationship to heavy alcohol consumption.[6] Temperance organizations did try to counter the popular myths associated with the nutritional qualities of alcohol – potato-schnapps being singled out for most attention – but even within some middle-class circles it was believed that beer had nutritional properties.[7] In the early nineteenth century, however, alcohol was a universal palliative; it was used as a cure for indigestion and as an anaesthetic; it relieved psychological problems and removed inhibitions. Mothers were even known to give babies schnapps to send them to sleep.

'The drinking house', writes Peter Clarke in his excellent study of the English ale house, 'was at the heart of the social world of pre-modern Europe.'[8] Certainly by the eighteenth century the public house had become the focus of numerous community activities, masquerading as a meeting place, labour exchange, recreational venue and communications centre. Situated on a convenient crossroads or on the outskirts of a town, the inn was a meeting place for stagecoach travellers. It was also the centre for local news and gossip, a reading room and debating chamber. Publicans were always more than purveyors of wines, beers and spirits. They were entrepreneurs – bartenders, restaurateurs, hotel managers, organizers of sports and games (the public house was often the venue for animal sports) and promoters of a variety of popular recreations such as dances and theatrical performances. In the towns during the early stages of industrialization, the public house was the source of rather more basic comforts and necessities. Whereas the home of the worker was frequently cold, cramped and noisy, the public house was warm and bright. Here one could enjoy good company, eat a hot meal, read the newspaper and discuss current affairs accompanied by a measure of beer or spirits.

Licensed premises came in all shapes and sizes. Working-class *Kneipen*, often situated in cellars, and neighbourhood corner pubs (*Eckkneipen*) were furnished with little more than a bar and two or three tables. Some were no more than a room adjacent to the family's living quarters. Others, like the infamous *Verbrecherkellern* in Hamburg, were notorious for their role as a focus for underworld activities or, like the *Animierkneipen*, were frequented by pimps and prostitutes. There were public houses associated with particular occupational groups and used as hiring centres, labour exchanges and wage offices, and there were those with known political affiliations.[9] Some only had one bar, others had several bars as well as meeting rooms and dance halls. The larger towns had beer halls capable of accommodating up to one hundred customers or more, and of course there were inns, restaurants and hotels for socially superior drinkers. Their customers were almost invariably male. Drinking in itself was not an exclusively male activity, but drinking inside a public house certainly was, fostering a kind of *Männlichkeit*. Abstinence was regarded as a sign of weakness.[10] Drinking was one way of gaining respect in the eyes of one's peers; drinking rituals further reinforced male group solidarity and many taverns became a kind of working man's club.

Punctuating their drinking and smoking, customers undoubtedly sang, told jokes, talked about sport and items of news.[11] They amused themselves in groups by playing pub games like cards, billiards and skittles, or by gambling on games of chance. Card games were the most popular forms of gambling but the stakes were rarely very high. Public houses were used as betting shops, and by the 1890s automatic games machines were beginning to appear. Such machines soon became almost a necessity as publicans believed they attracted custom, especially when competition in the drink trade was at its height, but they were sharply criticized and banned in some places for encouraging people to waste their money. In fact all games of chance were strictly controlled.

Throughout the course of the nineteenth century the publican's role as a commercial entertainment manager expanded, partially as a result of prowess in this area already, but also owing to a lack of alternative premises where acts at the lower end of the market could be performed. Thus itinerant performers, musicians, singers and dancers could be seen in the tavern, and small-time theatrical companies performed there along with a variety of speciality acts which constituted the infamous *Tingel-Tangels*. Dances were regularly held in those taverns that had the space. The next chapter will be devoted to a detailed discussion of these forms of entertainment; it is important to point out here that the presence of such amusements in the local tavern reinforced its place as the centre of or focus for working-class social life.

Alcohol, then, pervaded all spheres of urban working-class life. It was not just a social lubricant but a dominant feature at the workplace, in the home, in political life and in the recreational context. And it was this multi-functional role of alcohol and the public house that distinguished working-class drinking from that of other classes of society. If we are to understand this phenomenon and assess the contribution made by drink and the public house to the development of a distinct working-class culture in the period before the First World War, then working-class drinking has to be studied in all its contexts, not simply the recreational.

An increase in the number of outlets for the sale of alcohol shadowed the early stages of industrialization. In the course of the mid-nineteenth century in Prussia the ratio of licensed premises to every 1,000 inhabitants rose from 2.5 in 1852, to 3.7 in 1869, to 4.8 only three years later in 1872, virtually doubling the number of taverns and ale-houses in twenty years.[12] The more startling increases took place in the new industrial towns of the Ruhr. The massive population increase and the concentration of the working-class in the urban centres were preconditions of the enormous rise in the number of taverns during the second half of the nineteenth century.

It has been said that 'taverns existed in Bochum like sand at the sea-side', prompting one of the town's early historians to comment that 'a large section of our population prefers to seek its entertainment with a glass of beer rather than in the theatre.'[13] Düsseldorf had so many public houses it was rumoured that you could come out of one and fall immediately in to another.[14] The inner city was once described as the longest bar in the world. Neither town, it must be said, was ever a temperance paradise. The brewing of beer was a traditional craft dating back over 400 years in Düsseldorf. As early as 1828, there were 75 breweries operating in the town, employing 150 workers, and a number of taverns brewed their own beer on the premises, as many still do today.[15] In Bochum a number of private distilleries dating from the 1750s were joined a century later by two larger breweries. By 1858, 44 innkeepers were listed on Bochum's occupational census.[16] By the mid-1860s the multiplication of public houses was beginning to arouse police concern. Between 1862 and 1872 the number of taverns more than doubled in Bochum and the surrounding district.

The 1870s were certainly boom years in the public house trade. Between 1867 and 1875, Bochum's population almost doubled from 14,700 to over 28,000, whereas the number of licensed premises increased from 95 to 224, a 135 per cent increase.[17] Similar developments were apparent throughout the area and particularly in the new mining towns. Clearly the growth in the number of public houses coincided with the transformation of Bochum and its hinterland into an industrial metropolis, a point remarked upon by the Minister of the Interior in 1878: 'it has been revealed that in certain districts [of the Ruhr] with a dense working-class population, the population increase has been considerably surpassed by the increase of licensed premises.'[18] By the 1870s, however, the massive population expansion easily outstripped public-house provision and by the end of the century conditions were positively crowded, with a ratio of 363 persons to every one drinking establishment in 1898.[19] In Düsseldorf too there were more than 300 persons to every pub after 1882, thus underlining the fact that the fears of the authorities were not strictly justified by the statistics.[20]

If demand alone had determined public-house provision in this period then the number of taverns would have continued to increase until demand was satisfied, but all establishments had to apply for a licence before alcohol could be sold. Licensing became progressively stricter as municipal authorities and the police realized that this was one way of controlling the proliferation of taverns. An imperial decree of 1879 determined that licenses should only be granted if local need warranted another licensed establishment.[21] The decree was punctually applied in Bochum with effect from 1 October 1879, with the consequence that the number of new licences awarded decreased as licensing inspectors rejected applications on the grounds that the number of public houses corresponded with the needs of the public.[22] Far from regulating the licensing procedure, the decree allowed some rather arbitrary decisions to be taken in accordance with the prejudices of the licensing authorities. As late as 1900, the November meeting of the Bochum licensing committee, faced with more than 100 new applications, decided after many hours of discussion 'that the 336 public houses which exist in the Bochum district have been more than adequate to meet the existing demand for a long time and in no part of the district is there an appreciable need for the erection of new public houses.'[23] The decree was implemented in Düsseldorf too, where it clearly had some effect. In the ten years before the decree, the number of public houses in the city had increased from 377 in 1869 to 616 in 1879, or one for every 148 inhabitants.[24] Only six months later, after the introduction of the stricter laws, the number had decreased to 469, that is one for every 228 inhabitants. The decree was similarly effective throughout Germany.[25]

It is by no means clear whether the steady readjustment of public house-to-inhabitant ratios, which continued until the turn of the century, was due solely to stricter licensing procedures or to a gradual shift in the nature of the demand for alcohol as well. One suspects, however, that the reaction of the authorities in implementing the 1879 law roughly coincided with the early stages of a fundamental change in drinking habits among the industrial working-class, most notably in the decline of so-called instrumental drinking (estimated to have begun in the 1880s), along with the decline in popularity of schnapps and the concurrent rise of beer. On the other hand, the drink trade was not monopolized by licensed pubs. Until the 1890s the sale of bottled beer was not dependent on such a licence. It was sold in public houses but more often from the off-sales section, from booths at the side of the road and by private individuals. Bottled-beer sellers were frequently able to sell their liquor more cheaply than their licensed competitors could, the absence of overheads and a steady turnover facilitating a quick profit, and they sold to a wider market too. Women and children bought bottled beer along with the groceries from the corner shop and factory workers purchased it literally at the factory gates.

Bottled-beer sellers were anathema to the authorities precisely because of their freedom of trade and mobility. Owners of public houses, on the other hand, were regularly forced to defer to the decisions of the licensing committee who frequently refused to grant or renew a licence on the grounds that the proposed establishment was too close to an industrial or working-class residential area. The location of drinking establishments was directly related to their function; the clustering of taverns around transport centres and market places are clear examples. In Bochum the two major public spaces which were regularly used as market places, the Moltkeplatz and the Kaiser-Wilhelm Platz, had a tavern on every corner. Public houses also occupied all the available street corners in a town, particularly on busy thoroughfares. Most controversial, however, were those clusters of taverns near and on the major routes to industrial sites. Publicans were keen to capitalize on the thirsty factory labourers and mineworkers, recognizing that good trade was to be had from workers drinking in their breaks and on the way to and from the workplace. Efforts to gain licences for such locations were often thwarted by the licensing committees, and in the workers' colonies public houses were usually prohibited on the instructions of the company. Thus there was not a tavern to be seen within the Stahlhausen workers' colony in Bochum, owned by the Bochumer Verein, while drinking places lined the periphery and the approach road, within easy reach of the inhabitants.

This still tells us relatively little about trends in alcohol consumption. Did the growth in the number of outlets for the sale and consumption of drink imply a concomitant increase in the quantity of alcohol consumed per head of the population? Did the industrial working class drink more in this period than other sectors of the population? Certainly alcohol consumption dramatically increased from the 1850s on, reaching a high point in the boom years between 1870 and 1874 when expenditure on alcohol as a proportion of total household expenditure peaked at 14.5 per cent. Moreover, it has been calculated that the annual consumption of pure alcohol (mostly drunk in the form of schnapps) peaked at 10.2 litres per head in 1874.[26] But these calculations are not socio-economic group specific and therefore no firm conclusions about working-class consumption alone can be reliably drawn from them. What can be confirmed is the increase in the popularity of beer over schnapps from the early 1870s until the turn of the century and beyond. The consumption of beer reached a high point in 1900: in that year almost 119 litres per head were drunk throughout the Reich.

There is, therefore, a tentative relationship between the trend in alcohol consumption and the pattern of public-house provision during the second half of the nineteenth century. When alcohol consumption was at its peak in the 1870s, the growth in the number of public houses continued to meet the demand. As schnapps declined in popularity and beer took its place, and (equally significant) as living standards improved, the role of the public house began to change to meet these new drinking patterns. Making use of the terminology employed by Roberts, 'instrumental drinking', that is the consumption of alcohol for physiological reasons, became less significant and was gradually replaced by social drinking or psychologically induced consumption, coinciding with the rise in popularity of beer (a more sociable drink) over schnapps.[27] This trend is demonstrated most clearly by the changing pattern of alcohol consumption associated with work and the workplace.

Workplace drinking

Industrial labourers sought comfort and solace wherever they could; a flask of schnapps or a bottle of beer alleviated the physical and material discomforts experienced in extremities of heat or cold, dust and noise. In foundries and brickworks and other industries where extreme heat dominated the work experience, the frequent intake of liquids was a necessity.

Construction workers drank schnapps to keep themselves warm, while those working in dusty conditions, like miners and textile workers, believed they had to drink from time to time in order to flush dust particles from their lungs. Alcohol enabled workers to labour in conditions that would have been unbearable otherwise. Alcohol 'increased the feeling of strength, numbed the feeling of tiredness and alleviated the feeling of reluctance . . .'[28]

Officially, drinking was restricted to the regular breaks for breakfast and the midday meal. Breakfast was usually consumed on the factory premises, but the midday meal was an opportunity to venture out. Married men were often brought hot food by their wives or children, but single workers could be found in taverns and bars in the vicinity where meals could be purchased very cheaply. Local publicans who anticipated the profits to be made by trading in such a favourable location met the demand for refreshment by industrial workers, occasioning the observation of a number of Bochum employers in 1884 that *Schnappskneipen* were situated 'in a very handy situation for the worker so that he can get the necessary quantity to allay his "thirst", but also handy enough for whole bottles of liquor to be smuggled into the factory.'[29] Employers frequently bemoaned the fact that foundries and mines were generally surrounded by public houses; even 'walls and fences', they said, 'do little to prevent the craftiness of the landlords and workers' in managing to smuggle drink into the workplace.[30]

Workers were also able to satisfy their need for refreshment at the beginning and end of the working day in one of the many public houses lining the major routes to and from work. Many purchased bottles of beer or filled their flasks with schnapps to see them through the day. In Bochum in 1884, employers like the Bochumer Verein and the Bochumer Eisenhütte expressed their dismay at 'the sale of spirits as early as daybreak to factory workers and miners on their way to work', and said it was 'distressing to see so early in the morning, around 5 and 6 am . . . whole crowds of workers in these pubs.'[31] Some pubs opened especially early in the morning so as to catch workers from both the day and night shifts.[32]

Early morning drunkenness was probably rare but employers did express concern regarding their workers' fitness for the job and the increased likelihood of accidents. 'How many accidents have occurred as a result of the carelessness of colleagues who have come out of the watering-holes shortly before work?' asked the same Bochum employers.[33] The Association for the Prevention of Alcohol Abuse claimed that almost half of all industrial accidents were a consequence of excess alcohol consumption, but efforts to stem drinking at the workplace seem to have had little significant effect on the accident rate. At the Krupp steelworks in Essen spirits had been forbidden at the workplace since 1892 and after 1910 beer was only permitted outside working hours. The works canteen sold mineral water and bottled milk instead. A fairly significant decline in beer consumption in favour of the alcohol-free alternatives did take place. In 1906 over two million bottles of beer were sold to workers from the canteen, along with 421,000 bottles of mineral water and 207,000 bottles of milk. By 1912 beer consumption had fallen to under 200,000 bottles and mineral water and milk increased their share of the sales to 1,746,180 and 795,371 bottles respectively. However, the accident rate bears little relation to the changing pattern of consumption. In 1906 there were 445 non-fatal accidents recorded. The figure fell slightly to 398 the following year, but 417 accidents were noted in 1911 and 390 in 1912. The fatal accident figures are even less encouraging. Eighteen occurred in 1906, 25 in 1908 and only 10 in 1909; but in 1911 there were 26, and 16 in 1912.[34]

Night-shift workers were also criticized for rushing into the nearest pub on the way home, 'staying there until around midday and drinking away their money while the wife and child go hungry at home.'[35] The reality, however, was that workers were in need of a rest, a drink and a place to clean up and relax before their homeward journey. Miners were apparently fond of a measure of schnapps after work to protect them from catching a chill, it was said, after the heat of pit-working conditions.[36] Eventually, such pressure was exerted by employers' groups that police authorities in several areas, including Bochum and Düsseldorf, imposed a ban on the sale of alcohol before 8 am. This was strictly enforced and publicans were fined for contravening the new law.[37] It appears, however, that the law was not infallible. The Essen police force argued that it did not have sufficient manpower to keep watch on all the bars in the mornings and in Duisburg a rather ingenious method of avoiding the law was discovered; spirits could be obtained from the ships which arrived in the port during the night and so were exempt from the regulations.[38]

Workplace drinking was not indiscriminate. Drinking and drunkenness was particularly widespread on pay days and Mondays. A Düsseldorf factory inspector noted in 1876 that Saint Monday was still a 'widespread evil' among the workers of the city.[39] The picture painted by one Düsseldorf factory owner in 1883 was surely exaggerated but his view found widespread assent among the employers of the region:

> After each pay day a substantial part of the wages received finds its way into the *Schnapskneipe*; the women constantly complain that they only get a fraction of the wages from their husbands . . . in the pub until late at night and sometimes until early morning after the shift change there is carousing, uproar, insults against the employers, complaints about the low wages and debates about how they can be raised.[40]

As late as 1909, the Düsseldorf authorities were considering the implementation of restrictions on the sale of alcohol on pay days, following the example of their colleagues in Upper Silesia, where the Polish population was, according to the authorities in the area, given to frequent 'alcoholic excess'.[41] After considerable consultations, however, similar measures were not introduced in Düsseldorf, as wages were paid on a number of different days throughout the area and, according to the Essen authorities, it would only induce workers who 'cannot go without alcohol' to take the drink home instead.[42] Some employers changed the customary pay day from a Saturday to a weekday, but this only encouraged workers to indulge in longer drinking bouts.[43] Of course the problem was even more intractable when workers actually received their wages in the public house, as was common in the construction trade. Building workers were often forced to sit and languish for hours in a public house waiting for their money to be delivered while the publican plied them with drink.[44] Had the middlemen and the publican come to an arrangement, one wonders, to keep the workers waiting in the pub for as long as possible, as Brian Harrison suggests was common in England?[45]

Drinking incorporated a social dimension too. 'Drinking was an important manifestation of social life on the job', writes Roberts, '. . . it suggests the persistence of artisanal drinking customs and more casual forms of convivial drinking at the workplace well into the twentieth century.'[46] By and large, drinking was not an individual pursuit but a public and social activity, undertaken with friends and colleagues. Workplace ties reinforced friendship ties and vice versa. Perhaps nowhere is the close relationship between work and the public house more clearly illustrated than in the institution that emerged in the Ruhr in the 1890s as a response to the deficiences in public-house provision. The *Schnapskasinos*, as these establishments were known, filled the gap created by the strict licensing laws.[47] Although licensed premises were fairly numerous, they were often located at some distance from mining centres and their licensing hours did not coincide with the work-free time of the workers. This was particularly true in industries where a shift sytem operated. By the 1890s, most factories had two shifts, and the larger mines worked three. The incentive to found the *Schnapskasinos* was encouraged by the imposition of the ban on the sale of alcohol from licensed public houses before 8 am. The *Schnapskasinos* were set up in privately rented rooms by groups of workers, thereby constituting private clubs under the 1867 Law of Association and were not obliged to adhere to the licensing laws. Moreover, their status also enabled them to ignore the official opening and closing times that applied to all public premises. By 1894 there were, according to Franz-Josef Brüggemeier, 110 *Schnapskasinos* with 16,640 members in the Ruhr, mostly located in the north around Dortmund, Oberhausen and Recklinghausen.[48] As well as providing somewhere comfortable and warm, a place where workers could change their clothes and refresh themselves before their journey home, the *Schnapskasinos* were able to sell beer and schnapps to their members more cheaply than licensed public houses could. Moreover, they provided the opportunity to 'meet after work, to exchange information, to discuss things among themselves as well as to escape the confines of housing and everyday problems.'[49]

It is hardly surprising that these exclusively working-class institutions were attacked from their very conception by the police, local government and employers. At first they were depicted as wholly immoral establishments. The Arnsberg administration condemned them for encouraging drunkenness on account of the low price of alcohol, leading to 'the economic ruin of the worker'.[50] Dortmund's mayor described them as 'hotbeds of drunkenness, laziness, brutality, of household destruction and family poverty'.[51] Yet one could find similar reactions to a number of licensed public houses. What tended to distinguish the *Schnapskasinos* was their association, rightly or wrongly, with political organization. In Arnsberg they were regarded as 'hotbeds of Social Democratic efforts and agitation' and certainly in Dortmund it appears that Social Democratic meetings were regularly held in the *Schnapskasinos* as they were an ideal place in which to escape police harassment.[52] In 1896 the Reichstag decreed that such organizations must henceforth have a licence if they were to sell alcohol; of course the licences were not granted, thus signalling the demise of the *kasinos*. It is likely, however, that by this date the original justification for their existence was beginning to recede. With improved facilities within many of the larger industrial plants, including wash houses and refreshment stations, workers no longer needed the *kasinos* for instrumental reasons. Rather, they had become centres of working-class consciousness; they were an extension of workplace relations.

While students of the drink question in nineteenth-century Germany have been correct to emphasize the shift away from schnapps in favour of beer among the working class, far less attention has been paid to another shift in consumption patterns. Beginning around the turn of the century and gaining in momentum in the years before the outbreak of war in 1914, there was a gradual decline in the consumption of alcohol in favour of non-alcoholic beverages like mineral and soda water, lemonade and coffee. In the 1890s improved chemical analysis techniques and the establishment of hygiene institutes led to much tougher enforcement of laws regulating the purity of water and milk and the sale of adulterated and unhygienic soft drinks.[53] Between 1899 and 1913 a 25 per cent reduction in the per capita consumption of alcohol was recorded. While in 1900 9.1 litres of alcohol was consumed per capita, in 1913 this figure had fallen to 6.9 litres.[54] In 1913 a noticeble decrease in the consumption of alcohol among workers was observed in the Düsseldorf district. This was partially ascribed to economic hardship and particularly to the high price of foodstuffs, including beer and spirits. However, the question of expenditure provides an inadequate explanation.

As early as 1900 the temperance associations had begun to promote non-alcoholic beverages to urban dwellers, mainly by erecting water fountains in the streets and opening coffee houses, milk booths and the so-called reform restaurants or alcohol-free public houses. However, the secretary of the Düsseldorf branch of the Association for the Prevention of Alcohol Abuse reported in 1900 that despite the cooperation of several groups in the city, their efforts were having a negligible effect.[55] More significant, and probably more popular, were the stalls set up by private individuals with no obvious temperance affiliations. These *Trinkhallen*, usually just roadside booths, sold non-alcholic drinks like soda and mineral water, lemonade and coffee as well as cigarettes, tobacco and confectionery. Since the owners encountered little difficulty in obtaining a licence they were situated in very favourable locations, on street corners and crossroads, in competition with the neighbouring public houses. This development was encouraged by the local authorities and in Düsseldorf it was said that they 'restrain a proportion of the public from visiting the public house, there is no doubt about it, observations have shown that they are widely used by workers who are on their way to work or coming home.'[56] However, it was at the place of work that the revolutionary change in drinking habits was initially effected, at first with a combination of coercion and reform, later as a result of a mixture of social and economic changes on both sides of the industrial equation.

The measures introduced with pressure from employers and implementation by the police were, until the 1890s, seen as repressive mechanisms designed to work in the interests of industrial efficiency and profit. At one time employers had exploited workers' alcohol consumption by the operation of the truck system but by the 1880s they wanted drinking, or at the very least the consumption of schnapps, banished from the workplace. Grüttner estimates that by 1904 around 60 per cent of large factories in Germany had banned spirits from the workplace, although in a number of these beer continued to be consumed since, in the absence of alternatives, it was regarded as the lesser of two evils.[57] The physical needs of the workforce were disregarded. The workers' demand for liquid refreshment had not substantially declined, in spite of the reduction of the working day, largely because of the consequent intensification of the work process. By the turn of the century, however, employers were able to provide alternative thirst-qenchers in their canteens. These alternatives had the advantage of being cheap, palatable and, of course, alcohol-free and they seem to have dramatically reversed the consumption of beer in favour of mineral water and milk.[58]

By the end of the century the production process in a number of branches of industry had become increasingly mechanized and began to rely less on brute muscular strength and energy than on skill and mental alertness. The physical need for alcohol throughout the day thus diminished; moreover, employers wanted an efficient workforce whose senses were not dulled by alcohol. Furthermore, there is some evidence to suggest that the workers themselves were becoming more aware of the dangers of alcohol consumption. In the 1900s a new generation of industrial labourers manned the factories and the mines; a generation for whom the traditional drinking patterns of their fathers meant little, whose diet was more nourishing and satisfying owing to the more regular consumption of meat, fruit, sugar, milk and so on, and who regarded alcohol as a hindrance to efficient working.[59] In the first decade of the twentieth century Levenstein found in his survey that only 5.9 per cent of workers could not do without alcohol at work, while 65 per cent of all respondants replied that they were not dependent on alcohol.[60]

At the same time workers were subjected to pressure from temperance groups like the German Social Democratic Abstinent Workers' League (Deutscher Arbeiter Abstinenten Bund: DAAB) and the trade unions, which were instrumental in educating the workers in the medicinal and nutritional dangers of alcohol and at the same time working to ensure the provision of alternative refreshment at the workplace.[61] Employers' actions too are to be interpreted not merely as measures to further efficiency, but as part of a social reform ideology manifesting itself in factory welfare measures. The provision of canteens selling healthy and nutritious food and drink was just one aspect of this. In Elberfeld the municipal gasworks built a dining room where tea, coffee, cold peppermint tea and soda water could be purchased, and in Düsseldorf all municipal employees were strongly encouraged to avoid alcohol at work. Leaflets were distributed and posters hung proclaiming, 'The consumption of spirits at the workplace is strictly prohibited'. Workers in the city's parks and gardens were expressly forbidden to consume alcohol on the job. Construction workers employed by the building department were provided with hot water for coffee; and employees at the gas, electricity and water plants were able to purchase milk, lemonade and mineral water at a specially reduced price.[62]

How are we to interpret this and other shifts in working–class alcohol consumption from the 1870s through to the outbreak of war? A pattern can be detected. The working class adapted its drinking patterns to its economic and social circumstances. The change from schnapps to beer and then later in the century towards alcohol-free beverages must not be interpreted solely, in the work context at least, as a response to coercion from above. Indeed, repressive measures saw some spectacular failures and it proved impossible to prevent workers from smuggling alcohol into the workplace if they were determined to do so. The adaptation has to be seen as the result of a decision by the workers themselves. By the turn of the century alcohol had virtually lost its instrumental function, except in backward areas and branches of industry little affected by technological advances. In Roberts's words, alcohol had become a stimulant (*Genussmittel*) as opposed to a foodstuff (*Nahrungsmittel*). Once alcohol had been an intrinsic element of the working-class diet, a necessary dietary supplement, the source of essential nutrients and calories. Now it was an accompaniment to other activities, recreational and political, and consumption shifted away from the public into the private domain.

Drink and the family

In March 1880 the Bochum district court sentenced a local man to a year's imprisonment. His wife got three months, and the eldest son was placed under supervision. The father had spent all his wages on drink, leaving him unable to feed his wife and five children. Consequently the two eldest children had been encouraged to steal.[63] This was just one of a number of cases brought before the courts illustrating the extent to which alcohol could lead to the ultimate destruction of family life. Of course, for an individual to be taken to court indicated the presence of a serious alcohol problem and such instances were only the tip of the iceberg. Drink was not limited to the male work sphere but rather permeated all aspects of family life, affecting men, women and children in a variety of ways.

Contemporary observers – employers and temperance groups in particular – had made the connection between drink and the alleged decline of the family early on. In 1853, for example, the Mülheim/Ruhr authorities observed a 'growing need to take steps against the abuse of alcoholic beverages, in particular spirits', since 'day-to-day experience shows that families are affected and fall into great poverty.'[64] German temperance groups used the spectre of the destruction of the family as a major theme in their campaigns. The Association for the Prevention of Alcohol Abuse warned of the 'pernicious effect which sitting in a bar has on marriage and family life' and the stultifying effect on the family when 'the husband regularly spends his evenings at the pub.'[65] Bars in industrial areas did nothing more than 'take the nest-egg from the purses of workers and their families', in the opinion of the Winz authorities, who went on to say, 'that so much immorality, insecurity, need and poverty and other social evils of all kinds exist amongst the lower classes is all the fault of liquor which destroys family life.'[66] However, drink was only infrequently brought into the family home for consumption there, although the appearance of bottled beer and, according to publicans' groups, licensing restrictions, increased the likelihood of this. In fact, alcohol consumption within the family and the home was portrayed as a horror to be avoided at all costs. In 1884 the Association of Publicans in the town of Essen petitioned for the lifting of a ban on the sale of spirits before 8 am, not merely in their own interests, they argued, but:

If the worker comes home in the evening with spirits, or has a keg of spirits in the cellar, so the temptation to drink at home will be massive; the only part of the day in which the worker can devote himself to his family will be filled with the drinking of spirits, and soon the wife and perhaps also the children will take part in the consumption.[67]

As I have already indicated, alcohol occupied a fairly prominent place in the household expenditure of working-class families. While there is no evidence to suggest that working-class families in Germany spent excessive amounts on alcoholic beverages, a study carried out in 1909 showed that alcohol headed the list of non-essential expenditure, constituting 3.9 per cent of the total and more than the amount spent on health care, education, amusement and transport.[68] A survey in 1907 tells us that in the Ruhr 10.6 per cent of the total expenditure on foodstuffs consisted of alcohol and food purchased in public houses, plus tobacco and cigarettes.[69] While alcohol appeared on the weekly shopping list of many working-class families, consumption over and above the norm, usually by the male breadwinner, could be economically and socially dislocative. In a stable situation the woman usually controlled the financial affairs of the household; when excessive drinking was undertaken by one or more members of the family she lost this control. Moreover, in social terms, women tended to set the moral standards of the household, but this role too was undermined when the husband was given to drink.[70] In the last resort women could be forced to go out to work in order to maintain a standard of living. Drink, then, did have the potential to disrupt family life in a number of ways; certainly a high proportion of divorce cases cited drink as a contributory factor in the marriage breakdown. In this the moral reformers were correct. Where they were wrong, however, was in the extent to which alcohol abuse was a widespread problem within working-class society.

It was working-class wives and mothers who had the task of juggling weekly income and expenditure in order to provide nourishing meals for the family. Household budgets were extremely finely balanced and a few less pfennigs in the wage packet could have serious consequences. But women were severely criticized for their failure to adopt what experts regarded as sensible eating patterns. The petit bourgeois magazine, *Die Gartenlaube*, posed the question in 1888: 'How many thousands of working-class "housewives" are there today who cannot cook; how many thousands of men therefore go to the public house, and how many of the assets of the lower classes are wasted owing to the ignorance of women in kitchen matters?'[71] Others bemoaned the substitution of nutritious foods with alcohol, but who could blame hard-pressed housewives for trying to add variety in the form of alcoholic beverages to otherwise monotonous meals consisting of bread, potatoes, cabbage and sausage? Many women were forced to keep a close eye on their husbands' incomes. Few workers earned enough, 'to get drunk and still have enough to pay the rent and feed their family.'[72] Women who were not employed were sometimes able to exert limited control over the drinking habits of their husbands during the working day by ensuring they went to work with one breakfast inside them and another to be eaten at the workplace, thereby preventing the need to visit a bar or roadside booth. If the workplace was situated nearby, non-working family members would also take their menfolk a hot meal at midday.

A woman's control over the household budget and her husband's alcohol consumption was far more difficult, however, if he kept his earnings secret. It was said that in Hamburg the dockworkers there were very unhappy about trade union plans to issue all their members with wage books. They were afraid that their wives would find the books and compare the money they took home with their actual earnings.[73] Even if a worker did hand over his basic pay, any additional income such as commission or a bonus was often regarded by the man as his personal pocket money. In order to prevent workers withholding money from the household or spending it all on drink on pay days, some brave women were prepared to meet their husbands at the factory gates to collect their wage packets.[74] A miner's wife from Neumühl near Duisburg noted, 'after the men had got their wages they were often drunk, and the wives sat at home without any money. Many ran straight to the pit and caught hold of their husbands so that they didn't end up in the pub.'[75] In some cases employers were prepared to come to the aid of women. Ferdinand Heye, owner of the Gerresheim glass factory in the Düsseldorf suburbs, paid his employees' wages to their wives. In this way, 'women are given certain control in financial terms over their husbands.'[76]

For those workers for whom a visit to the public house was unavoidable, the purchase of alcohol on credit was a common practice and one which Heye wished to see abolished. Credit purchase was certainly encouraged by publicans who knew they could rely on repayment on pay day, but the accumulation of debt could eventually ruin a family if it got out of hand. Take the example of a miner from Wiemelhausen who ran up a debt of 27 marks 40 pfennigs with one publican. His son, although acknowledging that his father was a drunkard, placed the blame firmly on the shoulders of the local publicans for encouraging the practice.[77]

The problem of the proportion of the household budget spent on alcohol was apparently one of the major causes of marital conflict. Certainly, drink could throw a family into severe poverty or destitution and placed a number of women and children under great strain; in the worst cases they stood in fear of their lives. 'My father', wrote the son of a Wattenscheid man in 1850,

'is unfortunately very addicted to drink, perhaps like no other man in Wattenscheid . . . When he is drunk he sells not only the indispensable things in the house but even the shirt off his back for a small sum which is sufficient to quench his momentary thirst for the poisonous spirit.'[78]

After ten years of marriage and several hospital visits, Therese Zimmermann of Düsseldorf appealed to the authorities to protect her and her children from her alcoholic husband. 'On the 26 August', she wrote, 'I was discharged from the Grafenberg hospital and found my husband to be an even worse schnapps drinker than before. In a drunken condition he threatens the lives of the children and myself and acts like a raging monster.'[79] In a similar predicament was Frau Heinze from Eller in Düsseldorf who pleaded with the police to admit her husband to a clinic:

My husband is addicted to drink very badly, he is drunk day and night and gives us no peace. The police have picked him up twice this week . . . after he had drawn a knife out of his pocket because he wanted to kill me and my children. We are no longer safe with him. He doesn't provide for bread or rent, only for his schnapps. He does only three days' work and drinks for three days . . . Yesterday evening he hit me and my children again and threw me into the corner where my hands fell onto the red-hot oven and I burnt myself.[80]

Unfortunately, ignorance of the wider circumstances of these cases of alcohol abuse means it is impossible to say whether drinking was the cause or the consequence of tensions and dislocations within the family. Some may have been the victims of circumstance, of poverty, appalling housing conditions and unhappy marriages. Not all women were blameless, of course, and some were equally inclined to take to the bottle, although this rarely culminated in violence, but rather neglect of the children – regarded as just as heinous by temperance advocates. Women were accused of nagging and quarrelling and not leaving their husbands in peace. 'When you are at home', answered one respondent to Adolf Levenstein's survey of 1907, – 'the wife quarrels so and makes the husband even more despondent.'[81] However, the absence of a stable family structure in industrial centres may have created a gap to be filled by the public house. The 'half-open' family described by Brüggemeier and Niethammer, which included a variety of extra-familial members, was a necessary response to the conditions in the towns and the fault of neither husband nor wife, but of economic need and inadequate housing.[82]

The cases described above concerned men from a cross-section of the working class: artisans, miners and factory workers all appear to have had similar dispositions towards drink. But it has been suggested by contemporary observers and more recent historians that unskilled and poorly paid workers and labourers were those most likely to succumb to alcohol abuse.

Apart from the more trying working conditions experienced by the unskilled, the material living conditions of the lowest groups of the working class gave rise to the great attractiveness of alcohol and the public house and the low appeal of family life. Conversely, workers who were predisposed to spend most of their work-free time at home with the family were more likely to belong to the better situated groups of the working class. Forty-five per cent of the more skilled metalworkers in Levenstein's study preferred family amusements to the public house, compared with only 30 per cent of textile workers. This tentatively suggests that the skilled metalworkers were more family-oriented.[83] Such a simplistic and rigid categorization has been criticized, not least because of the exclusion of the role of women in the family. Martin Sodor, for instance, wonders why, when material circumstances are cited as a major factor in the creation of the pub-oriented worker, the wife did not succumb to drink as easily as her husband did?[84] There is no answer to this question except to suggest that women had limited access to alcohol and to the independent means with which to purchase it if they had wanted to. Perhaps more importantly women were not subjected to social pressure from their peers to drink.

Quite clearly, women tended to be on the receiving end of male alcohol abuse rather than indulging themselves, because of the exclusive nature of male sociability and the cultural importance of alcohol and the public house to industrial workers, at least until the 1890s. Male and female work and leisure spheres were still quite separate when non-working women's lives centred on the home and the children. Leisure was hardly a reality for married women workers; even Sundays were given over to housework. Men, on the other hand, experienced a more rigid separation of work, non-work time and leisure. We have already seen how non-work time was spent in the regeneration of strength by relaxing and drinking in the tavern. Real leisure time, which was effectively limited to Sundays, was the only time when men were able to choose between family- or pub-oriented activities. As a rule women did not accompany their husbands to the public house solely to drink. The pub remained a bastion of male sociability until the last decade of the nineteenth century, when the provision of alternative amusements on pub premises became widespread and women were able to attend dances, speciality performances and the like without being labelled fallen women.

The decline in drinking was perhaps the most significant factor in the transformation of working-class social life. With the decline of instrumental drinking and the replacement of alcohol at the workplace by soft drinks came the rise of social drinking and, simultaneously, a change in the function of the public house. Drinking began to be an accompaniment to other social activities, a number of which welcomed both men and women. Dancing became very popular and was enjoyed mostly by young, single men and women, but also by married couples. Those pubs which had the

space became venues for small-time speciality entertainment and performances by itinerant artists and theatre companies; men and women constituted the audiences in roughly equal numbers. Public houses were
increasingly used for club meetings and political gatherings which,
although primarily male-dominated, had an alternative *raison d'être*: the
focus was on the activities of the organization as opposed to drinking for
its own sake. Somewhat predictably, those who had condemned working-
class drinking for its effect on the family now managed to find fault with
the emerging leisure culture based on associational life; male participation
in clubs and societies could cause resentment on the part of the other family
members, it was said, while if the woman and children too were involved
in their own clubs, the stable family unit was threatened by this diversity
of interest and activity. This aside, one can only compare the quality of
working-class family life and leisure in the 1870s and 1880s with subsequent
decades and conclude that drink, while never ceasing to be a destructive
and dislocative factor in a minority of families, certainly lost its pervasive
influence over the vast majority of working-class men by the turn of the
century, a development that undoubtedly enhanced the quality of working-
class family life.

Drink and the labour movement

Alcohol may have been declining in importance as a stimulant among
members of the working class, but for the Social Democrats the pub
retained and even increased its significance at the centre of the political,
cultural and social life of the labour movement. It was a political lifeline, in
spite of the ambivalence of the SPD towards alcohol itself. A leading Social
Democrat, Karl Kautsky, wrote in 1890: 'the tavern is the only place in
which the lower classes can meet unmolested and discuss their common
affairs. Without the tavern, not only would there be no social life for the
German proletariat, but also no political life.'[85] Kautsky's observation was
made at the end of a period when the SPD had relied upon the goodwill of
publicans to carry them through 12 years of illegality. Pubs were the only
possible meeting places when other venues were out of bounds. Pubs had
traditionally been essential recruitment centres for the labour movement,
but throughout the outlawed years the local party organizations who were
fortunate enough to have the sympathy and support of a publican (who
risked a fine or imprisonment if collaboration with the SPD was discovered)
were those who survived and flourished. Where this was not the case the
movement suffered a severe setback.[86]

After the repeal of the anti-socialist laws the Social Democrats certainly
encountered less resistance when renting premises for meetings. Josef
Zielhoff's public house in the working-class suburb of Bilk was the regular

venue for meetings of the Düsseldorf Social Democrats. The room held up to 1,000 people and it was argued that far more would have attended from other suburbs had the premises been closer to the town centre.[87] However, publicans were not always so welcoming to those of a socialist persuasion. In Düsseldorf tavern owners seem to have been particularly reluctant, creating a state of tension between the two groups. The SPD sporadically boycotted individual publicans who had been disloyal or uncooperative and in 1906 a general boycott of publicans who refused their hospitality was proclaimed, with the party newspapers publishing lists of offenders.[88] In a large city such as Düsseldorf the cooperative publican was particularly important because the party could use him to spread their message to the working-class suburbs and neighbourhoods. Although the Düsseldorf Social Democrats had a trade-union meeting hall and in 1909 a *Volkshaus*, these were located in the city centre and not immediately accessible for regular visits to the majority of the workers who lived in the industrial areas of Bilk, Gerresheim and Flingern.

Not only was the tavern essential for the politically active side of the SPD, it was also the base from which the cultural offshoots of the labour movement began to develop. Just as the non-political gymnastic, choral, carrier pigeon and cyling clubs held their meetings in their *Lokal*, so the Social Democratic associations did the same, at least until the local party organization was able to provide alternative accommodation. Purely in terms of providing a roof over their heads, the tavern had grown into an indispensable aid to the successful operation of the Social Democrats' activities. Bearing this in mind, the official party attitude to the drink question at the end of the century is perhaps rather puzzling.

The party line on the drink question was established by Kautsky in a series of contributions to *Die Neue Zeit*. His appreciation of the central importance of the pub to working-class life, however, was not accompanied by an equally sympathetic attitude to working-class alcohol consumption. In response to Social Democrat temperance advocates Kautsky conceded that German society was afflicted with an alcohol problem and, moreover, it was the ignorant, uneducated section of the working class who were its main victims. The organized working class, he argued, was alert to the danger of excessive alcohol consumption, while the lumpenproletariat, along with the 'petty bourgeoisie and the peasantry and the wage-earners who still have not succeeded in realizing their own class-consciousness, who continue to vegetate in petty bourgeois or small farmers' ideas . . . form the majority of alcohol's victims.'[89] In some respects, of course, Kautsky was correct. Alcohol abuse tended to be more pervasive among the unskilled workforce and those employed in the heavy industrial sector, a group that the SPD failed to attract. It was said that workers in brick-works, for instance, regularly consumed two litres of schnapps a day.[90] However, although Kautsky blamed industrial capitalism for creating the conditions in which the working class was forced to resort to alcohol, the underlying message was a moral one: drinking and drunkenness were not compatible with the respectable image that the SPD was striving to achieve.

In 1907 the Essen Party Congress committed Social Democrats to the 'fight against the dangers of alcohol'. Popular drinking was to be tolerated while excess was explicitly rebuked. But the party line perpetuated the false distinction between the so-called respectable and rough elements of the German working class. This fatal flaw in the SPD's drink policy was to be exposed when the party chose to confront the problem head on. In 1909 at the Leipzig Party Congress a resolution calling for a schnapps boycott was adopted; this was a policy arising from the imperial fiscal reform which increased the tax on beer and spirits. The subsequent 'beer war', when workers throughout the country protested against the tax on beer and the price increase, was a popular cause and relatively successful, recalling the beer boycotts of 1873 around Frankfurt and Mannheim when an increase in the price of beer prompted the boycotting of certain public houses, public meetings and a number of acts of 'popular justice' against publicans who raised prices.[91] The popular nature of the protest and the boycotters' sense of a 'moral economy' (the political significance of the protest was secondary) were clear signs that beer still occupied an important place in working-class diets. The SPD's call for a boycott of schnapps, on the other hand, never became a popular cause. From the outset the boycott was conceived as a political struggle first and foremost, waged against the *Junker* schnapps barons whose profits were made from the hapless alcohol consumption of the working class; it was to be a concrete enactment of the class struggle. However, underlying the political dimension was an inadequately disguised moral message; some Social Democrats hoped a decline in schnapps consumption would be a welcome by-product. The entire campaign was wracked with confusion from start to finish. The leadership failed to get its message across to those who consumed the spirit, mainly the unorganized working class, demonstrating again how the party sought to distinguish between its members and the rest of the class. Although total schnapps consumption did decline, this probably owed more to the increase in price than to working-class adherence to the boycott.[92] Schnapps was far less popular by the 1900s and did not have the same capacity to rouse working-class emotions as beer had.

While one can blame the failure of this campaign on the weakness of the party leadership and its inability to see farther than party dogma, more significant is the reluctance of the workers to alter their drinking habits. Although schnapps consumption was already on the decline, it had not disappeared from working-class diets altogether, while the beer war supported by the Social Democrats illustrated the extent to which drinking continued to play an important role in the everyday lives of the industrial working class. As James Roberts argues, the majority of workers were not prepared to support a policy that made great incursions into their personal pleasures. Moreover, the failure of the boycott reveals a fundamental misunderstanding on the part of the SPD. Roberts says, 'The culture of the working class . . . was never precisely equivalent to the values and standards of behaviour espoused by the labour movement's local and national spokesmen.'[93]

Perhaps not, but it might be suggested that the SPD's policy towards drink was indirectly an appeal to working-class women, a group that the labour movement had been singularly unable to attract to its ranks. Women were not particularly active in the German temperance movement – around 80,000 were members of some sort of temperance organization – but there is reason to suppose that working-class women were passive sympathizers with the anti-alcohol stance.[94] In addition to the economic damage and violence excessive alcohol consumption could cause, the tavern was a peculiarly male republic, centre of male sociability and intercourse, impenetrable to most women. Yet the failure of the labour movement to find alternative meeting places only perpetuated the close relationship between the pub and politics. The situation in Düsseldorf was typical. In the early years of Social Democratic activity in the 1870s women were entirely absent from public meetings, largely as a result of the law forbidding their participation (not repealed until 1908). By the late 1890s women had begun to attend such gatherings but even on special occasions they were considerably under-represented. On 3 May 1899, for instance, the May Day meeting of the Düsseldorf Social Democrats was attended by around 500 men but only 25 women. A similar occasion the following year attracted 90 women as opposed to 360 men, but on the occasion of the 1900 Lassalle festivities – when the public meeting was billed as more of a social event with a lecture on Lassalle and performances by the choral society – only eight women were present among some 150 men.[95] Even when meetings took place in the trade union house in the city as opposed to a tavern, women were present in no greater numbers. On the social side the SPD did make piecemeal efforts to include women and children, in its May Day celebrations for example, but this did little or nothing to break down the barriers between male and female spheres of activity. However, around 1905–6 the SPD began actively to address the question of female recruitment in order to shore up the socialist family unit. In 1908 women were legally permitted to attend political meetings and join political parties. This entry of women into the previously male-dominated political scene may have had repercussions in the social arena too. The moderating influence that women probably exerted over their male comrades may have extended to alcohol consumption and reflected the growing family orientation of the SPD.[96]

Local party organizations were slow in obtaining alternative accommodation for their political and social activities. Only those in the larger cities were able to afford their own meeting halls when tavern rooms became inadequate for large functions.[97] In 1900 there were only around 15 *Volkshäuser* in Germany, although this number dramatically increased to 80 by the outbreak of war.[98] Alternative arrangements which fulfilled the need for relaxation and sociability appeared only slowly. The tavern continued in its role throughout the Weimar Republic; in between strikes and election campaigns, when it really came into its own, it was a solid and stable institution which represented continuity in workers' lives. However, as Anthony McElligott has shown for Hamburg, with the advent of extremist politics and the commandeering of taverns as strategic posts in the streets by Communists and National Socialists, the labour movement's use of and reliance on the public house began to work against them. The undermining of working-class social and political culture by the Nazis in Altona in 1932–3 took place primarily on the streets and, more specifically, in the neighbourhood taverns that had long been associated with Social Democratic and, more recently, Communist political activity and solidarity. The resistance encountered by the National Socialists in their attempts to take over these strategic taverns with physical violence attests to the extent of identification with the tavern by the organized working class.[99]

Cultural aid to social stimulant

It was some time before drinking became a truly recreational activity for the working class. Until the 1890s alcohol was consumed primarily for its perceived nutritional and narcotic properties and the public house was visited for more than social reasons. The consumption of all forms of alcoholic beverage gradually began to give way to non-alcoholic refreshment in certain contexts and, on the whole, overall levels of consumption declined from the turn of the century onwards. A quantitative decline in alcohol consumption, however, is not to be interpreted as a gradual rejection of alcohol *per se* by the working class. In fact, levels of schnapps and beer consumption were probably more a response to swings in the economy, changes in working-class budgets and social disciplining than indicators of fundamental shifts in basic working-class attitudes towards drink. It is safe to say that both alcohol in all its forms and the public house continued to play an important role in working-class life well into the Weimar Republic. Alcohol became an accompaniment to other activities, rather than a beverage consumed to transport the drinker away from reality. It is understandable, then, that consumption declined when visitors to the public house were, for the most part, not there solely to drink but also to participate in some other activity. This new social function of drink is discussed more fully in the following chapters – on dancing, which generally took place in the back room of taverns; on low-grade musical and theatrical entertainment, which found a receptive and captive audience in the public house; and on associational activity, which was wholly dependent on the goodwill of the local publican. It was not until the years preceding the outbreak of war in 1914 that alternative amusements began to divert the punters away from activities based on the tavern. At this time sport, for instance, began to attract thousands; not only did it become independent of public house patronage by taking place in purpose-built gymnasiums and playing fields, but it also emphasized healthy living, encouraging the young in particular to spend their free time on the sports field rather than in smoke-filled taverns. Allied to the sports movement was the growth in popularity of allotments which occupied whole familes in healthy activity in summer evenings and at the weekends. Less healthy, but certainly the most significant newcomer to the entertainment scene, was the cinema, which quickly became the most popular form of amusement among the working class.

The fact that the public house remained such a vital institution in workers' lives right up until the Great War suggests that it was more than just a convenient location for the welter of activities undertaken by the workers in their leisure time. Indeed, it is clear that the public house helped to foster a distinct culture by playing a crucial role in the socialization and integration of the new industrial workforce. Roberts describes alcohol and the tavern as a 'cultural aid which enabled the workers to withstand social changes . . .'[100] Certainly in towns like Bochum and Düsseldorf where thousands of migrants had made their homes the local neighbourhood tavern was the centre of social intercourse and integration.

On the other hand, in creating this culture based on the tavern, the working class set itself apart from other social groups who increasingly carried out their drinking in the privacy of their own homes. Workers' alcohol consumption became an easy target for social reformers who regarded the public house as a reflection of workers' day-to-day lives. This fact concerned the Social Democrats, fearing that they would be tarred with the same brush that marked the unorganized workers. Moreover, the culture of the tavern, which was predominantly male-oriented, hindered the early development of a more broadly based culture including not only women but other social and ethnic groups as well. It was not until the diversification of tavern activities that one could really identify a working-class culture as opposed to a working-class male tavern culture.

Notes

1 G. Gervinus (1839), cited in U. Jeggle, 'Alkohol und Industrialisierung', in H. Cancik (ed.), *Rausch-Ekstase-Mystik. Grenzformen religiöser Erfahrung* (Düsseldorf:

Patmos, 1978), p. 85. Cf. W. Schivelbusch, *Das Paradies, der Geschmack und die Vernunft. Eine Geschichte der Genussmittel* (Munich & Vienna: Ullstein, 1980).

2 A. Levenstein, *Die Arbeiterfrage* (Munich: E. Reinhardt, 1912), p. 264.

3 J. Roberts, 'Drink and Working-Class Living Standards in Late Nineteenth Century Germany', in W. Conze and U. Engelhardt (eds), *Arbeiterexistenz im 19. Jahrhundert: Lebenstandard und Lebengestaltung deutscher Arbeiter und Handwerker* (Stuttgart: Klett Cotta, 1981), p. 79.

4 U. Wyrwa, 'Der Alkoholgenuss der Hamburgischen Unterschichten', in *Bochumer Archiv für die Geschichte des Widerstandes und der Arbeit*, vol. 6 (1984), p. 51. See also Wyrwa's *Branntwein und 'echtes' Bier. Die Trinkkultur der Hamburger Arbeiter im 19. Jahrhundert* (Hamburg: Junius, 1990).

5 H. Bächthold-Stäubli (ed.), *Handwörterbuch des Deutschen Aberglaubens* (9 vols, Berlin & Leipzig: Walter de Gruyter & Co., 1927–42), vol. 1, 'Bier', p. 1269.

6 James Roberts states that the energy value of alcohol was considerably higher than that of most other dietary elements, *Drink, Temperance and the Working Class in Nineteenth Century Germany* (London: Allen & Unwin, 1984), but he is contradicted by A. E. Dingle, 'Drink and Working-Class Living Standards in Britain, 1870–1914', in *Economic History Review*, 2nd series, vol. 25 (1972), pp. 608–22.

7 StAB, LA 1175: 'Der Schnaps', Commission des Verbandes 'Arbeiterwohl', Köln, 27 November 1883; HStAD, RD 33194a: Deutscher Verein gegen der Mißbrauch Geistiger Getränke, Belehrungskarte No. 4, 'Was muss der Arbeiter von Alkohol wissen?', 1910.

8 P. Clarke, *The English Alehouse c.1200–1830* (London: Longman, 1983), p. 14.

9 M. Grüttner found pubs being used as hiring centres for dockworkers in Hamburg – see *Arbeitswelt an der Wasserkante: Sozialgeschichte der Hamburger Hafenarbeiter 1886–1914* (Göttingen: Vandenhoek & Ruprecht, 1984). Also see below p. 72 for pubs used as wages offices for building workers.

10 M. Wettstein-Adelt in her *3½ Monate Fabrikarbeiterin* (Berlin: J. Leiser, 1893) wrote, 'In the so-called workers' pubs I never found a female worker.'

11 R. J. Evans, *Kneipengespräche im Kaiserreich. Stimmungsberichte der Hamburger Politischen Polizei 1892–1916* (Hamburg: Rowohlt, 1989).

12 J. Roberts, 'Wirtshaus und Politik in der Deutschen Arbeiterbewegung', in Huck (ed.), *Sozialgeschichte der Freizeit*, p. 124.

13 W. H. Koch, *Bochum Dazumal* (Düsseldorf: Droste, 1974), p. 40; Seippel, *Bochum Einst und Jetzt*.

14 H. Müller-Schlosser, *Die Stadt an der Düssel* (Düsseldorf: Droste, 1949), p. 225.

15 Ibid., p. 226.

16 Crew, *Town in the Ruhr*, pp. 12–13.

17 StAB, LA 1166: Nachweisung der Verkaufstellen für geistige Getränke in einzelnen grösseren Ortschaften der Industrie-Distrikte des Regierungsbezirks Arnsberg, Arnsberg, 6 December 1878.

18 StAB, LA 1163: Berlin Ministerium des Innern re. Verkauf des Branntweins, 13 November 1878.

19 Ibid.: Bochum police statistics 1857–98; StAD, III 5111: Uebersicht von den Gast- und Schankwirtschaften und Kleinhandlungen, in denen Branntwein und Spiritus und damit gemischte Getränke verkauft werden dürfen, 30 June 1878. Clarke has discovered the same pattern in English industrial cities in the early to mid-1800s; *The English Alehouse*, p. 57.

20 StAD, III 5111: Uebersicht von den Gast- und Schankwirtschaften und Kleinhandlungen in denen Branntwein und Spiritus und damit gemischte Getränke verkauft werden dürfen, 30 June 1878.

21 StAD, III 5116: Düsseldorf police decree, 6 March 1902.
22 StAD, III 5113: Mitteilungen des Statistischen Amtes der Stadt Dortmund – Die Gast und Schankwirtschaften in den deutschen Gemeinden mit mehr als 15,000 Einwohnern – 1898.
23 MS, 16 November 1900: 'Wirtschaften im Landkreise Bochum.'
24 StAD, III 5111: Uebersicht von den Gast- und Schankwirtschaften und Klein-handlungen in denen Branntwein und Spiritus und damit gemischte Getränke verkauft werden dürfen, 30 June 1878.
25 Ibid.: Table showing ratios of public houses to inhabitants compiled by Rheinische-Westfälischen Gefängnis Gesellschaft, 3 April 1884.
26 M. Grüttner, Alkoholkonsum in der Arbeiterschaft', in T. Pierenkemper (ed.), *Haushalt und Verbrauch in Historischer Perspektive* (Sonderdruck: Scripta Merca-turae, 1987), p. 235; I. Vogt, 'Einige Fragen zum Alkoholkonsum der Arbeiter. Kommentar zu J. S. Roberts "Der Alkoholkonsum deutscher Arbeiter im 19. Jahrhundert"', in *Geschichte und Gesellschaft*, vol. 8 (1982), p. 137. Vogt's calcula-tions refer to the quantity of pure alcohol consumed per person, per annum; H. Wunderer, 'Alkoholismus und Arbeiterschaft im 19. Jahrhundert. Kritische Anmerkung zu James S. Roberts: der Alkoholkonsum deutscher Arbeiter im 19. Jahrhundert', in *Geschichte und Gesellschaft*, vol. 8 (1982), pp. 141–4.
27 J. Roberts, 'Der Alkolkonsum deutscher Arbeiter im 19. Jahrhundert', in *Geschichte und Gesellschaft*, vol. 6 (1980), p. 242.
28 A. Grotjahn cited in Grüttner, Alkoholkonsum in der Arbeiterschaft', pp. 245–6.
29 StAB, LA 1163: Bochumer Verein, Eisenhütte Westfalen, Bochumer Bergwerks Aktion Gesellschaft and Bochumer Eisenhütte to RPA, Bochum, 28 April 1884.
30 HStAD, RD 8971: Large employers in Mülheim/Ruhr to RPD, 20 February 1884.
31 StAB, LA 1163: Bochum employers to RPA, 28 April 1884.
32 HStAD, RD 8971: Re. Polizeiverfügung, 26 October 1883, Elberfeld, 27 November 1883.
33 StAB, LA 1163: Bochumer Verein, Eisenhütte Westfalen, Bochumer Bergwerks Aktion Gesellschaft and Bochumer Eisenhütte to RPA, Bochum, 28 April 1884.
34 HStAD, RD 33194a: Bekämpfung des Alkoholmißbrauchs – Verfügung 16. Oktober 1913 – Zusammenstellung für die Krupp'sche Gußstahlfabrik, Essen, 19 December 1913.
35 HStAD, RD 8971: Verabreichung von Branntwein vor einer gewissenen Morgenstunde, Mülheim/Ruhr, 15 September 1883.
36 StAB, LA 1168: Stratmann licence application, November 1886.
37 HStAD, RD 8971: Nachweisung über die auf Grund der Polizeiverordnung vom 16. 12. 1884 festgesetzten gerichtlich erkannten Strafen, 24 September 1884.
38 Ibid.: Den Erlass einer Bezirks Polizei Verordnung wegen Verbot der Aus-schankes von Schnaps in den Morgenstunden von 5 bis 8 Uhr betreffend, Essen, 3 November 1883. HStAD, RD 8972: Düsseldorf police, 14 August 1889. Cf. Lucas, on the function of alcohol at work in Hamborn and Remscheid, *Arbeiterradikalismus*, pp. 96–8.
39 J. Roberts, 'Drink and Industrial Work Discipline in Nineteenth Century Germany', in *Journal of Social History*, vol. 15 (1982), p. 30.
40 W. Martius, *Der Kampf gegen den Alkoholmissbrauch. Mit besonderer Berücksichti-gung des Deutschen Vereins gegen den Missbrauch geistiger Getränke* (Halle: Strien, 1884), cited in M. Hübner, *Zwischen Alkohol und Abstinenz. Trinksitten und Alkoholfrage im deutschen Proletariat bis 1914* (Berlin: Dietz, 1988), p. 65.

41 HStAD, RD 8973: Beschränkung an Lohntagen, Düsseldorf, 12 October 1909.
42 Ibid.: Schankbeschränkung an Lohntagen, Essen, 12 October 1909.
43 Roberts, 'Drink and Industrial Work Discipline', p. 31.
44 StAD, III 5112: RPD, 7 November 1889.
45 Harrison, *Drink and the Victorians*, p. 57.
46 Roberts, 'Drink and Industrial Work Discipline', p. 27.
47 The only discussions of the *Schnapskasinos* are the articles by F-J. Brüggemeier and L. Niethammer, 'Schlafgänger, Schnapskasinos und Schwerindustrielle Kolonie. Aspekte der Arbeiterwohnungsfrage im Ruhrgebiet vor dem Ersten Weltkrieg', in J. Reulecke and W. Weber (eds), *Fabrik, Familie, Feierabend* (Wuppertal: Hammer, 1978), pp. 135–76, and K-M. Mallman, 'Saufkasinos und Konsumvereine', in *Der Anschnitt*, vol. 32 (1980), pp. 200–6.
48 Brüggemeier, *Leben vor Ort*, p. 145; StAD, III 5112: RPD, re. Schnapskasinos, 3 August 1895.
49 Brüggemeier, *Leben vor Ort*, p. 144.
50 StAD, III 5112: RPD, re. Schnapskasinos, 3. 8. 1895.
51 Brüggemeier, *Leben vor Ort*, p. 145; Mallman, 'Saufkasinos und Konsumvereine', p. 204.
52 StAD, III 5112: RPD, re. Schnapskasinos, 3 August 1895.
53 On the purification of the water supply see R. J. Evans' account of the cholera epidemic in Hamburg and the measures subsequently taken by municipal authorities in his *Death in Hamburg* (Oxford: Clarendon, 1987).
54 Roberts, 'Drink and Industrial Work Discipline', p. 31.
55 HStAD, RD 8973: Verein gegen den Mißbrauch geistige Getränke, Düsseldorf, 22 October 1900.
56 StAD, III 5114: 2. Polizeibezirk Düsseldorf – Trinkhallen, 16 October 1905; StAD, III 5115: Nachweisung der in der Polizeibezirken am 1. Januar 1911 vorhandenen Wirtschaften etc., Essen, 1911.
57 M. Grüttner, 'Alkoholkonsum in der Arbeiterschaft', p. 244.
58 HStAD, RD 33194a: Bekämpfung des Alkohlmißbrauchs – Verfügung 16. 10. 1913 – Zusammenstellung für die Krupp'sche Gußstahlfabrik, 19 December 1913.
59 Grüttner, 'Alkoholkonsum in der Arbeiterschaft', p. 273.
60 Levenstein, *Die Arbeiterfrage*, p. 247.
61 J. Roberts, *Drink, Temperance and the Working Class*, p. 89.
62 HStAD, RD 38987: RPD to Minister des Innerns Berlin re. Bekämpfung des Alkoholmißbrauchs im Regierungsbezirk Düsseldorf, 14 January 1912.
63 MS, 22 March 1880.
64 HStAD, RD 8971: Mülheim/Ruhr, 24 February 1853.
65 StAD, III 5113: Verein gegen den Mißbrauch geistiger Getränke, Düsseldorf, 'Ein Krebsschaden am Deutschen Volkskörper', *Bürger Zeitung*, 12 October 1900.
66 StAB, LA 1163: Gastwirtschaftsgewerbe, Winz, 4 May 1883.
67 HStAD, RD 8971: Petition um Wiederaufhebung der Regierungs-Polizei Verordnung vom 26. 2. 1884 (Verbot zur Verkauf des Branntweins vor 8am), 26 February 1884.
68 Roberts, 'Drink and Working-Class Living Standards', pp. 78–9.
69 K. Pechartscheck, 'Die Veränderung der Lebenshaltung und ihrer Kosten bei deutschen Bergarbeiterfamilien in den Jahren 1876–1912' (dissertation, University of Freiburg, 1933), p. 61.
70 Cf. E. Roberts, *A Woman's Place. An Oral History of Working-Class Women, 1890–1940* (Oxford: Blackwell, 1984), p. 112.

71 *Die Gartenlaube*, 1888, cited in F. Dröge and T. Krämer-Badoni, *Die Kneipe* (Frankfurt am Main: Suhrkamp 1987), p. 105.

72 P. and R. Knight, *A Very Ordinary Life* (Vancouver, 1974), cited in J. Fout, 'The Woman's Role in the German Working-Class Family in the 1890s from the Perspective of Women's Autobiographies', in Fout (ed.), *German Women in the Nineteenth Century* (London: Holmes & Meier, 1984), p. 307. A similar tension between housekeeping and expenditure on drink was present in English working-class families, as shown by E. Ross, 'Survival Networks: Women's Neighbourhood Sharing in London before World War One', in *History Workshop*, vol. 15 (1983), pp. 4–27, especially pp. 7, 16.

73 Grüttner, 'Alkoholkonsum in der Arbeiterschaft', p. 256.

74 M. T. W. Bromme, *Lebensgeschichte eines modernen Fabrikarbeiters* (Jena: Diederichs, 1905), p. 249.

75 Duisburg Autorenkollektiv, *'Und vor Allen Dingen das is "Wahr!"' Eindrücke und Erfahrungen aus der Filmarbeit mit alten Menschen im Ruhrgebiet* (Duisburg Autorenkollektiv, 1979), p. 120.

76 HStAD, RD 8971: Glasfabrik Gerresheim, Düsseldorf, 19 December 1885.

77 StAB, LA 1168: Gesuch des Bergarbeiters H. Hulsemann junior mit der ganz ergebensten bitte um Abstellung nebenstehender Angaben, Wiemelhausen, 20 January 1889.

78 StAB, LA 1175: Wattenscheid, 1 November 1850.

79 StAD, III 4778: Frau Joseph Zimmermann (b. Therese Brebach) to Düsseldorf Oberbürgermeister, 11 December 1901.

80 StAD, II 1361: Frau Heinze to RPD regarding August Heinze, Trunkenbolde, 1 November 1911.

81 Levenstein, *Die Arbeiterfrage*, p. 248.

82 On the 'half-open' family structure see Brüggemeier and Niethammer, 'Schlafgänger, Schnapskasinos und Schwerindustrielle Kolonie'; F-J. Brüggemeier and L. Niethammer, 'Wie wohnten Arbeiter im Kaiserreich?' in *Archiv für Sozialgeschichte*, vol. 16 (1976), pp. 61–134; and Dröge and Krämer-Badoni, *Die Kneipe*, p. 106.

83 Levenstein, *Die Arbeiterfrage*, p. 270 and p. 282.

84 M. Sodor, *Hausarbeit und Stammtischsozialismus. Arbeiterfamilie und Alltag im Deutschen Kaiserreich* (Giessen: Focus, 1980), p. 54.

85 K. Kautsky, 'Der Alkoholismus und seiner Bekämpfung', in *Die Neue Zeit*, vol. 9 (1891), p. 107.

86 StAD, III 6918: Düsseldorf, 18 March 1891.

87 Nolan, *Social Democracy and Society*, pp. 128–9.

88 For example, see *Niederrheinische Volkstribune* on the boycott of 'Neue Welt', 11 February 1895.

89 Kautsky, 'Der Alkoholismus', p. 115.

90 Hübner, *Zwischen Alkohol und Abstinenz*, p. 98.

91 L. Machtan and R. Ott, '"Batzebier!" Ueberlegungen zur sozialen Protestbewegung in den Jahren nach der Reichsgründung am Beispiel der süddeutschen Bierkrawalle vom Frühjahr 1873', in H. Volkmann and J. Bergmann (eds), *Sozialer Protest* (Opladen: Westdeutscher Verlag, 1984), pp. 128–66. Also E. Turk, 'The Great Berlin Beer Boycott of 1894', in *Central European History*, vol. 15 (1982), pp. 377–97.

92 See J. Roberts, 'Drink and the Labour Movement: the Schnapps Boycott of 1909', in R. J. Evans (ed.), *The German Working Class*, pp. 80–107, and Roberts' *Drink, Temperance and the Working Class*.

93 Roberts, 'Drink and the Labour Movement', p. 101.

94 Roberts, *Drink, Temperance and the Working Class*, p. 61. On the involvement of middle-class women in the temperance campaign see E. Meyer-Renschhausen, *Weibliche Kultur und Soziale Arbeit* (Frankfurt am Main: Böhlau, 1990), especially ch. 3.

95 StAD, III 6923, 6924, 6925: Sozialdemokratischer Wahlverein, Düsseldorf 1896–1903.

96 See R. J. Evans, 'Politics and the Family: Social Democracy and the Working-Class Family in Theory and Practice before 1914', in R. J. Evans and W. R. Lee (eds), *The German Family* (London: Croom Helm, 1981), pp. 256–88.

97 W. Niess, 'Von Arbeitervereinslokalen zu den Volkshäusern (1848–1933)', in *Hessische Blätter für Volks-und Kulturforschung*', vol. 16 (1984), pp. 141–56.

98 Grüttner, 'Alkoholkonsum in der Arbeiterschaft', p. 253.

99 A. McElligott, 'Street Politics in Hamburg', in *History Workshop*, vol. 16 (1983), pp. 83–90. See also E. Rosenhaft, '*Beating the Fascists? The German Communists and Political Violence 1929–1933* (Cambridge: Cambridge University Press, 1983).

100 Roberts, 'Der Alkoholkonsum deutscher Arbeiter', p. 221.

4

From the street to the stage

Street entertainment

The industrial towns of the nineteenth century are often portrayed as cultural wastelands, the everyday monotony punctuated only by occasional high points like the festivals described in Chapter 2 or by frequent bouts of alcoholic stupor. In reality the towns were magnets for every kind of entertainment imaginable. Street musicians rubbed shoulders with hypnotists and escapologists. Singers and comedians found audiences in the hastily improvised music halls. Circuses were frequent visitors and one could guarantee finding a public dance somewhere virtually every night of the week. In this chapter we shall pursue the progress of organized amusements from their spontaneous street origins, via the improvised tavern music and dance halls, to the sophisticated theatres and ballrooms of the prewar years.

Düsseldorf was proud to possess one of the earliest cabarets in Germany and advertised itself as a *Kunststadt*. Bochum also established a name for itself in the classical theatre tradition. The Bochum Stadttheater was, and still is, widely acknowledged as one of the foremost provincial theatres in the country. But these were symbols of civic pride rather than venues for truly popular entertainment. Behind the classical facade stood a host of grassroots entertainers waiting to step into the limelight: organ-grinders, street musicians, jugglers and acrobats; itinerant family theatres, tumblers and gymnastic troupes; travelling menageries and circuses; hypnotists, spiritualists; a plethora of side-show owners with their card tricks and games of chance; strange and wonderful creatures, learned animals and freaks; waxworks and scientific discoveries. Then there were the performers who entertained audiences in the back-room tavern theatres, the *Tingel-Tangels* and *Polkakneipen* as these establishments were known. Throughout the eighteenth and early nineteenth centuries, these artistes made a living by travelling the country, performing at a moment's notice in a market square, following the fairs and festivals and entertaining the clientele of a tavern. By the second half of the nineteenth century they were a permanent feature of German urban life. They were the backbone of popular entertainment in the imperial period.

Their predecessors were the medieval wandering minstrels, professional entertainers patronized and admired for their art by the European nobility. There were also the less well-respected showmen, 'the ballad singers, bear-wards, buffoons, charlatans, clowns, comedians, fencers, fools, hocus-pocus men, jugglers' and so on, who wandered across early modern Europe.[1] Their stage was usually the street, and by the early to mid-nineteenth century musicians and performers were competing with the hustle and bustle of city life to entertain the urban populace. Organ-grinders were a permanent feature of many towns – at least 64 of them roamed the streets of Düsseldorf in the 1880s – and a large proportion of them had taken to their trade as a result of illness or injury that prevented them from gaining secure employment.[2] There is every reason to believe that the working class regarded street entertainers favourably. The latter had been part of a rural popular culture and thus were familiar to the early industrial migrant workers, who may also have sympathized with the plight of many of these involuntary descendants from their own ranks; indeed, it was suggested that the working class was quite likely to dip into meagre wages to find a few pfennigs for the itinerant musicians.[3]

There is little evidence to support the assertion of the bourgeois *Düssel-dorfer Anzeiger* that these street musicians were workshy. Their musical ability was also frequently criticized but such comments provided a smokescreen for the real concern of society's more fortunate groups. Space was at a premium in the increasingly crowded and noisy industrial towns and the streets were beginning to be regarded as threatening and dangerous by the new elite. Public performances created a disturbance. A crowd of onlookers would sometimes gather, blocking the passage of passers-by. At a time when the urban bourgeoisie was retreating into private clubs, it resented working-class domination of the streets that it had formerly controlled. From the 1860s on the police were empowered to limit the number of street entertainers. Permits were awarded less frequently. Some local authorities only licensed certain categories of performer, others restricted street entertainment to designated days in an attempt to control one manifestation of popular culture that appeared incongruous in the urban environment. The attempt to eradicate street entertainment was just one expression of a more fundamental transformation of public space in the new urban centres. Just as the gentry maintained its power over land in the country by the enclosure movement, so in the towns it attempted to retain control of the streets by introducing laws to cleanse them of undesirable elements.[4]

The gradual suppression of itinerant street entertainment signalled a number of changes within the popular entertainment scene as a whole. The first was a movement away from the streets into more private, enclosed spaces. The classless entertainment of the streets now became class-specific by appearing in ale-houses and taverns catering only to one sector of the population. And although the fairs remained a showcase for the variety of entertainment on offer, the fairground itself was increasingly dominated by commercial tradespeople and mechanical amusements. Musical and theatrical acts, as well as freaks, animals and so on, retreated to the public houses in the vicinity, encouraged by the publicans but perhaps also by the absence of a fairground fee. As a consequence of the move indoors individual entertainers began to surrender control of their own movements and their own acts to the new entertainment entrepreneurs, the publicans. Commercial considerations meant that artistes were booked at times and for acts designed to attract maximum audiences. Tavern entertainment met the demands of the urban working class more fully than the more spontaneous street amusements. The location of the performance was more convenient for industrial workers and, more importantly, the timing of the programme was designed to coincide with workers' free time. The new forms of entertainment thus complemented industrial lifestyles.

Having said this, developments within the popular entertainment scene did not follow a linear and logical process. The emphasis in this chapter on institutionalized entertainment in the circuses, music halls and dance halls unfortunately conceals the immense diversity of entertainment passing through the towns in the region. For example, during the 1880s Düsseldorf played host to Buffalo Bill's Wild West Company, an oriental magic show, several anatomical exhibitions, waxworks, siamese twins, rogues' galleries, panoramas and even a stuffed whale.[5] For a time, itinerant performers were equally at home on the streets, in the market place, at the fair or in a backroom *Tingel-Tangel*. Movement between venues was very fluid. The venues themselves constantly changed their identity; one night a room in a tavern would be a speciality theatre, on another a dance hall and in the daytime an exhibition room. A remarkable degree of persistence characterizes the popular amusements of the period 1860 to 1900. Most forms of entertainment did not die with the fairs or disappear when forced to vacate the streets. Indeed, industrialization and urbanization were lifelines to numerous entertainers in that they created a constant demand for amusement from all sectors of the working and lower middle classes. This demand, never satisfied, stimulated the development of a multitude of musical, theatrical and, one should add, spectacular entertainment before the end of the century.

The taming of popular entertainment

A fundamental shift in the sensibilities and attitudes of the wealthy and particularly the educated middle class affected more areas than street entertainment alone. The vulgar and cruel amsuements of the common people were regarded as anomalies in modern urban society and a threat to public order. A vast array of sports and games was submitted to scrutiny; football and pugilism, for example, were not governed by any fixed rules until the mid-nineteenth century and frequently involved extensive blood letting. But it was the popular diversions involving creatures of the animal kingdom – cock-fighting, badger- and bear-baiting, dog fights and bull-baiting – that aroused the most ferocious and also the most intellectual criticism on the part of the educated middle class, whose vision of the organization of society was beginning to be influenced by wider intellectual movements.

The anthropocentric view of the world had been challenged as early as the late seventeenth century by certain scientists, discoverers and philosophers.[6] Man's place in the natural order was gradually redefined. Animals began to be regarded as fellow creatures, although not quite deserving equal status. Unnecessary cruelty to animals, therefore, was seen as socially immoral when perpetrated by intellectually superior human beings. The people-centred point of view which condemned animal cruelty out of a concern for the brutalizing effect it had on the human character rather than compassion for the animal itself, gave way to a more general advocacy of the humane treatment of all inferior beings, whether they be animals or the insane or criminals.[7] In response to this movement the first German Animal Protection Society (*Tierschutzverein*) was founded in Stuttgart in 1837, closely followed by Dresden (1839), Hamburg (1841) and Berlin and Munich (1842). Measures to prevent cruelty to animals were implemented soon after.[8]

The urban middle classes, local authorities and the police experienced little difficulty in suppressing the amusements they found so objectionable. Some diversions were already on the decline in the towns before verbal attacks upon them were converted into concrete action. The reduction in the amount of open space in the urban centres signalled the demise of some amusements and at the same time there seemed to be little need or desire among the urban working class to retain customary amusements and games, not least owing to the proliferation of new diversions on offer in the towns by the middle of the century.

While active participation in 'cruel' animal sports was limited to pitching one dog against another at the fairs, more harmless amusements featuring animals were guaranteed to draw a crowd. Freaks, like two-headed sheep, 'unicorns' and 'gifted' creatures – usually horses and pigs – had massive appeal. 'Nature's mistakes and aberrations', notes one historian of popular entertainment, 'had a morbid attraction for a popular mind that was steeped in superstition and avid for cruel shocks, even outright revulsion.'[9] But members of the bourgeoisie could also be found among the crowds, satisfying their curiosity and claiming the pursuit of scientific knowledge to justify their presence.[10] At the same time, the popular mind continued to be fascinated by the barbaric side of animal life. As the baiting of animals receded as a popular amusement, feeding time at the menagerie emerged as a substitute, appealing to all sections of the populace. The bourgeois press in Düsseldorf urged its readers not to miss the gruesome spectacle of boa constrictors devouring live animals at a visiting menagerie.[11] There was a difference, however, between the satisfaction of idle public curiosity and the justification of such sights in the name of educational advancement, and herein lies a clue to the more basic and immediate cause of the change in attitudes towards popular amusements involving animals. While there was indeed a perceptible trend towards humanitarianism within the educated bourgeoisie, the real and more pressing motivation for the suppression of these sports and diversions derived from a more selfish desire 'to discipline the new working class into higher standards of public order and more industrious habits.'[12] Hence the reform movement for the humane treatment of animals and the abolition of cruel sports centred on urban areas and the majority of those prosecuted under the new anti-cruelty laws belonged to the lower classes. These people did not share middle-class humane values. Their relationship to the animal world was different. Animals were functional creatures used for work purposes (pit ponies and canaries, cab horses and other draught animals, including dogs who were frequently used to pull small carts in Imperial Germany), or they were pests, or were thought of as sources of food. Moreover, cruelty meted out to animals by working people was rarely premeditated and more a consequence of the pressures of urban life.[13] It was not until the 1880s that the urban working class began to regard animals as sympathetic creatures, as witnessed by the formation of numerous small animal- and bird-breeding clubs in the Ruhr at the end of the century.

Menageries were a fairly common sight in Europe throughout the course of the century, providing the public with an entertaining diversion without obvious cruelty or mistreatment of the animals on show, although the conditions in which they were kept would arouse concern today. Menageries had, of course, always been popular with royalty and the nobility, and private collections of unusual and exotic creatures were regarded as symbols of the 'civilized' human state, representing the triumph of the civilized and educated world over nature. By the mid-nineteenth century, several German cities had permanent menageries. Berlin was the first in 1843, followed by Frankfurt (1858), Cologne (1860) and Hamburg (1863). They became a symbol of bourgeois self-confidence, a sign of the bourgeoisie's perception of its own power and prestige, both in society and within the natural order of things. Menageries and their successors, zoos, demonstrated that people, particularly educated people, could tame the natural order by means of their civilization. Just as animals could be tamed or domesticated, so too could the lower classes, by being exposed to more instructive and edifying forms of amusement.[14] Düsseldorf's zoo, financed by an offshoot of the animal protection society Fauna, opened in 1876 and was conceived primarily as being for scientific investigation, not an amusement park. However, the educated middle class never entirely succeeded in repressing the working class's desire for spectacle, excitement and elements of entertainment verging on the gruesome. The continuing popularity of fairground attractions like rogues' galleries, and exhibitions of human and animal deformities and human anatomy satisfied a popular mind hungry for novelty.[15]

Popular fascination with the wild and unknown was exploited by a more institutionalized form of entertainment in the 1880s – the circus. Circuses had existed throughout Europe since the end of the eighteenth century in a variety of guises. The earliest circuses consisted of troupes of horse riders and gymnasts who set up wooden rings at the edges of fairs and markets. The first modern circus was Phillip Astley's Amphitheatre of Arts which opened in London in 1779. He was closely followed by Franconi in Paris, with his Cirque Olympique. Germany had to wait until 1847 for its impressario, one Renz, whose Olympic Circus established itself with three months of successful performances in Berlin in 1847–8.[16] By his death in 1892, Renz had established permanent circuses in Berlin, Hamburg, Breslau and Vienna; by then, however, the Renz heyday had come to an end in the face of the extremely high costs of running a circus of such quality.

This was circus at its most extravagant and sophisticated. Equestrian skills formed the backbone of the performances and even when new acts such as high-wire walkers, acrobats and trained animals were introduced, horseback riding remained the dominant art form. Every circus had its own style. Thematic productions were much admired, but equestrian acts still tended to headline the circus bill. Circuses such as these did not reach mass audiences. The style and sophistication of the acts were directed at the upper classes and in truth it was only they who could afford it. The Parisian circuses in Berlin, it was said, attracted an audience of 'the distinguished classes, the greatest part officers, diplomats and the cream of Society', and Renz, with his standards of 'order, punctuality and cleanliness in all things', was a particular favourite.[17] It was not until the late 1870s at the earliest that the middle and working classes began to visit the modern circus, housed in a big top.

The incursion into the circus programme of acts such as wild animal training, acrobatics and clowning more or less coincided with the transformation of the circus into a popular form of entertainment. The programmes became much more varied in content; variety and spectacle were the keys to success. Circus proprietors often had to change the programme more than once if they were playing a short season in one town. Acts involving animals were still prominent, but comedy now made its appearance. The clown had been a feature of the early Circus Renz, but this art form gained a larger share of the circus programme and won greater popularity around the turn of the century. Developments in the circus, and indeed in popular entertainment as a whole, undoubtedly reflected structural, social and intellectual changes in urban society. Acrobatic performances responded to the popularity of sport, one result being the obsession with the formation of higher and higher human pyramids. Wrestling and boxing found a home in the circus ring after the suppression of public combat sports and famous fighters made guest appearances. Even pre-First World War imperialism was echoed in Busch's Berlin circus, where it was said the pantomimes were 'sophisticated concoctions of chauvinistic-militaristic propaganda'.[18]

By the 1880s most cities and large towns in Germany were accommodating travelling circuses at various times throughout the year. In both Bochum and Düsseldorf it was possible to see many of the big and famous circus troupes like the Circus Corty-Althoff, Circus Wulff, Circus Schumann and Circus Krone, as well as The Greatest Show on Earth, the American Barnum and Bailey Circus. Most circus companies only remained in a town for two or three days before moving on, but occasionally they played a longer season, as in the case of the Circus Corty-Althoff which performed in Bochum throughout January and February in 1888. The travelling circuses were able to perform in more towns as industrial centres grew in number and a transport network began to develop. They were thus able to take larger profits and enable greater numbers of people to see their shows. Several thousand people filled the seats to see the Corty-Althoff Circus in Bochum in 1900, and two weeks later people were still packing in to the big top on the Kaiser Friedrich-platz.[19] Similarly, performances by the Barnum and Bailey Circus in Düsseldorf attracted 'vast masses of people'.[20] Even as late as 1919, when this type of entertainment was only just beginning to resurface after the stringencies of wartime, the Circus Krone attracted an 'enormous crowd' in Bochum; 'a thousand-headed throng pressed in front of the main entrance to the wooden circus building', necessitating police control.[21] While detailed evidence of the composition of circus audiences is not forthcoming it is fair to assume that a broad cross-section attended the performances, including town dwellers, visitors from the surrounding area and children as well as adults.[22]

'In the circus the forces of moral and progressive civilization always triumphed. Willpower subdued the wildness of life and brought order and high civilization in its wake', writes an historian of the American circus.[23] The moral values of the industrial age were reproduced through a popular medium for mass consumption. While this may be the case – and the bourgeois newspapers of the time found little to criticize and much to praise in the German circus performances of the later nineteenth century – it is also true that audiences reserved their greatest appreciation for spectacular and dangerous acts. Premeditated or thoughtless violence had been replaced, although it is clear that the excitement engendered had not been dulled. Middle-class intellectuals had impressed their values and ideals onto the popular entertainment scene but then they withdrew, leaving the entertainment entrepreneurs and artistes in collusion with the audiences to develop a form of entertainment that expressed their values and desires. The legacy of the change in middle-class sensibilities and the urbanization of the towns was the decline of amusements that no longer complemented industrial lifestyles, the emergence of distinctly urban-influenced entertainment, and the separation of the bourgeois and working-class entertainment scenes.

Tingel-Tangels and music halls

The circus was an escapist form of entertainment that only abandoned its bourgeois pretensions to become one of the most popular lower-class amusements in response to the demographic and structural changes transforming German towns in the mid to late nineteenth century. Theatrical entertainment, on the other hand, began its modern life segregated along class lines. Thus the working-class side of theatrical and music hall entertainment can be regarded as a positive and conscious response to the demand for amusement on working-class terms, as opposed to the compromising of bourgeois entertainment standards.

The 1860s and 1870s saw the emergence of a number of forms of variety theatre specifically catering to the urban working class. Previously, towns like Bochum, far from being cultural deserts, had frequently hosted itinerant theatre troupes performing classical works by famous German playwrights. By the 1860s the local bourgeoisie was organizing a packed programme of events all year round. The influx of workers into the town, however, stimulated Bochum's alternative entertainment scene. Primitive 'theatres' were set up in the back rooms of public houses, the so-called *Singspielhallen, Musikwirtschaften, Polkakneipen* and *Tingel-Tangel* saloons (it is said that the name of the latter was derived from the noise made when the public jangled spoons and forks against their beer glasses during the refrain of a song).[24]

The entertainment provided by the early tavern-theatres was scarcely distinguishable from the acts already familiar by their appearance on the streets and at the fairs. Magicians, musicians, jugglers and acrobats, to name just a few, appeared frequently. As their old 'stages' began to disappear, these itinerants found refuge in the new establishments. Simultaneously, new acts began to emerge that were better suited to the small, enclosed spaces, the close proximity of the audience and the limited time allowed. Thus comedians, ballad singers and recitation acts began to dominate the tavern circuit. More emphasis was placed on the linguistic content of the acts at the expense of spectacle and excitement. Audiences responded to what they heard as opposed to what they saw. In the towns the newcomers were surely optically bombarded anyway; with the advance of education and literacy the spoken word had a new significance. The crucial factor, though, was variety and as Peter Bailey has remarked on the entertainment seen by singing-saloon audiences in Bolton in England, it was 'diverse in its materials, illustrating the wide resources of popular culture; the songs, dances and tricks were derived from the travelling show and popular theatre, the village green and the street, the drawing room and the church.'[25]

Gareth Stedman Jones, in his seminal article on working-class culture in London, suggests that 'music hall appealed to the London working class because it was both escapist *and yet* strongly rooted in the realities of working-class life.'[26] Performers did not preach to their audience. Rather, they reflected and exaggerated the dominant values held by urban workers. Relations between men and women, marriage, sex, infidelity and the realities of everyday life expressed with an earthy humour dominated the comic acts and the popular songs. Audiences almost invariably knew the words to these songs, either because they were repeated so often, or because song sheets were on sale before the larger shows. The success of material like this was due, in no small part, to its roots in reality. As the Social Democratic Deputy Vollmar pointed out in the Reichstag during a debate on the proposed anti-pornography law, the Lex Heinze, in 1900: 'This corruption . . . really has its origins not in works of art but in social conditions.'[27] However, music-hall songs only reflected and parodied workers' experiences; they did not advocate social change, express political opinions or put forward alternative visions or solutions.[28]

The *Tingel-Tangels* were probably the most basic form of music-hall entertainment available in the towns. They were officially described as 'performances of songs and declamatory speeches, performances by persons or theatrical groups not serving the higher interests of art or society', a description not far from the truth.[29] The acts appearing were characterized by their down-to-earth humour and lively performances. According to Hans Ostwald, the Berlin *Tingel-Tangels* were ale-houses in which provocatively dressed women sang risqué verses in an atmosphere impregnated with bad language and beer fumes.[30] They were also known to be centres of the Berlin prostitution market. From the 1870s on the *Tingel-Tangel* was regularly attacked by the government and its supporters. A Reichstag decree on 'Performances in Inns, Saloons, Beer and Coffee Houses', implemented on 15 March 1879, pinpointed the *Tingel-Tangel* as a threat to public morality 'partly owing to the frivolous or suggestive content of what is performed, and partly because of the suggestive nature of the performances themselves.'[31] Familiar repressive measures were implemented: licences were often not awarded or renewed, early closing times were enforced and the owners of concert halls were obliged to pay a hefty entertainment tax for every performance. Yet the *Tingel-Tangel* was a popular and therefore resilient form of lower-class entertainment. Despite persistent criticism and police suppression throughout the course of the century, given impetus by the long-running debate in the Reichstag over the effect of pornography and immorality on public behaviour, the Minister of the Interior in Berlin still found it necessary to intensify police surveillance in 1895. That amounted to an admission that all previous measures had been ineffective.[32]

By the turn of the century it was not so much police repression of the *Tingel-Tangel* that signalled its gradual decline but intense competition within the entertainment industry itself. Not only had the number of tavern-theatres increased but larger, custom-made theatres and music halls had appeared in major towns, run by professional entertainment entrepreneurs with exciting programmes. The Düsseldorf public had enthusiastically patronized the city's two early speciality theatres, the Bockhalle and the Reichshalle, but by 1900, alongside the newly opened Apollo Theatre (1899), someone looking for amusement was well served by no less then eight sizeable entertainment venues, all featuring speciality acts and variety on their bills, not counting a number of venues for serious, classical entertainment like the Stadttheater (founded 1875) and the opera. Nevertheless it was the Apollo that was hailed as Düsseldorf's prime attraction. It was regarded not merely as an entertainment venue but even as a virtue of the city. Düsseldorf was the first town in the region to possess such a theatre, pre-empting Essen (1901), Dortmund (1902) Elberfeld (1904) and Bochum, whose own Apollo theatre did not open until 1919. By all accounts the Düsseldorf Apollo was an impressive structure, providing the prototype for many later variety theatres. It had an auditorium the size of which had never been seen before, seating 2,000 people and including stalls where the wealthier members of the audience sat at tables. The performance area was large enough to accommodate the most expansive of acts like trapeze artistes and animal dressage.

The Düsseldorf Apollo represented the apogée of German speciality theatre. Yet, while the acts booked to perform there were famous international stars on the variety circuit, their performances were not far removed from their predecessors in the *Tingel-Tangels*, street theatres and fairgrounds. One of the most popular and acclaimed artistes to perform at the Apollo was Paul Mündner, with his cycle act, 'Looping-the-Loop', which, it was said, 'held the audience in breathless nervous tension for several minutes and at the end caused them to break out into roaring applause.'[33] The moving pictures were the only part of the programme to anticipate future developments in the entertainment scene.

The Apollo served the Düsseldorf public and also people from miles around who took advantage of improvements in public transport to reach the city centre. However, although the authorities and the Apollo directors regarded the theatre primarily as a bourgeois entertainment establishment, it appears, in the absence of any concrete information on social stratification, that audiences were quite mixed.[34] When the Apollo opened in 1899, the two old speciality venues in Düsseldorf closed in the face of the competition, implying that their predominantly working-class audiences had transferred their custom to the new theatre.[35] But working-class attendance was restricted chiefly by the price of a ticket entitling one to a good (or any) seat. The cheapest tickets, at around 50 pfennigs, usually gained admission to the gallery providing standing room only. The high cost of tickets may have been the fault of the city governors, whose demand for the payment of an exceptionally high rate of entertainment tax indirectly forced prices upwards. On the eve of the First World War the Düsseldorf Theatre Association claimed that the existence of the theatre was under threat owing to the increased entertainment tax and declining receipts, as visitors took advantage of the number of new alternatives available to them, primarily the cinema.[36]

While the Düsseldorf entertainment scene was being made bourgeois, at least superficially, a similar process was at work in Bochum. In 1897 it was proposed that a new theatre be erected to be representative of the town, and that the town should contribute towards the costs of building, equipping and maintaining it. This was a relatively new philosophy that was only put into practice after the war. The Bochum Apollo opened in Bochum-Ehrenfeld in 1919 under the direction of Saladin Schmidt, who had been appointed by the culturally progressive councillor Wilhelm Stumpf.

Bochum was an unlikely home of what was to become perhaps the most famous provincial theatre in Germany. The presence of the theatre was certainly important for Bochum's future cultural development, although too much retrospective significance should not be attached to this one institution. The Bochum Apollo never became a popular threatre for it failed to attract working-class audiences in significant numbers, or at least in proportion to their numbers in society as a whole. With a capacity of over 1,500 less than a third of the places were designated as standing room. This segregation aroused the anger of the local Social Democrats who, while hailing the new theatre, vehemently criticized the seating arrangements. The Apollo

> arises out of the spirit of the class state, that spirit which separates the Prussian railway train into four classes, whereby the people in the overfilled stalls of the fourth are barred [from the more expensive seats] and besides still have to pay over the odds so that the fine ladies and gentlemen on plush seats can travel undisturbed and in comfort.[37]

Unlike its namesake in Düsseldorf, the Bochum Apollo produced classical, serious entertainment. If working-class inhabitants of the town wanted to enjoy a speciality show, they were more likely to travel to the neighbouring towns of Dortmund and Gelsenkirchen, whose variety shows were advertised in the local newspaper.

The middle-class reformers who had been so critical of early popular entertainment because of its vulgarity, immorality and sensationalism, would have been cheered by the building of large, commercially run theatres like the Apollos since, in appearance at least, they represented middle-class values: they were opulent, stratified, organized and sensible. However, the buildings were mere façades. In Bochum the new theatre directed attention away from the troublesome working-class amusements; the town used the Apollo as a symbol of bourgeois achievement and control. In Düsseldorf the Apollo was regarded as the acceptable face of popular entertainment; it legitimized speciality as a form of harmless amusement to be enjoyed by middle and working-class family audiences. In terms of the actual performances, very little had been compromised in either case. In the words of Gareth Stedman Jones, 'this [working class] culture was clearly distinguished from the culture of the middle class and had remained largely impervious to middle-class attempts to dictate its character or direction.'[38] Entertainment in the towns had become superficially bourgeois yet, beneath the surface, specifically working-class forms of amusement continued to flourish.

The dance craze

Despite the popularity of theatrical entertainment among the working class, it was surpassed by the new craze of the urban populace. In less than thirty years a dance craze had gripped the German people. By the end of the century even the music hall, the circus and other diversions found it hard to compete. Most small towns had at least one venue large enough to serve as a temporary dance hall for the few occasions during the year when public dances were officially permitted, usually at carnival and *Kirmes*-time and at the local shooting festival (dances were not generally allowed on religious holidays). In 1877 there were already 27 taverns with dance-cum-concert rooms in the town of Bochum alone, while by 1914 Düsseldorf had around 80 establishments where dances were regularly being held; there were probably many more less salubrious, unofficial dance-halls too.[39]

By the 1870s Sunday was no longer a day of rest as far as dance hall proprietors were concerned. In fact, apart from holidays, Sunday was the most popular day for dances, as the majority of workers were employed on Saturdays. Of course, the local police tried to control the frequency of dances in their districts as strictly as they could but, in the absence of any general guidelines from a higher authority, the distribution of dance licences appears to have been rather arbitrary: restrictions were not imposed fairly and there was little coordination between the police departments of neighbouring areas.[40] Even the constraints that did exist were not particularly effective, for they did not prevent people from attending dances in other towns where the authorities were more lenient. The popularity of dances was such that people were prepared to travel considerable distances in order to attend.

Above all, tavern dances attracted members of the working class.[41] While one cannot discount the fact that married couples and even families enjoyed dancing, the overwhelming number of regular dancers belonged to one distinct segment of the working class: young, single people. Teenagers and people in their twenties had more disposable income, more free time, were less inclined to observe the Sabbath, and by the early twentieth century were able to travel to neighbouring towns in search of a dance if nothing was available locally.[42] In 1910 Marie Bernays, in her study of the Mönchengladbach textile workers, noted that while on Sundays many workers enjoyed a walk in the fresh air, 'many young lads and girls get more pleasure from a wild gad-about from tavern to tavern, from dance hall to dance hall'.[43] Numerous other contemporary observers also bear witness to the popularity of the dance halls among young people. Dancing was one of the cheapest forms of amusement. Compared with the price of a ticket to see a variety show in one of the music halls, which one could purchase for not much less than 50 pfennigs, entrance to a tavern dance could cost only 10–20 pfennigs, well within the budget of many young people.

The tavern dances had their most basic roots in rural popular culture. Dancing traditionally marked the most important occasions in the rural community: weddings, harvest and religious festivals and even pilgrimages. One only has to look at the role of the dance at the *Kirmes* to realize that communal dances were more than just the popular pursuit of pleasure.[44] Supporters of fairs and the dances repeatedly expressed the opinion that dancing was a positive force, strengthening family and comunity ties, reaffirming the collective consciousness of the group. In the early stages of industrial development, when movement by workers between towns and the surrounding rural areas was still quite fluid, the communal dance gained even more significance as the only occasion during the year when all members of the community were able to be together. It can be argued that in the towns the local tavern dances had a similar socially integrative function. They encouraged group solidarity, particularly among young people, who tended to attend dances in large groups, often from the same street or residential area. Relationships begun there between two members of the local community further strengthened the ties binding that community together. But dancing was also an escape from and a compensation for the monotony of work.[45] Dancing was a reward and, at the same time, a release from everyday hardship.

The introduction of couple-dancing, epitomized by the waltz but soon followed by more intricate dances like the tango and the foxtrot, was revolutionary in its impact on working-class amusement, for it facilitated the development of dancing as a form of mass entertainment. Traditional folk dances had required plenty of space and a group of people who were familiar with the steps. The new dances sweeping Europe and the United States were danced by couples. The steps were simple and the dance forms encouraged greater intimacy on the dance floor. Attendance at a dance was, quite clearly, one of the best ways of meeting a future partner, as Paul Göhre observed in the suburban dance halls of Chemnitz:

> In one and the other were unbridled merriment, increasing tumult, sensual excitement, which reached its climax and its abrupt arrest when, at the stroke of twelve, the music stopped, the hall was emptied, the lights extinguished. Then couple after couple would silently withdraw for a midnight stroll to the fields, where the stars are their only witnesses, or to sweetheart's doorway, or straight to sweetheart's chamber and bed. For, according to my observation, such is, if not the universal, at least the vastly more common ending to the Sunday dance. In these halls, in the nights from Sunday to Monday, our labouring youth is losing to-day not only its hard earned wages, but its strength, its ideals, its chastity.[46]

But 'the association of dancing, music, liquor and sex' prejudiced official attitudes towards lower-class dancing establishments and provided an excuse for punitive measures designed to limit lower-class pleasure.[47] The dances that swept the dance halls in the immediate prewar years were regarded as immoral, lacking decorum and even, in some quarters, dangerous.[48] The dance halls themselves were also singled out for criticism, with the publicans often being accused of encouraging the *Vergnügungs- und Trunksucht* of their working-class customers in inadequate surroundings. The small halls scattered all over Düsseldorf caused the police great consternation. They were often connected to the bar, facilitating the free flow of people to and from the drinking and dancing areas. Until the turn of the century purpose-built dance halls were rare. Bars and club rooms were used instead, where dancers and drinkers were packed in together in a smokey, heady atmosphere.[49]

Moreover, these kinds of dance halls were rumoured to be centres of immorality and vice. Dance halls were said to be thronging with 'easy women'; in Berlin, certainly, a number of tavern dance halls did operate effectively as brothels.[50] The combination of large numbers of young people congregated in an enclosed space in the evening, the presence of alcohol, and the types of dances most popular in the tavern dance halls, caused widespread criticism of this form of entertainment.[51] Middle-class fear of the loss of control on the part of the young people who might form relationships away from any kind of supervision (unlike in traditional, rural societies, where sexual licence was publicly sanctioned, or in upper-class circles, where courtships were strictly controlled) and under the influence of alcohol, was justified to some extent.[52]. Suspicions prompted outbursts in the newspapers and measures imposed by the police on the dance-hall proprietors, like higher age limits for young people.[53]. It was, of course, in the interests of some dance-hall owners to comply. They were unwilling to risk losing their licences after having invested so much in their establishments, but their boast that 'contact between both sexes, apart from in the dance hall, is completely and utterly prohibited' must be viewed with scepticism.[54] Yet there is evidence that dances acted as a kind of safety valve in the towns as far as urban youths were concerned. 'Besides there being an increase of drunkenness and immorality if the supervised dancing occasions are reduced', observed the rural Malmédy authorities, 'the young people will be induced to go to bars and get together with girls in other places.'[55]

Reactions to the working-class dance craze smack of bourgeois hypocrisy. Criticism of working-class enjoyment in the tavern dance halls paralleled similar campaigns against other popular amusements, like the *Tingel-Tangel* or the variety show. In the broader context of late nineteenth century urban society, it was also analogous to the moral drives to control working-class sexual practices (which were thought to result in illegitimacy) and the efforts to regulate prostitution.[56] Similar undesirable bourgeois 'amusements' were largely left untouched. Few measures were implemented against the notorious *Animierkneipen* where male customers were served outrageously expensive drinks by young girls who received no wages; their income was derived from tips and payment for additional sexual favours. At fairgrounds and market places, men could satisfy their frustrated lust by visiting one of the 'secret' show booths where half-naked and naked women posed or offered themselves as prostitutes. Only the morality leagues concerned themselves with this outrage. And, of course, prostitution was regulated in Germany; the women were confined to certain areas of the town, which meant that 'respectable' men could visit them without fear of being seen by their wives.[57] The middle classes' double standard with regard to the amusements of the lower classes only emerged publicly during the debate over the Lex Heinze, when the prejudiced standpoints of various interest groups were aired openly.

It was not until the outbreak of war in 1914 that the authorities finally bowed to the pressure and banned all forms of popular entertainment, including dancing. Until then, reform and control had prevailed over abolition and local police forces were only able to place limits on the frequency and duration of dances. In Düsseldorf by 1912 the police had succeeded in establishing a 10 pm closing time on public dances and had restricted publicans to holding events on weekdays or Sundays – but not both. In 1914, however, dances were banned in the name of moral regeneration and wartime prudency.[58] The authorities had wanted an excuse to introduce such measures for years and had previously shrunk from acting largely on account of a fear of the bitterness this would arouse in the working population. But the 1914 regulations, which stayed in force for the duration of the war, in no way dampened people's enthusiasm for dancing. Rather, they resulted in an even keener desire to visit the dance halls once the war was over.

The dance craze was said to be of epidemic proportions in the early 1920s, once the ban on public dancing and entertainment had been lifted in January 1920. Düsseldorf workers had suffered particularly severely throughout the war. Inefficient local government policy had exacerbated the already serious situation; inadequate rations, food shortages, high food prices, illness and disease were the unhappy results.[59] The return of some of the prewar amusements must have come as a partial relief. Throughout the Rhineland and Westphalia there was a noticeable increase in the number of dances held in 1920–21 in comparison with the prewar years. And this was not confined to the cities like Düsseldorf and Cologne; even the small parishes in these districts experienced a dramatic increase in dances, both public and private. However, this state of affairs did not arise without a struggle by publicans, dance-hall proprietors and the dance-crazy public against an officialdom which continued to act as if the war was still in progress. At the end of hostilities the authorities were extremely reluctant to reintroduce public entertainment on a large scale, constantly referring to the 'gravity of the times' and with the memory of the 1918–19 revolution firmly in their minds. The government was supported in its puritan stance by a number of organizations such as the Christian trade unions. The Cologne cartel expressed disbelief at the 'daily opening of new places where orgies are celebrated' (meaning ballrooms and variety theatres) when, in their view, building materials would be better utilized in the construction of housing and food was of more importance than dancing.[60] In fact it was a commonly held view that any outward sign of public enjoyment and gaiety would give both foreign governments and the occupying powers a false impression of the condition of the German people and economy. Few local government authorities were prepared to admit, as the Bonn government did in 1921, that it was in their interests and indeed was their duty to 'raise the sunken morale of a large proportion of the German people'.[61]

Even bearing in mind the almost incalculable problems faced by the government in the immediate postwar years – the severe food shortages, the homelessness and the presence of an occupying force – it was stalling with regard to the reintroduction of public entertainment. All its problems in controlling such amusements before the war seemed to have been solved in 1914, and it was not prepared to sacrifice these gains easily. By the early

1920s people were flocking to legal and illegal dances, held throughout the area. This new dance epidemic was not, however, merely a result of postwar frustration or a response to influences from abroad (particularly the United States), although these factors did play their part. The desire by many dance-hall owners and publicans to revive their businesses was a more decisive factor. The effect of the war and the ban on dances had dealt a devastating financial blow, and they wished to see a return to normal conditions as soon as possible.

The popularity of dancing was a clear indicator of a number of developments in the provision of leisure activities in urban areas. The proliferation of dance halls and the frequency of legal and illegal dances reflected not only the entrepreneurial spirit of publicans and businessmen but also a new self-consciousness on the part of the urban proletariat, who began to demand the provision of amusements. Dancing signalled the separation of leisure from work, it introduced large numbers of women to public entertainment and, perhaps more significant for the future, it established the idea of popular amusement for young people. Dancing was, as Wilhelm Brepohl has rightly stated, a barometer of wider trends in society. For example, new dance forms reflected a new permissiveness among the younger generations. Although the majority of dances were beyond moral reproach, they did offer young people the opportunity to engage in public relationships with the opposite sex, leading to greater openness and frankness in sexual relations.[62] On a different level the immense popularity of the dance hall was a sign of the future complexion of the leisure market. On the one hand popular amusements increasingly became dominated by organized interest groups, and on the other leisure activities were guided more and more by business considerations. Without a doubt, dances would not have been held on such a scale if they had not been profitable. In the final analysis the dance craze was just as much engineered by the fledgling leisure industry as it was an expression of a greater desire for amusement on the part of the urban working class.

Real entertainment

It is difficult to sum up the changes in the provision and enjoyment of entertainment described in this chapter because the emergence of more modern forms of amusement represented a watershed in urban working-class leisure in so many ways. The appearance of theatrical and musical performances in theatres, circuses in big tops and dances in ballrooms signalled the existence of real leisure activities for urban inhabitants. In a number of respects all the forms of entertainment described above represented a more modern concept of leisure. Performances and events took place in venues specifically set aside for the purpose. While taverns remained the primary focus of lower-class amusements, at least until the turn of the century, the diversions provided in them were organized and planned in advance by publicans as totally separate events, unlike previously, when itinerant performers appeared spontaneously to supplement the drinking and conversation. With the advent of purpose-built speciality theatres and dance halls entertainment began to be self-sufficient, adequate as an activity in itself. Moreover, working-class leisure and entertainment stepped into the modern world when performances were timed to coincide with the work-free time of the audience and participants. Festivals and fairs were extraordinary occasions, essentially involving the transposition of pre-industrial work-leisure patterns onto the industrial system. Drinking evolved as an activity transcending both work and leisure. But the new forms of amusement were designed to complement the daily routine of industrial workers. Leisure activities began to be perceived as a real alternative to work, not just a means of recuperation or recreation.

Perhaps even more significant than changes in the nature of the entertainments on offer was the changing composition of the audiences and participants. Women entered the recreational scene in large numbers for the first time. Young people became probably the most voracious consumers of all kinds of entertainment. The new leisure opportunities in the towns played a role in the socialization of these girls and boys in their teens and early twenties; they were the new generation of urban inhabitants who grew up with more time and money than their parents and whose initiation into and wholesale acceptance of the popular entertainment of the final decades of the nineteenth century paved the way for the mass commercial leisure activities of the postwar years. Moreover, the treatment of leisure as a right, especially by young working girls in this period, challenged the traditional home-based 'leisure' of the working-class wife and mother. Finally, the innovations in entertainment for the working class created an environment in which a distinct working-class culture could begin to develop, by means of the convergence of groups within that class (up until now divided by ethnic origin, occupation, religion, neighbourhood, and so on), through the common experience of laughing at the same jokes, identifying with the lyrics of the same music-hall song or dancing the steps to the same modern dances. However, whereas in England, or at least London, the music hall played an important role in shaping working-class consciousness, albeit an unpolitical one, in Germany it would appear that provincial variety entertainment did not have the same effect. No evident challenge to authority emanated from either the music-hall performances or the audience; indeed, the values expressed were what Stedman-Jones has termed 'inward-looking', preferring to parody working-class life than to question the status quo. It may well be the case that variety entertainment in the larger cities broke out from this provincial pattern, but research on the cabaret would suggest the absence of political satire in Germany, in contrast to Britain and France.[63] Further research is required to illuminate this area of German working-class life.

Bourgeois fear of working-class amusements did not abate, but while they had made some impression on the more brutal and unruly elements of popular diversions it is clear that middle-class sensibilities only made the advance of popular entertainments falter slightly. Amusements like the *Tingel-Tangel* and the dance halls were peculiarly suited to working-class industrial life styles and their popularity can be attributed to the ability of the working class to influence and guide its own leisure activities. The only popular amusements 'abolished' as a result of middle-class pressure and government legislation were those that were on the decline anyway. Their incongruity in the urban environment found them few supporters. Attempts to clean-up the music halls and the dances, on the other hand, ran up against a wall of interest groups, including publicans and entrepreneurs who had invested their savings and their lives in the new entertainment industry. Bourgeois arguments foundered in the face of the business ethic to which the bourgeois critics adhered themselves, and of the hypocrisy of their class which operated a double standard that was clear to all.

Working-class patronage of public entertainment signalled an important shift in the perception of leisure, or use of work-free time, and of the workers' place in urban society. Previously, only the public house had offered solace. The music halls, circuses and dances were an alternative to this rather insular and separatist institution. The entertainments they provided parodied reality and were escapist at the same time and they gradually introduced the working class to a more active form of leisure activity, anticipating the formation of working class organizations which placed the initiative firmly in their own hands.

Notes

1 On the early modern tradition see Burke, *Popular Culture in Early Modern Europe*, p. 94; C. Küther, *Menschen auf der Straße: Vagierende Unterschichten in Bayern, Franken und Schwaben in der zweiten Hälfte des 19. Jahrhunderts* (Göttingen: Vandenhoek & Ruprecht, 1983); F. Irsigler and A. Lassota, *Bettler und Gaukler, Dirnen und Henker. Außenseiter in einer mittelalterlichen Stadt* (Cologne: dtv, 1989).

2 HStAD, RD 8948: *Düsseldorfer Anzeiger*, 9 September 1867.

3 HStAD, RD 30474: Essen Strassenaufführungen, 27 September 1893.

4 M. Gailus, 'Berliner Strassengeschichten', in H. C. H. Ehalt (ed.), *Geschichte von Unten: Fragestellungen, Methoden und Projekte einer Geschichte des Alltags* (Vienna: Böhlau, 1984), p. 108.

5 StAD, III 5756: Oeffentliche Vergnügungen 1902–9; 5833, 5834: Schaustellungen 1886–1908.

6 K. Thomas, *Man and the Natural World* (London: Allen Lane, 1984), p. 167.

7 Ibid., p. 150.

8 The first formal laws against cruelty to animals were implemented in the 1830s: by Saxony (in 1830), Prussia (1838), Württemberg (1839).

9 R. Altick, *The Shows of London* (Cambridge, MA: Belknap, 1978), p. 39.

10 Ibid., p. 34.

11 StAD, III 5833: *Düsseldorfer Anzeiger*, 30 November 1886.

12 Thomas, *Man and the Natural World*, p. 185.

13 See B. Harrison, 'Animals and the State in Nineteenth Century England', in *English Historical Review*, vol. 88 (1973), p. 802.

14 See D. Blackbourn's discussion of zoos in Germany in D. Blackbourn and G. Eley, *Peculiarities of German History* (Oxford: Oxford University Press, 1984), especially p. 200.

15 StAB, LA 1158: Bochum-Crange, unidentified newspaper cutting, 18 September 1882, Crange *Kirmes*; followed by reaction of the Königliche Landrath des Landkreises Bochum to Amtmann und Bürgermeister des Kreises und Bürgermeisteramt Witten re. Verbrecher-Kabinett/Wachsfiguren-Kabinett.

16 G. Bose and E. Brinkmann, *Circus: Geschichte und Aesthetik einer niederen Kunst* (Berlin: Wayenbach, 1978), p. 108.

17 Ibid., pp. 107–9.

18 H. Königstein, *Die Schiller-Oper in Altona* (Frankfurt am Main: Suhrkamp, 1983), p. 36.

19 MS, 1–8 August 1900.

20 StAD, III 5837: Schaustellungen, 10 November 1899; *Düsseldorfer Volkszeitung*, 25 January 1905.

21 *Bochumer Volksblatt*, 7 January 1919.

22 See M. West, 'A Spectrum of Spectators: Circus Audiences in Nineteenth Century America', in *Journal of Social History*, vol. 5 (1981–2), pp. 265–70; *Bochumer Volksblatt*, 9 January 1919.

23 L. A. Erenberg, *Steppin' Out. New York Nightlife and the Transformation of American Culture 1890–1930* (London: Greenwood, 1981), p. 16.

24 Königstein, *Die Schiller-Oper*, p. 53. An alternative explanation given by E. Gobbers in *Artisten. Zirkus und Varieté in Alter und Neuer Zeit* (Düsseldorf: Droste, 1949) is that the name derived from the title of a well-known song, 'Zum Tingelingling'.

25 Bailey, *Leisure and Class*, p. 31.

26 Stedman Jones, 'Working-Class Culture and Working-Class Politics', p. 491.

27 *Kölnische Zeitung*, 16 March 1900, report on the debate during the third reading of the Lex Heinze in the Reichstag.

28 J. Pelzer, 'Satire oder Unterhaltung? Wirkungskonzepte im deutschen Kabarett zwischen Bohemerevolte und antifaschistischer Opposition', in *German Studies Review*, vol. 9 (1986), p. 46. For a comparison with the content of British music hall songs see Bailey's chapter on music hall in his *Leisure and Class*; L. Senelick, 'Politics as Entertainment: Victorian Music-Hall Songs', in *Victorian Studies*, vol. 19 (1975–6), pp. 149–80. For France see T. Zeldin, *France 1848–1945*, vol. 2, *Intellect, Taste and Anxiety* (Oxford: Clarendon, 1977), ch. 13, 'Happiness and Humour', p. 700 for a brief discussion of the content of the songs in the concert cafés.

29 StAB, B 328: Ministerium des Innerns, Berlin, 13 January 1895.

30 H. Ostwald, *Großstadtdokumente*, vol. 6, 'Prostitutionsmärkte' (Berlin: H. Seemann, 1905), pp. 44–5.

31 HStAD, RD 30463: Ministerium des Innerns, Berlin, 30 March 1879.

32 See R. Lenman, 'Art, Society and the Law in Wilhelmine Germany: the Lex Heinze', in *Oxford German Studies*, vol. 8 (1973), pp. 86–113.

33 StAD, III 5819: Vergnügungs-Anzeiger für Düsseldorf, 13–16 April 1904.
34 The Düsseldorf Oberbürgermeister distributed a questionnaire asking which social classes used the Apollo Theatre but no reply was received or filed; StAD, III 5873: 29 December 1899.
35 J. Neuhausen, *Damals in Düsseldorf* (Düsseldorf: Hoch, 1964), p. 89.
36 HStAD, RD 30480: Theater-Betriebs Gesellschaft, Düsseldorf, 4 December 1912.
37 *Bochumer Volksblatt*, 18 March 1919.
38 Stedman Jones, 'Working-Class Culture and Working-Class Politics', p. 479.
39 StAD, III 5872: Düsseldorf, 23 January 1914.
40 StAD, III 5872: Düsseldorf Saalbesitzern, 22 May 1905.
41 StAD, III 5872: 2. Polizeibezirk Düsseldorf, öffentliche Tanzlustbarkeiten, 10 October 1905.
42 The same situation prevailed in the United States, or at least in Chicago where, in 1911, around 86,000 young people attended dance halls every night, the boys between the ages of 16 and 18, the girls slightly younger, between 14 and 16 years old; R. B. Nye, 'Saturday Night at the Paradise Ballroom: or Dance Halls in the Twenties', in *Journal of Popular Culture*, vol. 7 (1973), pp. 14–22.
43 M. Bernays, 'Auslese und Anpassung der Arbeiterschaft der geschlossene Großindustrie – dargestellt an den Verhältnissen der Gladbacher Spinnerei und Weberai', in *Schriften des Vereins für Sozialpolitik*, vol. 133 (1910), p. 238.
44 Zeldin notes that the faces of dancers in pre-industrial France were often serious rather than cheerful – see his *France 1848–1945*, p. 656; J. M. Phayer, *Sexual Liberation and Religion in Nineteenth Century Europe* (London: Croom Helm, 1977), p. 90.
45 Göhre, *Three Months in a Workshop*, trans. A. B. Carr (London: Swan Sonnenschein & Co., 1895), p. 202.
46 Ibid., pp. 201–2.
47 Cf. Nye, 'Saturday Night at the Paradise Ballroom', p. 14.
48 StAD, III 5872: Düsseldorf police re: Apache and Schiebe dance, 12 June 1912.
49 StAD, III 5872: Düsseldorf Großsaalbesitzern, 15 July 1912.
50 Ostwald, *Großstadtdokumente*, vol. 4, 'Berliner Tanzlokale' (Berlin: H. Seemann, 1905).
51 Cf. the American Congress of Dancing Teachers who said in 1921, 'The road to hell was paved with dance steps'. See also Nye, 'Saturday Night at the Paradise Ballroom', pp. 18–19; E. Perry, '"The General Motherhood of the Commonwealth." Dance Hall Reform in the Progressive Era', in *American Quarterly*, vol. 37 (1985), pp. 719–33.
52 Cf. rural society – see Phayer, *Sexual Liberation and Religion*, p. 90.
53 In 1907 a regulation forbade boys under 17 and girls under 16 to attend public dances in Düsseldorf; StAD, III 5872: Düsseldorf Polizeiverwaltung, 16 December 1907.
54 StAD, III 5872: Großsaalbesitzer von Düsseldorf um Aufhebung der polizeiliche Bestimmungen bezuglich Einschränkungen der Tanzlustbarkeiten, 17 May 1900.
55 HStAD, RA 22753: Abhaltung von Tanzlustbarkeiten, Malmédy, 29 May 1900.
56 On illegitimacy among the working class see Bajohr, 'Illegitimacy and the Working Class'.
57 HStAD, RD 30457, 30458: Prostitutionswesen 1885–1922; RD 8935: Prostitutionswesen 1885–98; RD 8938: Prostitutionswesen 1909–19; Evans, 'Prostitution, State and Society'; R. Schulte, *Sperrbezirke: Tugendhaftigkeit und Prostitution in der bürgerlichen Welt* (Frankfurt am Main Syndikat, 1979); Abrams, 'Prostitutes in Imperial Germany'.

58 HStAD, RK 7653: War regulations in Düsseldorf, Düsseldorf, 19 August 1914.

59 E. Tobin, 'War and the Working Class: The Case of Düsseldorf 1914–18', in *Central European History*, vol. 18 (1985), pp. 257–98.

60 HStAD, RK 7653: Kartell der christliche Gewerkschaften Köln to Regierungspräsident Köln, 17 October 1919.

61 HStAD, RK 7653: Einschränkung von Tanzlustbarkeiten, Bonn, 17 November 1921.

62 W. Brepohl, *Industrievolk im Wandel von der Agraren zur Industriellen Daseinsformen dargestellt am Ruhrgebiet* (Tübingen: Mohr, 1957), p. 238.

63 Pelzer, 'Satire oder Unterhaltung'.

5

The organization of leisure

Preconditions of organization

From the 1880s onwards workers' leisure assumed a more organized and collective profile, a progression from the spontaneous and embryonic forms of recreation enjoyed by working people in the first few decades of industrial development and in many respects an improvement upon the commercial amusements served up by unscrupulous music-hall proprietors. By 1914 a network of clubs and associations had extended its tentacles so wide that to the casual observer it must have seemed that everyone was a member of one society or another and that working men in particular were choosing collective sociability in preference to family life. Of course, historically it has frequently been said that probably no other nation has shown such a sustained preference for collective activity as the Germans have. Everyone is familiar with the saying that when three Germans get together they will form an association. One only has to have a brief acquaintance with German history to notice the nation's love affair with corporatism; witness the student corporations, the journeymen's associations, the miners' *Knappschaftsvereine* and the political associations of the more recent past. Associational life was a feature of all classes, religions and ethnic and political groups. Its high point was reached around the turn of the century when *Vereinsmeierei* (clubbishness) became a term of derision. Yet despite a certain weariness (*Vereinsmüdigkeit*) detected among the German people since the 1920s and a more cautious approach to joining such groups following the Nazi period, around 40 per cent of the population in the western part of Germany today still belong to more than 150,000 voluntary associations.

The voluntary leisure associations adopted by the working class in the imperial and Weimar eras are probably the prime feature distinguishing workers' culture in Germany from its British counterpart, despite the strength of the working men's club movement in Britain. Certainly the range of clubs serving the interests of workers and their families was more extensive in Germany; by 1914 socialist, Catholic, Protestant, Polish and non-party affiliated movements competed for members in the densely populated towns and cities. Within these separate movements were a

114

plethora of associations, from supportive groups like the sickness insurance and cooperative clubs, to recreational societies like the choirs, gymnastic and ramblers' clubs, to educational forums like the reading societies and libraries. But it is important to note that there was nothing inevitable about the emergence of this working class voluntary association movement. Statements on the national prediliction for corporative life have little substance to them as they ignore the fundamental realities of the structure of German urban society in this period. The reasons for the relatively sudden proliferation of clubs and societies catering to the needs of the working class may be found in the circumstances of German industrialization, the peculiarities of the Prussian political system and the dynamics of public life.

Notwithstanding the presence of a rich associational life in the eighteenth century, the voluntary association movement assumed real public prominence in the early decades of the nineteenth century, the era of bourgeois self-confidence and public participation. For the middle classes the voluntary association was the key to their adaptation to a society where the basic structures were undergoing change. As Vernon Lidtke has remarked, they founded associations 'as a way of restructuring their social existence'.[1] Or, as Otto von Gierke wrote in 1868,

> In the associations . . . society organizes itself to correspond to the needs of individuals, freeing them from the old dependencies and patronages. The association movement was the answer to the disbanding of the old order, to the abolition of feudalism and the 'decorporation' of society.[2]

The movement facilitated the elevation of the bourgeoisie as a class to positions of power and influence.[3] The corporate organization of the pre-industrial era, with its emphasis on birth and status, began to recede in the face of a new individualism, encompassing more all-embracing concepts like humanism, libertarianism, individual merit and equality before the law. To active members the association represented their world, merito-cratic rather than status-ridden, democratic rather than authoritarian, emancipated from the old corporate institutions like the church and the guild. For the bourgeoisie the voluntary association was not simply an agency of socialization and integration. Membership of a society was probably the best way of exerting influence on any number of social, economic and political issues, especially in the local community but also nationally when the absurdities of the Prussian political system denied an effective voice to those groups displaced by the triumph of the industrial elites. In political terms the associations have been described as 'mini-republics', preparing the ground for middle-class participation in democratic government.[4]

Thus the bourgeois example provided a blueprint for the movement of the working class towards collective sociability. A second reason for the growth of working-class groups was the status of the voluntary association *vis à vis* the state. A voluntary association is, by definition, independent. Membership is entirely voluntary and the execution of activities and protection of members' interests are regulated by a constitution. Politically affiliated associations aside, voluntary clubs in the Wilhemine era had a freedom not granted to individuals. Once an association had registered with the local police department and had submitted its constitution for scrutiny it was free to conduct its affairs in relative freedom. It was a form of organization understandably favoured by the working class whose activities were constantly regulated and controlled.

Thirdly, voluntary associations appealed to workers for practical reasons too. Forming a club was a means of sharing resources and it was one way of coping with social change. Sociologists have long recognized the connection between urbanization and the development of voluntary associations. Joining a club was not always a political statement but could be a reaction to the psychological stress imposed by the comparative anonymity of urban industrial society. Voluntary associations were formed by the middle and working classes in Imperial Germany at certain stages in their respective processes of adaptation to the capitalist, industrial economy. The working class of the final two decades of the nineteenth century followed the path forged by its bourgeois conterpart several decades earlier. Caught up in a cycle of economic change, threatened with alienation, looking for a means of expression and identification with the new society, individuals from both classes attempted to solve the problem by forming or joining a club. As Hans-Ulrich Wehler remarked:

> The reproach *Vereinsmeierei* which is commonly used against the migrants from the Eastern Provinces is only a pejorative description of the important socio-psychological function performed by the various associations, in which totally alien agrarian workers and linguistic groups in the Ruhr were helped to adapt to everday life.[5]

So far there has been little attempt to distinguish between party political and non-affiliated associations. However, as far as the majority of historians of the German working class are concerned the workers' club movement was part and parcel of the labour movement and therefore, in Lidtke's words, 'few if any Germans would have joined workers' clubs unless they were workers, perceived themselves as workers, or belonged to or sympathised strongly with the Social Democratic movement.'[6] It is true that the German labour movement did succeed in creating a cradle-to-grave network of workers' recreational, educational, cultural and welfare organizations. A working-class family could purchase its groceries at the socialist cooperative, borrow books from the Social Democratic library, exercise at a workers' sports club, sing in the workers' choir, if necessary call on the workers' Samaritan Association in the event of an accident, and draw on the workers' burial fund upon the death of a family member. Yet it was not until the Weimar Republic that the true extent of the socialist-affiliated voluntary association movement was realized. Certainly up until the outbreak of war in 1914 associational life in Bochum and Düsseldorf was multi-dimensional; competition between the various strands of the voluntary association movement for working-class membership was immense in the area of recreational provision.

The beginnings of associational life

The 1870s signalled the beginning of organized associational life on a large scale in Bochum and Düsseldorf. At least 150 new clubs were registered in Bochum between 1874 and 1889, the majority formed for musical purposes but a fair proportion patriotic, sporting or philanthropic in nature.[7] The pattern was similar in Düsseldorf, although military and war veteran associations were more prolific here. Sheer numbers are quite deceptive, however. Many of these clubs were inconsequential, masquerading under important sounding names. Few clubs managed to attract more than 50 members and 20 was closer to the norm. Moreover, the number of passive members often exceeded those who actively participated in the club. In 1877 the Bochum gymnastic club boasted 79 members but only 24 of these were active.[8] Longevity was not guaranteed. In Bochum clubs were constantly being formed and re-formed; they changed their names, affiliated with other organizations, merged with similar clubs and frequently disappeared altogether.

Perhaps the most significant feature of Bochum associational life in this period was its domination by professional, commercial and artisan classes. Without doubt, the voluntary association movement was predominantly (although not exclusively) a bourgeois phenomenon here until the turn of the century. Few associations managed to transcend class divisions; rather, they deliberately sought to represent particular interests either openly, like the overtly bourgeois Harmonie club, or more discreetly, like many of the sporting organizations, which levied high subscription rates and held their meetings and practice sessions at times of the day when potential working-class members were unable to attend. The Bochum gymnastic association, for instance, met on Wednesdays and Saturdays at 4.30 pm, well before workers on the day shift returned home.[9] In 1860 it had 84 members who without exception hailed from the middle classes of the town: white-collar workers, small businessmen, professionals and artisans. By 1899 little had changed. White-collar workers still accounted for a third of the membership, the proportion of businessmen had slipped to almost 30 per cent, and the remaining 20 per cent were classified as graduates and academics.[10] By 1901, however, Bochum workers had formed their own gymnastic club, the Arbeiter-Turnverein Altenbochum 01, closely followed by the Freie Sportvereinigung Bochum two years later which, after a slow and difficult start, could boast 80 members by 1906.[11] In Düsseldorf the situation was no different. The gymnastic association admittedly made no pretence of being representative, boasting in 1910 that its members came 'almost exclusively' from bourgeois families, and none of its 353 adult male members could be said to have been working class.[12]

It was not until the late 1880s at the earliest that the working class began to participate in Bochum's associational life on any significant scale, although small numbers had joined bourgeois singing societies before there were any workers' singing clubs. The 1850s and 1860s had already seen the entrance of the working class into voluntary associations, although in these early days they joined largely for instrumental reasons. Many of the first associations were supportive, for instance sickness and invalidity clubs and burial funds like the miners' *Knappschaftsvereine* in the Ruhr. By the late 1860s, however, the early stages of a working-class voluntary movement were evident; that is, workers were forming and joining associations that had a considerable social and recreational element.[13] By the 1870s Bochum workers were joining recreational and social associations describing themselves as *unparteiisch*. The membership of the singing association, Wachtel, seemed to consist largely of workers; the majority of the 39 members of Germania, another singing society founded in 1877, were mineworkers and factory employees; the male singing association Eintracht had a mixture of factory workers and artisans among its 42 members, and the reading club had 20 members, most of whom were factory workers. The first explicitly workers' clubs were the Christian-Social Workers' Associations formed by the Catholic Church in the 1860s and 1870s, followed by the Evangelical Workers' Organization around ten years later.[14]

Owing to the restrictions placed on the activities of the Social Democratic Party by the anti-socialist legislation, the cultural initiatives favoured by the socialist leadership were delayed until local party structures were able to function effectively. A Social Democratic culture, it was thought, would not only create an alternative value system to those imposed by the bourgeois state and, in Düsseldorf in particular, by the Catholic church, it would also go some way towards breaking down the barriers that divided worker from worker. But, as Nolan emphasizes, 'cultural activities were to strengthen commitment and raise consciousness, not to supplant politics',[15] and the party political framework had to be in place before cultural initiatives could be explored. The twelve years of repression between 1878 and 1890 saw the virtual cessation of all Social Democratic activity in Bochum and Düsseldorf, although it is fair to point out that neither town could boast a solid base of grassroots support on the eve of the law's implementation. Following the repeal of the laws, workers' recreational clubs were almost the last branches of the socialist movement to appear. Even in predominantly working-class districts of Düsseldorf like Oberbilk, associational life was dominated by the bourgeois shooting clubs and war veterans. After 1890 this began to change with the formation of a workers' singing association, Liederlust, followed by a workers' gymnastic association, Freiheit, in 1893. In 1895 the Gymnastic and Sports Association of Düsseldorf had branches in Rath, Unterrath, Eller, Gerresheim, Erkrath and Benrath and by 1898 there was a cycling club named Solidarität.[16] By 1907 the workers' athletic associations had a membership of 350; 200 belonged to singing groups; another 70 were active in the cycling club, and the theatrical society had around 80 members.[17] Still more workers belonged to recreational clubs attached to their places of work. By 1907 the workers at the Gerresheim glass factory had formed nine associations spanning gymnastics and athletics, cycling, singing and music.[18] In Bochum, too, the Social Democrats extended their cultural and educational activities after 1890 and by the end of the Weimar Republic they had built up an impressive range of over 60 clubs, from workers' chess and rambling societies to youth and women's groups.[19]

Clearly workers' associational activity was in its infancy until the turn of the century. Only 9 per cent of the Düsseldorf working class were organized in trade unions in 1900.[20] The combined membership of four of the most popular recreational associations in 1907, around 700, represented a mere 1.3 per cent of the male working class in the city, although 7 per cent of organized workers and 25 per cent of SPD members belonged.[21] This was hardly an impressive figure and certainly not significant in terms of the formation of a class-conscious culture, as some have claimed. In comparison with Düsseldorf's burgeoning middle class, who 'had established their economic position and social identity' by the 1890s, aided in no minor way by their association network, the working class of Düsseldorf was slow to develop its own cultural and political alternative.[22]

Bochum and Düsseldorf are not exceptional. In spite of their relatively weak socialist movements compared with cities like Leipzig, Hamburg and Berlin, membership of Social Democratic cultural organizations was hardly more impressive in the Reich as a whole. There were around 62,000 members of the Arbeitersängerbund in 1903–4, about 51,000 workers in the Arbeiter Turn-und-Sportbund and around 19,000 worker cyclists. It is estimated that some 600,000 workers belonged to one or more socialist cultural organizations by 1914. 'According to these rough calculations', argues Josef Mooser, 'the socializing effects of the subculture . . . were limited to a large minority of the workers, mainly those in the cities and particularly the more highly skilled.'[23] In this respect the social composition

of the voluntary association movement reflected that of the SPD membership as a whole. Although it has been calculated that 98 per cent of the
membership of the SPD in Düsseldorf was working-class in 1906, almost
all were skilled and semi-skilled workers.[24]

In Bochum the situation was somewhat different; semi- and unskilled
miners and factory workers were in the majority here. Although the data
enabling us to determine the social and occupational composition of the
SPD membership in Bochum are unavailable, Hickey has calculated that 71
per cent of the party leadership between 1891 and 1906 were employed in
the mining industry.[25] Perhaps the relatively large number of workers'
welfare associations, as opposed to recreational clubs, in Bochum is a
reflection of the occupational structure within the town. Unskilled manual
workers were more in need of financial support than cultural edification.
Although manual workers far outnumbered the middle-class presence in
Bochum the latter continued to strengthen its organizational presence,
prompting one of the town's historians to write:

> Bochum, the town of industry and the working class, almost had a
> bourgeois appearance . . . The workers' associations which gradually
> developed in Bochum, creating a lively workers' culture, still, for the
> time being, led a life on the social margins of the new town.[26]

Why then, in the absence of a strong socialist associational network in
these towns before 1890, is the history of working-class collectivism in
Germany dominated by Social Democratic recreational, educational and
cultural organizations at the expense of working-class voluntary associations with no political affiliation, confessional clubs and ethnic organizations? The answer lies in the historiography and methodology of labour
history in Germany. Since the 1950s a deluge of studies of the German
labour movement have adopted as their central thesis the assertion that the
Social Democratic Party was never as revolutionary as its adoption of the
Marxist Erfurt Programme in 1891 suggested; indeed it has been argued
that the labour movement was a stabilizing force in the imperial system,
aided largely by its dense associational network. According to this thesis,
the workers' clubs reinforced bourgeois values such as 'the necessity of
authority, discipline, skill and good work performance' and hence became
the prime agents in the 'embourgeoisement' of the working class, blunting
the revolutionary edge of the labour movement. Subsequently a number of
historians of the labour movement, through detailed studies of individual
workers' organizations, questioned the existence of an alternative Marxist
culture, accepting along the way that the associational movement was an
accurate and representative guide to the views and beliefs of the grassroots
membership of the SPD.[27]

The following survey of working-class associational life in Bochum and

120

Düsseldorf points out the inherent limitations in this approach for the understanding of a workers' culture, as opposed to a labour movement culture, in the imperial period. Indeed, labour movement associations were outnumbered by clubs and societies that were not party political. This fact owed something to the relatively late development of Social Democracy in these towns, and something to the impact of Bismarck's anti-socialist legislation which effectively prevented the formation and operation of associations affiliated to the labour movement until 1890. It also reflected the intensity and variety of individual interest in the voluntary organization as a way of pursuing a collective goal. Social Democratic clubs and associations contributed positively to the development of a working-class consciousness and the emancipation of the proletariat. But this perspective can also be extended to some of the non-party voluntary associations. Workers began to use the voluntary association form and structure outside the party political or instrumental context before the labour organizations gained any real strength. Members of the socialist clubs learned to express themselves, accept responsibility and develop leadership potential. Workers' associations based on similar principles, with identical organizational structures, were no less effective in this respect.

An 'alternative' associational movement

In 1892 an evangelical pastor writing in the *Düsseldorfer Zeitung* articulated a common attitude towards the apparent proliferation of clubs and societies at the end of the century. 'Berlin alone', he wrote, 'has 969 associations and everyone is a member of at least one . . . The association movement of today is overdone . . . Many healthy people have become tired and rundown as a result of their associational activities.'[28] Similarly Max Seippel, a chronicler of Bochum life, noticed in 1900 that 'the association movement has reached a peak that one would hardly have imagined fifty years ago.'[29] To what were they referring? Franz-Josef Brüggemeier in his study of the Ruhr before the First World War has alluded to the wider dimension of associational life present in all German towns and cities. 'It is very difficult to find out anything about the numerous skittle and lottery, goat-breeding and pig-insurance associations, and there is even little to say about the better-organized singing, gymnastic and sport associations', but he goes on,

> their loose organizational structure, the simple entrance requirements and the modest degree of obligation corresponded in particular ways to the needs of a mobile working class who sought opportunities to meet each other and be relatively undisturbed among their own kind.[30]

121

It was not long before the urban working class formed its own clubs and societies, having been denied access to what was already on offer. A rich associational life based on confessional identity, ethnic origin and common hobbies and pastimes developed quite independently of the bourgeois clubs and the labour movement. 'There was a whole host of associations', wrote the glassworker Germanus Theiss in his memoirs. 'Singing associations, gymnastic clubs, the cycling club "Wanderer 1892", besides the confessional clubs like the Catholic Workers' Association. In contrast the trade unions hardly made an appearance before 1914.'[31] In order to demonstrate that the working class in Bochum and Düsseldorf created its own social-cultural milieu which was not tainted by middle-class involvement or directed by socialist idealists, three broad areas of associational life will be discussed in detail: the Polish clubs, the Catholic and Protestant social movements, and the recreational societies which were closer to the environment than to cultural edification.

Industrial towns like Bochum contained a surprising number of animals as well as people. Small animals which required only a small space, like goats, pigs and rabbits, were kept by a large number of miners and factory workers. In spite of the overcrowded housing, many working-class families had at least a backyard or a communal courtyard, and those lucky enough to reside in company housing possessed a small garden and shed. The breeders of goats, pigs and rabbits had their own clubs, as did the poultry breeders and canary fanciers. By 1912 there were 39 associations representing goat, rabbit and poultry breeders in the Bochum district, with a total of 1,818 members. A year later the League of Small Animal Breeders in Rhineland-Westphalia calculated that it had 468 member associations which, in turn, had over 23,000 individual members, an increase of 36 and 53 per cent respectively over the previous year.[32] The goat was known as the miners' cow. This was an appropriate description. A good goat, it was said, could give two or three litres of milk a day and with around 6,000 goats in the district in 1905 the Bochum Association of Goat Breeders calculated that the needs of a substantial proportion of the population were being met.[33] The vast majority of members of all these animal clubs were workers. While the Bochum middle and upper classes were not entirely aloof from this land-based associational movement (they formed a horse breeding association in 1911 and a branch of the Society for the Prevention of Cruelty to Animals in 1899), they had little to do with the interests of the working class. The presidents of five of the nine small animal associations in Bochum in 1912 were miners (the others were factory workers, artisans and a teacher). This indicated a grassroots movement within the working class creating its own autonomous structure of voluntary associations around its own particular interests.[34]

While members may have kept their animals chiefly for practical purposes – as a regular source of nourishment and protein and an insurance against food shortages or hardship – the majority enjoyed the social side of their activities too. After all, one could keep a goat without joining a club. All the clubs had their own *Vereinslokal* (tavern meeting place) where they met at least once a month, and they frequently organized exhibitions and competitions on a local as well as a regional level. Similarly, owners of the poor man's racehorse, the carrier pigeon, joined clubs for the sociable and competitive elements of their hobby, pigeon breeding and racing. In Bochum this was said to be a mass sport; every miners' colony had at least one pair of pigeon fanciers. There were still enough old houses with lofts in the roof in Bochum, while in the colonies pigeon lofts could be erected in the yard or garden.[35] 'On summer Sundays the pigeon fanciers sat in front of their houses waiting for the return of their birds in order to get the number of the incoming bird to the clock as quickly as possible', reminisced a resident of Bochum.[36] It was in Langendreer, a mining suburb of Bochum, that pigeon racing was by far the most popular working-class recreational activity. By 1901 there were around nine clubs there, with miners forming the majority of members. The primary function of the clubs, in addition to coordinating breeding, was to organize races. The birds were often taken several hundred kilometres away and released so they would (hopefully) arrive back home on a Sunday. As the *Märkischer Sprecher* reported in 1885, this was often a family occasion:

On the day of the release of the pigeons the pigeon owners, often accompanied by their relatives, stand around the lofts [to see] whether or not one or other of the pigeons has arrived . . . The excitement among the pigeon fanciers increases still more when the flight involves other honourable decorations as well as money prizes.[37]

Miners were often attracted to pigeon fancying, not just in Germany but also in Britain, Belgium and France.[38] It was a hobby particularly well suited to densely populated residential areas. It could involve the whole community but at the same time it was a peculiarly personal pastime for the miner, who would often spend hours in the pigeon loft with his pigeons. It was a total contrast to work in the mines. The bird represented freedom, light and peace and it has been suggested it compensated workers for the time they spent underground.

Not only were birds and animals common among the smokestacks; there was also a surprising amount of open space, particularly on the edges of towns, that was commonly cultivated into small plots for growing fruit and vegetables. 'There were allotments everywhere', wrote a former resident of Bochum:

Inbetween the industrial plants there were spaces everywhere for small plots of land. The allotment gardeners were a cheerful lot. Competitions for the biggest cabbage head and the fattest kohlrabi took place. And a hut on the allotment, nailed together from planks and metal sheets, was often exactly the right place for a communal bottle of beer on a Saturday evening.[39]

The first allotment associations were formed in Bochum in 1909 by those who could afford to rent public allotments from the town council, primarily members of the professions, shopkeepers and owners of small businesses. As well as helping members with equipment, tools, seed and advice, the *Schrebergartenvereine* organized competitions, exhibitions and festivals. In the workers' colonies, however, it is likely that informal allotment clubs were formed. Like pigeon racing, allotment gardening was a family and community activity. Wives and children were frequent helpers, binding the community together around a common interest in its leisure hours. The allotments were 'not only places where we grew a few potatoes', remembered Walter Pape of the 1900s,

> they were also community centres. There developed these allotment associations with their central club huts, their garden festivals and their own personal networks. So that many people who had a very hard life found a place of leisure and personal freedom.[40]

Workers' voluntary associations formed around interests connected with rural life were a response to the need for collective identity and support in the urban environment. They helped workers to adjust by supporting an activity that bridged the gap with their past as well as acting as a form of insurance against misfortune. The clubs really came into their own during the First World War when fresh vegetables, meat and milk were hard to find. Similarly, the confessional associations represented stable values in an otherwise unstable, alien environment. Indeed, religious loyalties and identities were generally stronger than the political affiliations of the new industrial working class. 'The religious barrier was not simply an ideological question', writes Stephen Hickey, '. . . religious loyalties and religious organisations formed the basis of the community and the social life of many workers in the district.'[41]

In Bochum and Düsseldorf, as in most other towns in the area, the Catholics were the first to organize workers. A long tradition of Catholic voluntary association, going back to the brotherhoods and sodalities of the early nineteenth century, gave them a head start over the Protestant church.[42] The Christian Social movement appeared in Bochum in the 1870s, partly as a defensive reaction to the emergence of a 'godless radicalism' preached by Social Democrats, but in a more positive sense it addressed itself to the 'social question' too.[43] First and foremost the movement aimed to raise the religious and moral standards of the working class, but this was combined with a call for an improvement in social conditions. Members were not difficult to come by, even in the early stages. The first Christian Social Association, formed in Düsseldorf in 1871, soon had 500 members, far more than the membership of the Social Democrats at this time.[44] By 1910 the Catholic workers associations had been highly successful with their combination of social welfare, mutual aid, self-help and sponsorship of social and cultural activities. The Western German League of Catholic Workers' Associations, with its headquarters in Mönchengladbach, boasted 171,302 members in 961 affiliated associations by this date.[45]

The Protestant church was comparatively slow to adapt to the new social and economic conditions emerging in the industrial towns. Unlike its Catholic counterpart, it had no tradition of working-class activism or even of concern with social issues.[46] The first Protestant workers' club in Bochum was founded in 1882. By 1885 its membership of between 1,100 and 1,200 men was in line with that of neighbouring towns: Essen had 1,450 members in 1885, Dortmund 1,305 and Gelsenkirchen 800.[47] It was not until 1891, however, perhaps in response to the legalization of the SPD the previous year, that the Protestant hierarchy seized the gauntlet and acknowledged that an extension of the boundaries of its activities was necessary. Its effort to recruit workers was subsequently intensified and by 1909 Protestant workers' clubs in the Bochum/Gelsenkirchen district numbered 69 with around 12,500 members, while there were 47,000 members and 213 associations in the Rheinisch-Westfälischer Verband.[48] In Düsseldorf the movement was somewhat weaker, owing to the minority position of Protestants there. In contrast to the Catholic workers' associations the Protestant movement was far more conservative and patriotic in its outlook. It was always much more outspoken in its opposition to social democracy and in Bochum it consistently supported the National Liberal canadidate in elections. Yet on the social and recreational level there was little to choose between the two denominations; in both cases the emphasis was on education and self-improvement, with lectures on topical subjects, promotion of libraries and good reading matter, clubs for women and young people and the occasional dance and excursion.

The strength of the confessional associations is perhaps surprising in a period usually seen as characterized by an advancing secularization in the towns, particularly where the working class was concerned. The secularization of holidays and festivals has been commonly cited as evidence for this trend, and the fall in church attendance has been seen as a sure sign of the decline in religious belief among the urban proletariat. But while church attendance certainly did suffer (among Protestants more than Catholics), this was not necessarily an indication of a loss of faith.[49] Many factors accumulated to prevent workers attending Sunday services: shiftwork, Sunday working, the sheer length of the working week necessitating a lie-in on Sunday mornings, and limited leisure time.[50] Religious loyalties could be expressed in other ways. The working class continued to patronize the church and its rituals on the major occasions in the lifecycle, baptism, marriage and death.[51] Moreover, many aspects of everyday life were still dominated by the presence of the church; in Bochum there was an equal number of Catholic and Protestant primary schools, and the hospitals and orphanages were divided along denominational lines. The role of the religious associations was multi-faceted. As Hickey has noted for Bochum, 'religious organizations could offer not only a familiar language for the expression of important personal emotions and events but a framework for the establishment of social and community ties and even for the definition of social identity.'[52]

The positive advantages gained by working-class members of confessional organizations outweighed the negative aspects of social control inherent in the ideology of the clerical hierarchy. Participation in these clubs taught many workers the skills necessary for an active public life. Some societies initiated their members in the practice of democratic assembly and in some areas the Christian Social Movement was quite radical in its support of the working class.[53] Demands for social improvements were also high on the agenda; the edge was only blunted by the clerical leadership. Jonathon Sperber has suggested, nevertheless, that 'for a minority of the working-class adherents . . . the radical wing of the Christian Social movement was just a way station on the road to the socialists.'[54] And Vernon Lidtke has acknowledged that by the turn of the century 'working-class consciousness began to manifest itself in the Catholic Workers' Clubs' although it was almost entirely absent from the Protestant associations.[55] Confessional organization, then, was not the absolute antithesis to socialist organized activity that it has been alleged to be. The confessional associations also provided a leisure space for women. It was they who maintained their allegiance to the church the longest in the urban community. In the absence of suitable alternatives, the church offered women a territory that was their own, away from their husbands and fathers and in which they were free to express particular female concerns. For the first time, women's leisure was catered for as a separate activity.

Although the Catholic and Protestant workers' associations were instrumental in the integration of the working class into German industrial society, at the same time they helped to perpetuate the divisions which already existed within the working class. 'Black' (Catholic) and 'Blue' (Protestant) continued to dominate the economic, social and political life in Bochum well into the 1880s. In the political arena the National Liberals and the Catholic Centre Party dominated the elections in Bochum until 1887, when the SPD began to make headway.[56] Black and Blue even distinguished one public house and its clientele from another.[57] And in Düsseldorf it was said that workers 'divide themselves according to confession and the furtherance of this division does not serve to strengthen a consciousness of the unity of the state.'[58]

Yet the unity of the state, and even of the working class, was undermined further by the existence of another variable manifested in the voluntary association. The urban proletariat of the 1880s and 1890s was an ethnic mix, and among those of non-German extraction the Poles and Masurians were the most numerous. While it is difficult to determine exactly how many Poles were resident in any one area owing to the vagueness of the definition 'Polish speaking', some towns and districts experienced the inward migration of workers from eastern Europe to a greater extent than others. Bochum belonged in this category, the proportion of Polish speakers here outnumbering those in Düsseldorf by almost three to one.[59]

Poles in the district began to organize on a significant scale in the 1890s and the first Polish associations were essentially religious ones. Although Poles were Catholic, they were also fiercely independent and had little to do with the German Catholic church associations in spite of strikingly similar aims. As new clubs formed, however, the promotion of Polish nationalism through secular activities became increasingly important. Henceforth the Polish associational movement began to imitate its German counterpart in many respects. Singing and gymnastic clubs were by far the most popular. By 1905 there were no fewer than 65 Polish singing associations in the Herne, Oberhausen and Recklinghausen districts. They were affiliated to the Federation of Singing Associations in Rhineland-Westphalia, with almost 3,000 members.[60] The singing associations addressed the nationality question indirectly by promoting Polish music and songs. 'The Polish melody', proclaimed one of the Langendreer clubs, 'is the best means [in the struggle] against Germanization.'[61]

The gymnastic associations, *Sokolvereine*, were arguably more aggressively nationalistic. Certainly the Arnsberg authorities thought so, characterizing them as political organizations whose main purpose was not gymnastics but the strengthening of a national consciousness, a charge that could equally have been levelled at the German middle-class gymnastic clubs.[62] In numerical terms the *Sokol* were smaller than many other branches of the movement, but their emphasis on the nationality question prompted the police to regard them as enemies of the state, or *Reichsfeinde*.[63] However, the Polish associational movement did not assume a party political slant in Rhineland-Westphalia until the late 1890s, and even then its support was behind the Polish Party and the Catholic Centre Party rather than the Social Democrats.

The primary significance of the Polish associational movement was not its political dimension. It should be assessed in terms of its role in the adaptation of the Polish workers to their adopted country and environment and, in the final analysis, in terms of the so-called Germanization of the migrants and their families. By 1910 there were 660 Polish associations, with around 60,000 members, in the Ruhr, that is almost 22 per cent of the entire Polish population in the region. Two years later these figures had increased to 875 and 81,532 respectively.[64] Poles, or at least those active in the associations, seemed to be deliberately perpetuating their isolation from the rest of German society. They purposefully spoke the Polish language at their meetings even though this was forbidden. They remained residentially separate, often living in company housing and creating small-scale Polish communities. Moreover, the associations were largely self-sufficient. They maintained no contact with similar German clubs and societies; national boundaries were not crossed. Polish gymnastic clubs competed against other Polish gymnastic clubs. Polish singing festivals were attended only by Polish singing associations. It could also be argued that these associations were inward-looking; their emphasis on Polish Catholicism hardly helped their members adapt to a society that was becoming increasingly secular, and their nationalism held out false hopes in a society trying to come to terms with an imposed unity. But when the Poles and their associations are studied in the wider context of the German working class and the voluntary association movement as a whole, it becomes clear that in spite of its religious and nationalist tendencies the Polish associational movement had the same functions as the clubs and societies to which German workers belonged. Just as German workers identified with their rural or semi-rural origins or their confessional allegiance, so Poles found that their associational network gave them an identity in a pluralist society. As Richard Murphy has shown for Bottrop, the Polish associations did preserve Polish ethnicity but at the same time they conducted their activities along the lines of conventional German associational life.[65] Their network of associations mirrored that created by other working-class groups and thus must be interpreted as a typical mechanism created to cope with membership of an alien society.

By 1914 the associational movement in Germany was as diverse as the pluralistic society within which it operated. The social and cultural associations of the labour movement were just one element in this multi-coloured picture. By the outbreak of war Social Democratic associations were attracting an increasing proportion of the working class but, throughout the final three decades of the nineteenth century, Social Democratic clubs were just one of a number of interest groups competing for working-class membership. The relative weakness of the Social Democratic organizations in this period, unlike the apparent strength of the confessional and ethnic movements, points to the instability and insecurity of the majority of the working class. The Social Democratic movement was, compared with the churches, an unknown factor. In contrast, the church and nationalist organizations, and even those clubs founded around environmental interests, were known quantities.

Club life

Franz-Josef Brüggemeier was perceptive when he remarked upon the difficulty of discovering anything about the activities of these workers' clubs and societies, for it was the unofficial and unorganized nature of the pigeon fancying clubs and the societies of animal enthusiasts that governed the ephemeral quality of the records they left behind. Indeed, it is the detailed papers kept by the SPD and the excessive interest the authorities showed in the party that partially explain the over-representation of labour movement cultural and recreational associations in the literature. Nevertheless, it is possible to piece together a picture of the social life of the workers' groups from a wide variety of sources.

The popular image of a workers' social club was based on misapprehensions and prejudices. Bochum's Max Seippel echoed the feelings of many who were disturbed by the dominance of German social life, or at least that is how it seemed, by the *Vereinsmeierei*:

> We live in a time in which the pulse of life is much faster than before, in which individuals in the intensified struggle for existence have to cope with far greater demands with regard to work and production than used to be the case and was possible. Everyone who works should also rest, but one does not have to seek this only in the associations. It is really not advisable that the evenings of many people are spent only with the associations and for many, seven days a week are not enough to comply with their associational duties. [66]

Many were convinced that club membership was a pretext for an evening in the local tavern. It is true that most associations held their regular meetings in public houses; these were the only establishments sufficiently spacious to accommodate 20 or 30 members of a club. Few clubs owned their own halls, although confessional associations made full use of churches and church halls. Publicans encouraged patronage of their establishments and often did not discriminate between one club and another. While some were reluctant to accommodate SPD groups, most were far more pragmatic. One Elberfeld landlord opened his doors to 15 different clubs and societies representing a variety of economic and political interests. Publicans often insisted, however, on an agreement which obliged the club to consume a certain quantity of beer in return. On the day-to-day level most clubs held weekly or monthly general meetings which all members were invited to attend. These were normally concerned with routine business, although some clubs organized lectures and talks for these events while others treated them purely as social occasions.

It was said that the primary purpose of most of the associations in Bochum was 'convivial entertainment and collective amusement'. Moreover, in the summer this social life was allegedly carried out almost exclusively in the beer gardens of the town.[67] The statutes of the majority of clubs and societies committed them to at least one annual festival, in commemoration of their foundation day, and frequently more. District and local festivals were soon pencilled in to secretaries' diaries, as were competitions and participation in local events like the shooting festivals and carnival, and in national celebrations like Sedan Day when processions consisting of members of all the major local associations were common-place, accompanied by all the trappings of ritual and pageantry. The Düsseldorf gymnastic association organized and participated in 14 events between January and October 1910, including several area competitions and recruitment, foundation and jubilee festivals in addition to the regular meetings and practice sessions.[68] This pattern was imitated, for the most part, by the workers' associations, whether ethnic, confessional or indepen-dent. For instance, in 1910 the Polish gymnastic association in Bochum held 21 meetings during the course of the year, including eight lectures. It also had a constitution celebration, a foundation day festival, an evening commemorating the nationalist Kosciuszko Rising, and two excursions; several members also took part in a district gymnastic festival.[69] Voluntary associations were very keen to hold fundraising events throughout the year. Dances were the best way to raise money, but the frequency of *Tanzlustbarkeiten* prompted the charge that the associational movement had got out of hand, had become self-perpetuating and was a threat to the family. 'Where is their historical, familial, local or religious justification?', asked the *Kölnische Volkszeitung* in 1898. 'They are a parasite on the present factory and commercial times. They condemn the family to death and have a pernicious influence on the population of the entire area.'[70]

The notion of the all-embracing club life representing a threat, not only to the stable family unit but to the whole fabric of society, was a relatively common one in the 1890s, in contrast to the enthusiastic reception that had greeted the bourgeois associations several decades earlier. At first sight it is fairly easy to see why this opinion was so widespread. From the mid-1880s on the number of festive occasions organized by the voluntary associations increased dramatically. In one area of Düsseldorf 108 club events (excluding regular meetings, foundation festivals and so on) took place in the year 1882–3.[71] A further 118 dances organized by various associations took place in the whole of the Düsseldorf city police district between October 1885 and April 1886.[72] But critics were mistaken in assuming that the numbers of workers participating in associational activities were as great as the number of events taking place might suggest.

Owing to the paucity of associations' membership lists, it is impossible to say how many workers belonged to one or more clubs, but it was certainly not until the turn of the century that a majority of workers were members of even one or two associations and they certainly would not have been committed every night of the week, despite allegations to that effect. Moreover, the participation rate of working-class members was likely to have been lower than that of their middle-class counterparts. Although some clubs statutorily demanded regular attendance at general meetings, this may only have amounted to once a month. Attendance by workers would also have been sporadic if they were engaged in shiftwork. As recent research among modern American urban dwellers shows, actual attendance is far more infrequent than one would perhaps expect: only 1.02 times a month per membership held; 2.65 times for each person in the survey.[73] At the same time, mere membership of a club and attendance at meetings and events bears little relation to the actual amount of time a person spends pursuing a hobby or interest. Those who belonged to organizations with a supportive function (like the animal breeders and gardeners) probably spent comparatively little time in formal associational activities, but caring for animals or tending a vegetable plot could be extremely time-consuming in the informal sense. Moreover, those most likely to join voluntary associations were skilled workers. Semi-skilled and unskilled workers were the least likely to be members of any organization, yet it was they who were on the receiving end of the critics' complaints. Furthermore, the voluntary association movement was overwhelmingly male-dominated. There were few complaints about women spending all their free time in club activities.

Two assumptions were implicit in the arguments of those who criticized the burgeoning associational life of the working class: first that there was such a thing as a stable family unit and an identifiable family life; second, that workers automatically rejected this way of life for one based on a series of impersonal contacts when they became involved with clubs and societies. Certainly in Bochum and Düsseldorf, as in most newly industrialized towns, a large proportion of the workforce had no family life in the sense of a residence shared with members of the nuclear or extended family. The picture is one of high-density, unsanitary accommodation and a surplus of single men, offering little chance of a real family life in the sense envisaged by the middle-class critics of the associations. It is within this context that the importance of formal, secondary group associations grew in relation to the absence of extended kinship groups in the urban community. For single persons, the clubs and associations may have acted as a substitute for family life; informal contacts made here could have taken the place of the kinship network. And for those families living in the conditions described, clubs and societies were more likely to have had a beneficial effect on relations within family groups by providing individuals with the chance to escape, rather than contributing to the break-up of the family. While public houses had fulfilled this function in the past, voluntary associations did the same and more towards the end of the century. They were instrumental in siphoning off potential and actual tensions

131

(whereas retreat to the pub for a drink alone may only have added to them). Women eventually formed associations of their own which acted as spaces to which they could escape from household duties and male company, thus lessening their resentment of male leisure activities. Rather than acting as a substitute for family life, as contemporary observers believed, associational activities could enrich it.

For workers and their families the voluntary associations filled a gap in the urban leisure market by creating a bridge between sociable, informal gatherings and individual interests. Since most clubs made the public house their regular meeting place, workers would not have felt intimidated by the location and may already have been acquainted with some of the members. But the emergence of voluntary leisure associations, particularly of autonomous, non party political groups, signified a new departure in the development of workers' leisure. In contrast with the 'instrumental' associations that dominated the early years of the workers' associational movement, like the *Konsumvereine*, these 'expressive' associations represented the workers' active involvement in the organization of their own leisure.[74] In this respect, voluntary associations complemented urban working-class lifestyles. They grew out of interests and activities already being pursued informally by isolated individuals. The growth of expressive voluntary associations also signified a change of emphasis in the lives of workers, away from recognizing work as the central life interest and source of identity, and towards leisure interests.

Bourgeois contemporaries struggled to find an answer to the ambiguous effect the voluntary associations were having upon the working class. On the positive side there was a recognition of the benefits of associational life: if the associations helped workers to adapt to urban society (including the industrial factory system), if they engaged them in useful, rational activities in a controlled environment away from the streets and bars, then working-class membership had to be a good thing. On the other hand, if they sharpened the workers' sense of proletarian identity, if they replaced the family as the source of stability and, most dangerous of all, if they provided them with a forum in which to formulate and practise an alternative political ideology, then the workers' associational movement was a dangerous influence that had to be controlled and combatted.

Spontaneity to organization

Imperial Germany has been described as a culturally pluralist society and the voluntary association movement did little to challenge this state of affairs. Class, religious, ethnic and political divisions were all reflected in and perpetuated by the network of clubs and societies. Stephen Hickey proposes that we should begin to think in terms of a number of 'mutually exclusive sub-cultures' to replace the obsession with the search for an all-embracing working-class culture:

> There was thus not one working-class sub-culture in the Ruhr, rather there were a number of rival ones, outwardly similar in many respects (notably in the love of clubs and associations which was common throughout the district) but characterised by profound mutual suspicion and incomprehension.[75]

Although clubs and societies were gregarious by nature, few, if any, managed to transcend these more fundamental boundaries. The exclusivity of club life was common throughout Germany. This social differentiation within the associational movement was not simply a middle class phenomenon. Workers in Bochum and Düsseldorf, enthusiastic joiners of clubs as they were, failed to create an integrated movement, preferring to organize according to their perception of where they belonged: with Catholics or Protestants, with Germans or Poles, and eventually with socialists or communists.

The relative strength of the alternative, non-socialist associational network was not a temporary feature of the period of the anti-socialist laws. There is little evidence to suggest that had the labour movement been able to develop its associational network in the 1880s these workers would have joined them in preference to confessional, ethnic or other groups. The Social Democratic constituency was relatively small compared with, for example, that tapped by the Catholic associations, and there were few areas of overlap. It was not until the turn of the century that membership of the SPD or an affiliated organization was even considered by the majority of workers. Moreover, even after 1890 membership of confessional and ethnic workers' clubs continued to rise – a fact that paralleled developments in the political arena. In Düsseldorf, while the Social Democrats steadily increased their share of the vote in Reichstag elections from 1890 onwards, Centre Party support remained strong and by 1912 both parties polled around 42,000 votes in the second ballot.[76] Similarly, in Bochum, although the Reichstag seat was held by a Social Democrat from 1903 to 1912, National Liberal, Centre and Polish Party support prevented the SPD from winning more than a third of the vote in the first ballot.[77]

The period from 1900 to the outbreak of the First World War can confidently be described as the dawn of the heyday of the socialist associational movement. Until then the labour movement was in a state of re-formation and consolidation. Despite the heroic efforts of underground clubs during the years of illegality the SPD was in no position to challenge the social-cultural affinities of rival interest groups. Until the 1900s it remained just another facet of what had become a rich and diverse associational life in German towns and cities. Thus the workers' associational movement is perhaps best studied within the context of a number of social milieux, notably Catholic, Protestant, Polish, socialist and occupational. While there was manifest antagonism between them the tactics they employed were remarkably similar. One could indeed distinguish a distinct associational lifestyle common to all. Of course they all had their own guiding ideologies – the raising of the cultural level and collective consciousness of the working class in the case of the socialists, the preservation and promotion of religious and moral values for the confessional groups, the raising of Polish national consciousness for the Poles – but the organizational forms and the ways in which they tried to achieve their goals were remarkably similar. There would seem to be a case for proposing that associational life in general, by providing members with common experiences and models of democratic participation, formed the basis of a workers' culture that was to transcend more fundamental differences. Certainly, socialist and non-socialist, confessional and ethnic associations had some things in common, as Dieter Langewiesche has recently recognized.[78] Cultural improvement was a prominent aim of all clubs and societies. Amateurism was rejected in favour of excellence and professionalism, even by the allotment societies and animal breeding clubs by means of their competitions and shows. Socialist clubs with their lofty claims were not the only proponents of cultural improvement; most of the associations modelled themselves on their bourgeois predecessors and, in so doing, rejected popular cultural forms as plebeian and unrespectable.

By emphasizing the respectable side of their activities and rejecting those working-class elements they defined as rough or 'lumpen', argues Roth, the Social Democrats effectively blunted the edge of their revolutionary potential. The picture is, I would suggest, rather more complicated. It is no longer sufficient to explain the weakness of labour movement culture in terms of its bourgeois patina and the negative effect of its rejection of popular cultural forms. The internal diversification of the working class before 1914 continued to determine the social identity or consciousness of the majority of workers. As Stephen Hickey rightly points out, 'Loyalties for many remained focused on particular groups, often defined in terms of ethnic origins or religious allegiance, and not on a broader concept of the workers at large.'[79]

Finally, the relationship between the association movement and workers' leisure must be examined. In their study of voluntary leisure organizations in Britain today Jeff Bishop and Paul Hoggett have criticised the attitude of those who 'talk about leisure as if it were the modern opium of the masses – a form of mindless escapism or orchestrated passivity.' The association is, crucially, in Bishop and Hoggett's view, ' a place to be' as well as 'a place to do'. Leisure does not have to be a means to an end (class consciousness, political organization and activism) but can be 'an end in itself'.[80] If this analysis is applied to German workers' associations at the turn of the century they begin to appear as more central and dynamic elements in the lives of workers and communities. Activities undertaken in this context were not so much consumerist as involving 'cultural production' by the individual. This emphasis on the positive and meaningful value of voluntary association activity must also involve a re-examination of workers' central life interests. Workers who made a positive effort to organize their own leisure activities were suggesting that it was outside the work sphere that they were really able to express themselves.

The appearance of workers' recreational associations in the 1890s marks the start of the transition of popular leisure culture from spontaneity to organization and of the adaptation of leisure forms to the urban environment, albeit in a more future-oriented fashion than previously. Although many associations reaffirmed links with the pre-industrial past their methods and organizational forms were distinctly modern. In contrast with the consumer-oriented popular entertainment described in Chapter 4, the voluntary associations involved independent organization, active participation and, frequently, democratic decision making. They also initiated many women in to active leisure – confessional groups were particularly prominent here, but most other clubs and societies encouraged women and children to attend their extra-curricular events. And while in their early stages the leisure associations reflected and perpetuated divisions within the working class, in the long term they introduced a large number of working people to active leisure pursuits which eventually coincided, paving the way for the mass commercial leisure sector of the postwar years.

Notes

1 Lidtke, *The Alternative Culture*, p. 25.
2 O. von Gierke (1868), cited in R. Rürup, *Deutschland im 19. Jahrhundert 1815–1871* (Göttingen: Vandenhoek & Ruprecht, 1984), p. 100. More generally see G. Iggers, 'The Political Theory of Voluntary Associations in Early Nineteenth Century German Liberal Thought', in D. B. Robertson (ed.), *Voluntary Associations. A Study of Groups in Free Societies* (Richmond, VA: John Knox Press, 1966).
3 Blackbourn and Eley, *Peculiarities of German History*, pp. 196–7.
4 F. A. Hoyer, 'Die Vereinsdeutsche – Karikatur oder Wirklichkeit?', in *Deutsche Rundschau*, vol. 90 (1964), p. 19; O. Dann, 'Die Anfänge politische Vereinsbildung in Deutschland', in U. Engelhardt (ed.), *Soziale Bewegung und Politische Verfassung. Beiträge zur Geschichte der modernen Welt* (Stuttgart: Klett Cotta, 1976), pp. 197–232; T. Nipperdey, 'Verein als Soziale Struktur in Deutschland im späten und frühen 19. Jahrhundert', in Nipperdey, *Gesellschaft, Kultur, Theorie. Gesammelte Aufsätze zur neueren Geschichte* (Göttingen: Vandenhoek & Ruprecht, 1976), pp. 174–205; H. Groschopp, 'Bürgerliches Vereinswesen und Lebensreformbewegung vor 1914', in *Weimarer Beiträge*, vol. 30 (1984), pp. 1852–69.

5 H-U. Wehler, *Krisenherde des Kaiserreichs* (Göttingen: Vandenhoek & Ruprecht, 1969), p. 444.
6 Lidtke, *The Alternative Culture*, p. 38.
7 StAB, B 283, 284, 285, 286, 287: Vereinswesen 1875–89, contain all the association statutes submitted to the Bochum police.
8 R. Koch, 'Die Entwicklung des VfL Bochum auf dem Hintergrund der deutschen Turn-und Sportbewegung des 19. und 20. Jahrhundert' (thesis, Ruhr-Universität Bochum, 1977), p. 136.
9 A. Jagusch, 'Die Entwicklung des V.f.L. Bochum 1848 e.V. unter besonderer Berücksichtigung der Fußballabteilung' (thesis, Ruhr-Universität Bochum, 1975), p. 8.
10 Koch, 'Die Entwicklung des V.f.L. Bochum', p. 151.
11 J-L. Malvache, *Arbeitersport in Bochum* (Bochum: DGB, 1984).
12 HStAD, RD 33301: Düsseldorf Turnverein gegr. 1847. Bericht über Vereinsjahr 1908–9.
13 See K. Tenfelde, 'Bergmännisches Vereinswesen im Ruhrgebiet während die Industrialisierung', in J. Reulecke and W. Weber (eds), *Fabrik, Familie, Feierabend* (Wuppertal: Hammer, 1978), pp. 315–44.
14 Hickey, *Workers in Imperial Germany*, pp. 86–7.
15 Nolan, *Social Democracy and Society*, p. 135.
16 W. Matull, *Der Freiheit eine Gasse: Geschichte der Düsseldorfer Arbeiterbewegung* (Düsseldorf: Schwann, 1979), pp. 75–8
17 Nolan, *Social Democracy and Society*, p. 135.
18 H. Seeling, *Geschichte der Gerresheimer Glashütte – Ursprung und Entwicklung 1864–1908* (Studien zur Düsseldorfer Wirtschaftgeschichte, vol. 1, Düsseldorf: Lintz, 1964), pp. 48–9.
19 J-V. Wagner, *Hakenkreuz über Bochum. Machtergreifung und Nationalsozialistischer Alltag in einer Revierstadt* (Bochum: Studienverlag Brockmeyer, 1983), pp. 450–3.
20 Calculated from Nolan's figures, *Social Democracy and Society*, p. 309.
21 Nolan, *Social Democracy and Society*, pp. 312–13.
22 Ibid., p.18.
23 J. Mooser, *Arbeiterleben in Deutschland 1900–1970* (Frankfurt am Main: Suhrkamp, 1984), pp. 188–9.
24 Nolan, *Social Democracy and Society*, pp. 100–2.
25 Hickey, *Workers in Imperial Germany*, p. 255.
26 L. Dingwerth, *Mit dem Zeichenstift durch Bochum* (Bochum: Studienverlag Brockmeyer, 1984), p. 17.
27 Roth, *Social Democrats in Imperial Germany*; Ritter, 'Workers' Culture in Imperial Germany'; D. Dowe, 'The Working Men's Choral Movement in Germany before the First World War', in *Journal of Contemporary History*, vol. 13 (1978), pp. 269–96; H-J. Steinberg, 'Workers' Libraries in Imperial Germany', in *History Workshop*, vol. 1 (1976), pp. 166–80.
28 StAD, III 5890: Vermischte Vereine 1875–80; *Düsseldorfer Zeitung*, 20 May 1892.
29 Seippel, *Bochum Einst und Jetzt*, p. 288.
30 Brüggemeier, *Leben vor Ort*, p. 151. Tenfelde remarks, 'Pigeon associations and allotment societies, dog or rabbit-breeding clubs often arouse little more than sympathetic laughter!' – see 'Bergmännisches Vereinswesen', p. 315.
31 H. Glaser (ed.), *Von der Kultur der Leute* (Berlin: Ullstein, 1983), p. 389.
32 StAB, B 312: Zur Hebung der einheimischen Kleintierzucht, Bochum 1912; StAB, B 312: 6. Jahresbericht der Kleintierzüchter im Industriegebiet, 1913.
33 StAB, AL 176: Ziegenzuchtvereine Stadt- und Landkreis Bochum, Altenbochum May 1905.

34 StAB, B 312: Verzeichnis der im Stadtbezirk Bochum vorhandenen Kleintier-zuchtvereine, Bochum 1912.
35 M. Grän, *Erinnerungen aus einer Bergarbeiterkolonie im Ruhrgebiet* (Münster: F. Coppenrath, 1983), p. 35; Koch, *Bochum Dazumal*, p. 99.
36 Koch, *Bochum Dazumal*, p. 99.
37 MS, 25 June 1885.
38 Tenfelde, 'Bergmännisches Vereinswesen'; Hickey, *Workers in Imperial Germany*, especially pp. 156–68; J. Mott, 'Miners, Weavers and Pigeon Racing', in M. A. Smith, S. Parker and C. S. Smith (eds), *Leisure and Society in Britain* (London: Allen Lane, 1973), pp. 88–96.
39 Koch, *Bochum Dazumal*, p. 80.
40 W. Pape (b. 1903) in S. Bajohr, *Vom bitteren Los der kleinen Leute. Protokolle über den Alltag Braunschweiger Arbeiterinnen und Arbeiter 1900 bis 1933* (Cologne: Bund, 1984), p. 198.
41 Hickey, 'Class Conflict and Class Consciousness', p. 336.
42 J. Sperber, 'The Transformation of Catholic Associations in the Northern Rhineland and Westphalia 1830–70', in *Journal of Social History*, vol. 15 (1981), pp. 253–63; Sperber, 'Roman Catholic Religious Identity in Rhineland-West-phalia 1800–70: Quantitative Examples and some Political Implications', in *Social History*, vol. 7 (1982), pp. 305–18.
43 Sperber, *Popular Catholicism*, p. 177.
44 Ibid., p. 179.
45 *Statistisches Jahrbuch für das Deutsche Reich*, vol. 32 (1911), p. 466.
46 See Sperber, *Popular Catholicism*, for details of early Catholic tradition of social organization, especially pp. 280–2.
47 MS, 26 February 1885 and 16 June 1885.
48 A. Kraus, 'Gemeindeleben und Industrialisierung. Das Beispiel des evange-lischen Kirchenkreises Bochum', in Reulecke and Weber (eds), *Fabrik, Familie, Feierabend*, pp. 292–3; Hickey, *Workers in Imperial Germany*, p. 105; *Statistisches Jahrbuch für das Deutsche Reich*, vol. 32 (1911), p. 466. For a detailed analysis of Evangelical Workers' Associations in Gelsenkirchen see G. Brakelmann, 'Die Anfänge der Evangelischen Arbeitervereinsbewegung in Gelsenkirchen 1882–1890', in K. Düwell and W. Köllmann (eds), *Rheinland-Westfalen im Industriezeitalter*, vol. 3 (Wuppertal: Hammer, 1983), pp. 40–55, in which he identifies a dilemma within the movement: 'They had formulated none of their own social-political demands. They relied totally upon the initiatives and enforcement strength of the state. When it came to actual social conflicts, to robust fist-fights, confusion was the inevitable consequence' (p. 54).
49 On secularization and the decline in church attendance on the part of the working class, see H-J. Brand, 'Kirchliches Vereinswesen und Freizeitgestaltung in einer Arbeitergemeinde 1872–1933: das Beispiel Schalke', in Huck (ed.), *Sozialgeschichte der Freizeit*, pp. 207–22; Kraus, 'Gemeindeleben und Industriali-sierung'. By 1910 over 650,000 people demonstrated their allegiance to one of the main churches in a tangible form by becoming a member of one of the 4,775 Catholic or Protestant workers' associations, – see *Statistisches Jahrbuch für das Deutsche Reich*, vol. 32 (1911), p. 466.
50 Kraus, 'Gemeindeleben und Industrialisierung', p. 278.
51 Ibid., pp. 275–6; Hickey, *Workers in Imperial Germany*, p. 77.
52 Hickey, *Workers in Imperial Germany*, p. 106.
53 Tenfelde, 'Bergmännisches Vereinswesen', pp. 338–9.
54 Sperber, *Popular Catholicism*, p. 267.
55 Lidtke, 'Social Class and Secularisation', p. 32.

56 StAB, Nachlass Küppers, vol. 5, p. 329; StAB, 1887 Flugblatt, 'An die Wähler des Reichstagswahlkreis Bochum' from Gustav Lehmann – Die Arbeiter-Wahl Comité des Reichstagswahlkreis Bochum; for the election results in 1887 see Hickey, *Workers in Imperial Germany*, p. 254.

57 Crew, *Town in the Ruhr*, pp. 129–30; Hickey, *Workers in Imperial Germany*, p. 81.

58 HStAD, 8950: Kirchweihfeste 1870–93, 6 December 1890.

59 In 1871, 0.9% of local inhabitants of Bochum were from foreign countries, by 1907 the figure was 1.5% – Crew, *Town in the Ruhr*, pp. 60–1.

60 StAB, AL-D 68: Polen Gesangverein Julius Slowacki Dahlhausen (1909–12).

61 StAB, AL 350/6: Polnische Gesangverein 'Lutnia' in Langendreer (1902–14), 4 May 1902.

62 StAD, AL-D 71: prosecution of Schildberg Turnverein, 13 August 1907.

63 K. Klessmann, 'Kaiser Wilhelm's Gastarbeiter. Polen als Bergarbeiter im Ruhrgebiet', in L. Niethammer, B. Hombach, T. Fichter, U. Borsdorf (eds), *Die Menschen machen ihre Geschichte nicht als freien Stücken* (Berlin/Bonn: Dietz, 1984), p. 106; R. Murphy, *Guestworkers in the German Reich: A Polish Community in Wilhelmine Germany* (New York: Columbia University Press, 1983), p. 155.

64 K. Klessmann, *Polnische Bergarbeiter im Ruhrgebiet*, p. 103.

65 R. Murphy, *Guestworkers in the German Reich*, p. 168.

66 Seippel, *Bochum Einst und Jetzt*, pp. 288–9.

67 StAB, Verwaltungsbericht 1860–1.

68 HStAD, RD 33301: Düsseldorf Turnverein, provisional programme 1910.

69 StAB, AL-D 71: 31 March 1911; cf. Lidtke's descriptions of associational events, *The Alternative Culture*, pp. 50–74.

70 HStAD, RA 22753: *Kölnischer Volkszeitung*, 18 December 1898.

71 StAD, III 5753: Nachweisung der von geschlossenen Gesellschaften abgehaltenen Vegnügungen.

72 Ibid.

73 J. C. Scott, 'Membership and Participation in Voluntary Associations', in *American Sociological Review*, vol. 22 (1957), p. 318.

74 On the sociological theory of instrumental and expressive voluntary associations see C. Wayne Gordon and N. Babchuk, 'A Typology of Voluntary Associations', in *American Sociological Review*, vol. 24 (1959), pp. 22–9; A. P. Jacoby and N. Babchuk, 'Instrumental and Expressive Voluntary Associations', in *Sociology and Social Research*, vol. 47 (1963), pp. 461–71.

75 Hickey, *Workers in Imperial Germany*, p. 120. Cf. J. Bishop and P. Hoggett, *Organising around Enthusiasms. Patterns of Mutual Aid in Leisure* (London: Comedia, 1986), a study of voluntary associational life in contemporary Britain which concludes that the 'search for pure, oppositional, working-class sub-culture . . . is misplaced . . . Rather we see a series of sub-cultural formations infused with contradictory values' (p. 129).

76 Nolan, *Social Democracy and Society*, p. 309.

77 Hickey, *Workers in Imperial Germany*, pp. 252–4.

78 D. Langewiesche, 'The Impact of the German Labor Movement on Workers' Culture', in *Journal of Modern History*, vol. 59 (1987), p. 516.

79 Hickey, *Workers in Imperial Germany*, p. 291.

80 Bishop and Hoggett, *Organising around Enthusiasms*, pp. 121–7.

6

The struggle for control

The social question and 'rational recreation'

All the working-class leisure activities discussed thus far provoked an overwhelmingly negative response from those fearful of the imminent disturbance of the precariously maintained social order. Traditional fairs and festivals were suppressed and curtailed. Drinking was made illegal in factories, outlets for the purchase of alcohol were closely monitored and tavern opening hours were continually being interfered with. The streets were gradually cleared of irksome entertainers, small-scale theatrical entertainment was strictly controlled and even dancing was frowned upon. A series of measures was introduced to clear up the towns and cities from a moral point of view. And when workers joined associations to pursue their interests collectively they were accused of neglecting their family lives. For the most part these negative perceptions and repressive actions adopted by the police, city councils and employers arose out of specific local conditions and were not masterminded by the state on a nationwide basis. The Reichstag passed surprisingly little legislation regulating the amusements of the common people, leaving local elites considerable discretion.[1] Local officials were assumed to have a clearer view of the particular problems in their area and were relied upon to act responsibly. Working class recreation, therefore, increasingly became a local political issue, a focus of struggle for control between various interest groups, while the working-class voice was drowned out by the louder and more influential arguments emanating from the mouths of employers, small businesses, the church, members of the town council and the police. The interests of the group that stood to lose or gain the most – the workers – were largely ignored.

Most of those who had already made their views public on the issue of lower-class leisure retreated to an idealized image of a traditional society with a morality to match. The suppression of popular amusements, from fairgrounds to schnapps drinking, gambling and dancing the tango, failed to address the forward march of change in modern urban society. A combination of *naiveté* and lack of imagination meant that any conception of a future social consensus was conspicuous by its absence. Instead, a combination of paternalism and law enforcement was relied upon to maintain a fragile equilibrium. It was not until the 1890s at the earliest that any members of the middle class began to advocate positive improvements in the provision of leisure and recreation. While the absence of a central policy allowed local political and economic power blocs considerable room for manoeuvre, it also created an immense sphere of influence and activity for national and regional extra-parliamentary pressure groups. Indeed, since the 1840s liberal concern with the problems of an industrializing society was played out through the voluntary association, the first of which made its appearance in the wake of the weavers' uprising in Silesia in 1844. The Central Association for the Welfare of the Working Classes (*Zentralverein für das Wohl der arbeitenden Klassen* – ZWAK), a pressure group which saw its role as being the head of a social reform lobby and an intermediary between antagonistic social classes, was founded by a group of bourgeois intellectuals, liberal-minded adminstrators and educated middle classes. Its concept of reform was not interventionist, but it was progressive. Through education and self-help, the elevation of the culture of the working class would facilitate its integration into bourgeois society, it was thought.[2] A reform ideology that addressed deep-rooted social inequalities, while stressing amelioration rather than change, found a fertile soil among the frightened German business and educated classes. They warmed to this utopian vision emphasizing brotherlinesss and the 'conquering of the barriers between capitalists and proletarians' that was to be achieved initially through the establishment of savings banks, insurance and friendly societies and sickness and accident funds.[3]

Towards the end of the nineteenth century the ZWAK began to jettison its utopian social welfare ideology and increasingly became a tool of the large employers. Krupp and the Bismarck-Hütte were just two of the large industrial concerns with influence within the organization.[4] Some of the more liberal reform measures proposed by the educated middle classes (or *Bildungsbürgertum* as they were known) such as the introduction of social amenities which would lead to workforce contentedness and, theoretically, to higher production and profits for the company, were subjugated to employers' self-interest. 'The wild, fanatic phantom of socialism must be opposed', argued the ZWAK in 1870, and replaced by 'realistic ideas'.[5] The ZWAK was not alone in its aversion to socialist ideology. Even the prominent Society for Social Reform (*Gesellschaft für Soziale Reform*, founded in 1901), which maintained links with the trade union movement, saw itself as a mass, broad-based organization offering protection against the further expansion of the SPD, while the Association for Social Policy (*Verein für Sozialpolitik*, founded 1872) also believed that the introduction of social improvements would blunt the revolutionary edge of the working class and the labour movements.[6]

Employers' involvement in social reform associations were often little more than tokenism designed to salve their own consciences, since the profit motive was always higher on their list of priorities than genuine social improvements were. The 1906/7 annual report of an employers' association in the Barmen district stated that 'the most effective means of the improvement of the material condition of the working class is, next to the encouragement of thrift, a vigorous, stronger industry.'[7] A rise in wages would have been more effective than the establishment of savings banks, according to the SPD.[8] 'Under the guise of friendliness to workers and the declaration of social reform', wrote the socialist *Freie Presse* in 1891, 'bourgeois social reform efforts only work to the advantage of the capitalists.'[9]

Some of the larger employers had already begun to introduce company welfare schemes for their workforces. Krupp and the Bochumer Verein were at the forefront of this movement and, indeed, were unusual in the extent of their social provision. Krupp began to introduce workers' insurance schemes in the 1860s, and company housing was provided in the following decade. The welfare available to Krupp employees extended beyond health and disability insurance and pension schemes. Health facilities were provided on site; there was also a cooperative store, a school, library, reading rooms and recreational amenities (but no licensed premises selling alcohol). In Bochum, around 5,000 workers lived in the Verein's Stahlhausen colony by the turn of the century; in Gerresheim, a suburb of Düsseldorf dominated by the glassworks which employed 2,800 people in 1900, a total of 1,014 apartments were available to house 5,438 employees and their families.[10] By 1903 there were 72 Düsseldorf firms operating their own insurance schemes and 25 provided housing in 1910.[11] As Elaine Spencer has noted with reference to company housing in the Düsseldorf area, 'employers viewed company-owned workers' colonies . . . as a means of establishing an orderly and controlled environment conducive to the molding of orderly and controlled lives.'[12] Certainly there was a negative side to the social welfare provided by employers. Reform was tempered by control and activities thought detrimental to productivity were not permitted.

Company welfare paternalism, then, was part of the same movement, a mixture of welfare and control, the balance often weighing more heavily towards the latter. A similar point could be made about the involvement of municipal councils in welfare schemes and reform measures. They publicly subscribed to the liberal ideology that concerned itself with working-class living conditions, influenced by the ideas of people like Karl Bücher, a professor at the University of Leipzig in the 1890s, who prescribed the introduction of municipal socialism along English lines as an answer to the fragmentary nature of urban life. Similar practical proposals involving increased public ownership of services were recommended by Adolf Weber, one of Bücher's successors.[13] However, in a period when the socialists were gaining ground in municipal elections, local councillors had an eye to the future of their seats. It is clear that by the turn of the century social reform was no longer a minority concern fuelled by the desire to maintain a social order. Rather, the advocates of *Sozialpolitik* had found a much wider audience, not just among proclaimed liberals but within business and administrative circles too.

The growth of the labour movement and the revival of the Social Democratic Party in 1890, coupled with the reverberations of Bismarck's social insurance schemes and Caprivi's New Course, clearly rekindled interest in both sides of the social question. Pioneered by the *Bildungsbürgertum*, a group consisting primarily of academics, professionals, civil servants and members of the Protestant clergy, what has been called the 'socialization of the conscience of the educated middle classes' found expression in a plethora of voluntary associations on a nationwide scale: the German Education Association, the Society for the Spread of Public Education, the German Association for the Prevention of Alcohol Abuse and a host of others addressing problems of housing, poverty, health and leisure.

The social reform advocated by the *Bildungsbürgertum* derived its ideological basis from a more humanist evaluation of modern society that also found echoes in less well-known social movements of the period, like the Humane Association and societies promoting garden towns, vegetarianism, anti-vivisection and non-smoking. Reformers expounded a more profound philosophy; a mixture of social responsibility, humanitarianism and utilitarianism supplanted the earlier desire to maintain the status quo by outmanoeuvring working-class radicalism. Their primary aim was to create a more efficient society by promoting harmony between the classes; self-discipline was essential to the ideology of the liberation of the working class. However, the working class could only hope to attain this state by exposure to bourgeois example. 'Steeped in an ethic of social responsibility and believing in their . . . mission as bearers of a higher "Kultur"', writes James Roberts, 'they sought to open the path of social advance and cultural attainment to the new working class.'[14] It was bourgeois conduct in the private sphere that dictated what was acceptable, respectable and correct.

The approach of Protestant and Catholic reformers mirrored these trends, although their respective church hierarchies were less enthusiastic. Neither ever managed to abandon the missionary mentality completely, but genuine attempts to improve the way of life of the urban proletariat were made. The Christian Social movement reached its peak in the 1880s and 1890s with the formation of the Workers' Welfare League in 1880, 'the most significant Catholic-confessional employers' organization in Germany', and the Catholic German People's Association was founded in 1890 with around 100,000 members.[15] The subsequent establishment of Catholic workers' associations and the Catholic-dominated Christian trade unions emphasized the movement's commitment to the welfare of the working class. In contrast, the Protestant social reform movements like the

Innere Mission and the Central Association for Social Reform (*Centralverein für Sozialreform*) advocated state socialism based on a 'relationship of trust between the monarchy and the working class' and government interventionist policies in favour of workers' welfare.[16] Neither proposed socialist solutions; most Christian reformers restricted themselves to alleviating conditions rather than suggesting radical change in the capitalist system.

Working-class recreations appeared on the social reform agenda a little later than the more pressing problems of housing and health. The first public acknowledgement of this particular 'social problem' was a conference convened in 1892, prompted by a reduction of the working day and the repeal of the anti-socialist laws shortly before. For the first time alleged misuse of leisure time was not entirely blamed on the worker. Five years later the first Congress for Public Entertainment was held in Berlin. In the words of the journal *Die Volksunterhaltung*, this 'was the first attempt to gather together the powers which work in this important area of public charitable activity and bring into the open the exchange of opinions, and clarification of methods in the field of public entertainment.'[17] Leisure was treated as a problem arising from the conditions of industrial society, one which intensified as work became more mechanized and the length of the working day was reduced.[18] Reformers like Viktor Böhmert, leading light of the social reform movement and editor of *Der Arbeiterfreund* (*The Workers' Friend*, journal of the ZWAK), at least formulated a constructive approach to the problem, with the emphasis on raising the working class from 'coarse, sensuous enjoyment to unadulterated, spiritual pleasures.'[19]

Popular amusements such as drinking, music hall and so on were still frowned upon. But it was publicans and other entertainment entrepreneurs who found themselves the principal recipients of the reformers' ire. The working class, depicted as the victim of environmental pressures, became the innocent objects of the new ideology which aimed to wean them away from 'coarse, sensual enjoyment'.[20] Certainly temperance reformers, believed that state legislation to alter this environment, along with the provision of counter-attractions, would lure the drinker away from the public house.[21] Indigenous working-class amusements were clearly not compatible with industrial society. According to the critics, they only contributed to disharmony in society and in the workplace in particular. So, work discipline had to be projected into play. Thus emerged one of the most important underlying concepts of the reformers' philosophy. Harmony could be attained if the classes would join together in morally uplifting and socially useful pastimes.

The views held by people like Böhmert, Bücher and Weber signified a departure from the mainstream reform movements of the nineteenth century. Earlier philanthropic organizations had looked for solutions to problems like poverty, poor housing and ill health within the parameters of the existing social order. They emphasized the importance of the family and the home, the provision of 'sufficient, healthy, pleasant accommodation', the care and rearing of children, and regular church attendance.[22] Böhmert and his supporters, on the other hand, advocated a more positive and active approach to the social problems of the day. In *Der Arbeiterfreund* Böhmert put forward his plans for a system of *public* welfare, public entertainment, public leisure facilities and so on. Transactions between the classes were thought to be of paramount importance, although workers and their betters were never expected to meet on equal terms. 'Manners travelled downwards' in Germany too and the working class was to learn 'by better example from the top down' in order to wean it away from 'widespread bad habits'.[23]

Although the ZWAK had members throughout the Reich by the 1880s, with a particular foothold in Prussia, reformers like Böhmert could only hope to implement far-reaching reform of working-class recreation with the support of a countrywide network of voluntary organizations with the same aims. There was no shortage of socially concerned individuals prepared to meet the challenge. In 1897 at the Congress for Public Entertainment it was confidently stated that 'in almost all parts of Germany, associations and individuals are devoting themselves to the task.'[24] Education and welfare associations pressed for and implemented policy at the grassroots level, often in association with the local councils. Support from the state in the form of legislation and finance had always been a prominent feature of philanthropic activity in Germany, and the recreation reformers took advantage of this generosity. Municipal support and aid was particularly welcome, and it was not long before some politically sympathetic town councils were initiating action in this area themselves. 'Conceived as a measure of humanitarian relief and an antidote to political subversion', writes Peter Bailey with reference to the early British movement from which its German counterpart undoubtedly drew some inspiration, 'rational recreation . . . became part of the ongoing and fundamental re-socialisation of the working class', by means of its cultural and moral elevation.[25]

The translation of the rhetoric of social reform into the reality of rational recreation found early expression in public entertainment evenings (*Volksunterhaltungsabende*). Usually organized by local education associations, they were regarded as 'a particularly suitable means of spiritual and moral improvement of the mass of the population and of reconciling the common and painfully lamentable rift between the educated and the populace.'[26] According to the Düsseldorf Education Association these events, which typically featured classical and traditional music, recitations and public singing, were a tremendous success, attracting an audience representing all sectors of the population, from top government officials and tradespeople to factory workers and domestic servants, but in truth few members of the

144

working class attended.[27] Although the price of a ticket was only a few pfennigs the content of the entertainment did not appeal and workers and their families were not keen on making the long journey into the city centre where the events usually took place. Moreover, in spite of the public pronouncements of the reformers, political motives were not that easy to disguise. The entertainment evenings were conceived as an alternative to Social Democratic activities, thus driving away members of the SPD who might otherwise have attended. After the repeal of the anti-socialist laws in 1890 it is hardly surprising that the main tenets of middle-class reform – working-class self-improvement, respectability, harmonious class relations – should take second place to the combat of the socialist threat.

The public entertainment evenings were really only fringe events. More central to the social reform ideology were leisure activities capable of reaching large numbers of the working class. Libraries and parks fulfilled this requirement and at the same time had the potential to raise the manners and morals of working men and women in an environment where they could be physically controlled and morally educated. After the turn of the century the energies and finances of reform agencies were increasingly concentrated in these two areas of leisure provision. Workers' minds *and* bodies became the objects of rational recreation.

Useful pursuits

At a meeting of the Bochum town council in February 1900 the discussion turned to the proposed erection of a public library. The assembled representatives were agreed that 'one must give the citizens the opportunity to rest in a place other than the public house', thus echoing the sentiments of those engaged in the reform of working–class recreational habits.[28] The public entertainment evenings, although fairly successful, were only sporadic events attracting relatively small numbers of people. Libraries and other elevating institutions, on the other hand, would be permanent fixtures, and it was hoped, utilized by a large proportion of the general public, including the working class.

The importance of the role of educational institutions in the policy of the recreation reformers was paramount. Reading certainly fell into the category of useful and improving recreation and libraries were the natural extension of and accompaniment to other efforts like educational courses and lecture evenings. Reading was the ultimate regulated amusement. The supply of material could be controlled and it was a fine advertisement for the self-help philosophy, for those who used the libraries were said to be actively seeking to improve their knowledge rather than being in passive receipt of welfare. Libraries were potentially key institutions, of 'great worth . . . in the framework of the whole of public life, particularly in the struggle against trashy literature, alcoholism and criminality', according to a contributor to *Der Arbeiterfreund* in 1912.[29]

Literacy rates in Germany, especially among the working class, were relatively high, largely on account of the early development of compulsory primary education. Between the eighteenth and the mid-nineteenth centuries the literacy rate improved from around 10 to 70 per cent of the adult population.[30] Official statistics can be misleading, however. Schooling only left people with a minimal ability to read and write and *Hochdeutsch*, the official German language, was 'a foreign language for the majority of the population.'[31]

> Until the second half of the nineteenth century the majority of factory workers could only read with difficulty [writes Rudolf Braun]. It was not until the second half of the nineteenth century that education also reached the working population to a greater degree and their reaction to education began to change.[32]

The change was slow. Rudolf Schenda is correct in drawing attention to the discrepancy between those who were able to read and those who made use of this skill. Literacy levels only indicate the optimal number of potential readers. 'They do not mean that such a percentage of the population really read.'[33] Needless to say, the lower classes rarely purchased books and if they did they were commonly the Bible or prayer books, calendars and technical works.[34] Expenditure on reading material had to compete with other demands on the working-class budget, and it has been argued that women resented their husbands' attempts to educate themselves because they felt the money could have been better spent on household items.[35] Even the reading of newspapers was an infrequent pastime for the lower classes. They rarely purchased newspapers on a regular basis and were most likely to find one in the local pub. It was the urban middle class who accounted for the rise in newspaper consumption. In short, money was scarce and books and newspapers were luxuries.

If the social reformers had been faced with a situation of widespread literacy combined with working-class indifference to reading material their task would have been a simpler one. But a sudden increase in the availability of cheap, popular fiction, and a concomitant rise in working-class consumption of the products of the new commercial publishing houses, meant that recreational reformers found they were no longer preaching to the ignorant. Rather, they were having to influence a more sophisticated market. The revolution in the popular fiction market was spearheaded by the production of cheap pamphlets containing illustrated short stories, colporteur novels, or *Hintertreppenromane* (novels sold in innumerable instalments by door-to-door salesmen) and, gradually replacing the multi-story volumes, the *Groschenheft*. While a complete novel could have cost the reader upwards of 10 marks to buy, instalments could be purchased for 10 pfennigs each. Needless to say, the cumulative cost if one purchased every instalment exceeded the price of the complete book, but few could ever afford 10 marks at once and few subscribed to the end of a series. Both pamphlets and colporteur novels began to appear in the 1860s; by the mid-1870s they had achieved widespread commercial success, becoming the 'primary reading matter of the lower classes in the 1870s and into the 1880s'.[36]

Many were initially attracted to this type of literature by the pictures on the pamphlet covers reflecting the thrills and spills in the text. The content deviated little from tried and tested formats: adventure and sensation were the watchwords of most stories. They were full of heroes and villains, murderers and maidens, cowboys and Indians, criminals and detectives. The perceived tastes of female readers were catered for by romantic interludes between the violence and action.[37] The most popular of all the pamphlet fiction series were the Nick Carter American detective stories, introduced to the public in 1886. The popularity of this series surpassed all others and it was bought at the rate of 45,000 pamphlets a week.[38] In total, between 25 and 30 million pamphlets a year were sold in the half-decade before 1914.[39]

But it was the reading patterns of young people that gave rise to the most serious concern among reformers. Allegations were rife that trashy literature encouraged juvenile crime. The connection between this type of reading material and an alleged rise in the youth crime rate was a tenuous one, however. The excitement to be found within the pages of a Nick Carter pamphlet was, suggests Schenda, an escapist form of entertainment. 'The un-literary reader looked for actions, not ideas.'[40] These stories provided a form of consolation for the hardships of everyday life, and as such can be regarded as having a diversionary effect, siphoning off tensions that might otherwise have been expressed in more active, perhaps violent or deviant ways. Moreover, in spite of the action and violence contained within these pamphlets, the story-lines rarely challenged the status quo. Good triumphed over evil; nationalistic ideas were freely expressed; ethnic minorities and alien races were discriminated against.[41] Nevertheless, popular fiction was still judged to be a dangerous influence on young people and school libraries, children's reading rooms and campaigns to combat the so-called trash literature were at the front line in the attempt to encourage young people to appreciate 'good literature'.

Bourgeois-liberal voluntary associations threw themselves into the battle against filth and trash literature, the so-called *Kampf gegen Schmutz- und Schund*. The People United Against Trash in Print and Picture and the Society for the Mass Distribution of Good Literature were just two such organizations. But in contrast to those whose opinions were formed during the 'moral panic' era of the 1890s when, as Robin Lenman has pointed out, the distinction between trash and pornography or obscenity was a fine one and the debates around the Lex Heinze dominated all practical proposals, the 1900s saw the proliferation of national and local associations which regarded the radical anti-obscenity movement as counter productive.[42] Active groups like the Society for the Spread of Public Education, the Education Association, the Central Association for the Founding of Public Libraries and the Public Library Association advocated positive alternatives to the negative suppression of the mass literature markets, mainly in the form of public libraries and reading rooms.

It was a sign of more enlightened times, the adherence to a *Sozialpolitik* and the creation of acceptable alternatives as opposed to the suppression of an irritant, that public libraries were regarded by many as one of the best possible solutions to the problem. In rational recreation terms too, public libraries were the ideal institution. As well as playing a key role in the education of the working class it was hoped that libraries would

> encourage diligence and thriftiness . . . domesticity and sobriety, awaken [in the ordinary man] his domestic instinct and love of the fatherland and by these means counteract the dissemination of morally damaging and poisonous. . . reading material, as well as tavern life and coarse entertainment.[43]

The public library was envisaged as a neutral arena for communication between all social classes. In the words of the major proponent of the public library, Ernst Schultze, the *Volksbibliothek* was 'an institution which should serve *all* classes of the population'.[44]

Such libraries did already exist in the region. In Prussia as a whole there were 451 lending libraries in 1837, a figure which had almost doubled by 1858, to 824.[45] Moreover, branches of the Public Education Association in northwest Germany had established no less than 370 youth and public libraries in the area by 1873, each holding between 60 and 100 volumes.[46] Düsseldorf boasted a municipal public library as early as 1886, adding a reading room ten years later. This was the exception, however, and what libraries existed in smaller towns were mostly in schools or run privately by religious organizations, voluntary associations and trade unions.

But this network of libraries was hardly able to cater to a public apparently hungry for reading material, whose demand steadily increased as literacy improved and the supply of popular fiction escalated. The libraries were hampered by the low level of their book stocks. Most private libraries lent to members only and some levied high subscription fees. Of the 25 libraries in the district of Bochum only two had collections of more than 500 volumes.[47] There was clearly a need for a form of free public library, administered by the local authorities and with steady financial input. On 18 July 1899 a circular from the Prussian Minister of Culture gave considerable impetus to the public library movement. Along with public libraries, school and travelling libraries were to be encouraged, the latter playing an important role in the education of the rural population. Central government endorsement of the rational recreation policy, although not as decisive as the 1850 Libraries Act in Britain, sparked off a wave of library mania that was to continue throughout the first ten years of the twentieth century.[48]

Central government adopted an advisory but limited financial role compared with local government and private associational efforts to provide a public library service. Elberfeld's municipal librarian observed that the decree had 'caused hitherto slow corporations' to recognize public education as an important question.[49] Local authorities did not linger long over a decision on this score, bearing in mind the dangerous developments they saw looming on the horizon. Moreover, a public library was an important civic asset for a town in a period when municipal provision of public facilities was high on the agenda. The Society for the Spread of Public Education was also quick to react to the minister's announcement: in 1899 it founded and supported 352 libraries with a total of 16,627 volumes throughout the Reich.[50] But it was not until finance from central government was forthcoming that a comprehensive programme could be implemented. Initially the Prussian Ministry of Education provided 50,000 marks per annum, later increased to 100,000 marks, for the building of public libraries. District governments responded quickly. Indeed, even after the first burst of enthusiasm, financial assistance continued to be forthcoming. In 1904 the Düsseldorf government paid a total of 5,890 marks for the 'erection and expansion of public libraries' in the district, individual libraries receiving between 50 and 300 marks apiece.[51] Of course, central funding was supplemented by contributions from clubs, associations and private individuals.

Libraries were certainly the flavour of the decade in the 1900s, not only in Prussia but throughout Germany. By 1906, in 40 cities with a total of around 11.5 million inhabitants, 1.4 million registered library users borrowed 5.4 million books.[52] By 1906 almost all the major towns in the Ruhr and northern Rhine area had a public library: Bochum's was founded in 1902, Düsseldorf had three by 1900 with another added in 1908, and Dortmund, Barmen, Elberfeld, Hagen, Mülheim/Ruhr and Solingen also had public libraries.[53]

In view of the motives behind the establishment of a library network in Germany, it is hardly surprising that considerable emphasis was placed on the provision of 'good literature'. The religious organizations were particularly active in this regard. In 1896 the Christian Journal Association published a number of attacks against the Social Democratic press and colporteur literature and hoped to combat these bad influences through the distribution of their pamphlets, *German Worker's Friend* for male readers and *Leisure Hour* for women. Almanacs like *The Worker* and *Busy Hands* intended for women workers, peasant-oriented publications stressing the pleasures of the countryside and conjuring up an idyllic existence, supplemented the evangelical literary output.[53]

The religious organizations were supported by local authorities who, in setting up public libraries, wanted to see them put to good use. As early as 1879 the Arnsberg district administration had selected a number of books considered suitable for the new libraries. Censorship at this level was later codified in the 1899 Library Decree, which excluded from public libraries confessionally and politically biased publications and those in which deviant views were expressed in harmful ways.[54] 'Good literature' was promoted at the expense of so-called trash by individual voluntary organizations like the German Poets' Memorial Foundation (founded in 1901) which circulated pamphlets promoting 'good and cheap books' and supplied them to libraries.[55] In an ironic twist to the tale, it is interesting to note that while Social Democratic literary output was censorially excluded from the shelves of public libraries, the Social Democrats themselves were unwitting allies of the liberal middle-class reformers in their battle against trash literature. 'Without underestimating the importance of light reading', wrote one of the foremost supporters of workers' libraries, 'our major objective still must be to interest workers in serious literature.'[56] Moreover, as Lidtke points out, librarians in charge of workers' libraries applied their privilege of censorship far more widely, excluding works by authors unsympathetic to the socialist cause.[57]

Did policies like these mean that the public libraries were full of patriotic literature and 'good books' for the education of the working class? Hardly. The three in Düsseldorf held more fiction than anything else: 8,248 fictional works out of a total of 13,334.[58] Even in socialist and trade union libraries the largest part of the holdings consisted of *Unterhaltungsliteratur* (fiction). The same was true of libraries across Germany. Fiction, humour and satire exceeded not just every other category but, in many cases, the total of all other categories put together.[59]

The primary purpose of establishing the libraries was to ameliorate the moral and educational condition of the working class, and once they were in place it was assumed that a large proportion of workers would patronize them. Indeed, the foundation of libraries in several towns in the area was justified by reference to a 'particularly great reading demand' on the part of the working class (in Essen), or to a significant increase in the working-class population in the area (in Krefeld).[60] But did the reformers and philanthropists assess the situation correctly? Would workers, whose taste for reading had been stimulated by pamphlet fiction and serialized stories, transfer their allegiance to the more serious and demanding material held in public libraries?

The short answer is no. Estimates of the proportion of working-class borrowers from public libraries vary considerably but certainly no more than one third of the library members belonged to this group. When one looks at the proportion of workers using these libraries in a number of different cities in Germany around the turn of the century, substantial differences are immediately apparent. Figures vary from 33 per cent working-class users in Danzig in 1899, to 23 per cent in Hanover, to only 12 per cent in Düsseldorf and 6 per cent in Leipzig.[61] Working-class membership was undoubtedly dependent on a number of variables, such as the composition of the population and workforce and the profile of local industry. Other important influences relate more directly to the provision of reading and borrowing facilities, notably the location of public libraries and the presence of alternative libraries like those run by the trade unions, the SPD and the large employers.[62]

By 1908 Düsseldorf was the proud owner of four public libraries. The first was situated in the centre of the city. Subsequent libraries, however, were built on the outskirts; a factor that had considerable influence on the social class of users. But despite the location of two of these libraries in working-class areas of the city, working-class membership never even reached 10 per cent of the total number of borrowers in Düsseldorf throughout the period 1897 to 1908. It is clear that artisans, shopkeepers and those running small businesses were the principal users of the public libraries, followed by tradespeople and, by mid-decade, civil servants; in short, members of the Düsseldorf *Mittelstand* were the chief patrons of the public library service. Generally speaking, not much more than one third of library members in this period belonged to the working class, which in turn means that only a tiny proportion of the working class as a whole used the facilities. Schenda estimates that only 0.6 per cent of Frankfurt's working class made use of public libraries in 1895.[63] Evidence from the Krupp factory library in Essen shows that even with a captive audience, only 40 per cent of the company's 24,000 employees belonged to the library in 1902–4. Over 60 per cent of higher and middle white-collar workers had lending cards whereas only 37 per cent of blue-collar employees joined the library, a figure which is more in keeping with the statistical evidence derived from public library reports.[64]

Membership and borrowing levels within the working class varied considerably according to occupation. The amount of reading a person did was related to the intensity of the work process, the length of the working day and the level of skill involved. Skilled workers like bookbinders, printers, painters and decorators were more likely to join a library and borrow books than their unskilled counterparts.[65] In a study of organized trade union workers in Bremen, Engelsing found that those least likely to use the trade union libraries were brewery, dock- and factory workers, sailors and those employed in the tobacco industry.[66] These observations are largely supported by a more contemporary study of the reading habits of the organized workers of Leipzig in 1898 where wood- and metalworkers were the least likely to use trade union libraries: only 305 volumes were borrowed by a small percentage of the 3,020 members of the metalworkers union. On the other hand, printers borrowed books far more frequently, 3,155 volumes being lent to 703 of these readers, 7,488 times: an average of 10.6 books per person, per year.[67]

Women were more avid readers than men. They consistently accounted for around a third of public library members in Düsseldorf. But although working-class women were keen readers of commercial popular fiction, there is little evidence to suggest that they took advantage of the literature available in public libraries. Few libraries maintained occupational statistics on their female readers, but in general those women employed in semi-professional occupations and married women from the middle classes made use of the library far more than their working-class sisters did.

Public library usage was not constant. Understandably, it was heaviest during the winter when the weather was inclement and fewer alternative forms of amusement were available. In the summer, walking, visiting friends and working on the allotment were preferable pastimes. Consequently, most books were borrowed during the months of December, January, February and March, while the lowest figures were recorded during the summer.

The fact that usage also varied according to the condition of the labour market should not surprise us. We already know that the amount of work-free time enjoyed by a worker influenced his or her reading habits. Indeed, Paul Göhre remarked that only the introduction of the eight-hour day would enable the working class to read more (therefore assuming that the desire to read was being frustrated). Hence library usage increased during times of high unemployment; in Elberfeld it was noticed that 'unemployment straight away brings about an increase in the usage of the reading room', and Engelsing comments that 'unemployment nurtured an increase in the desire to read at the beginning of the twentieth century.'[68] Reading was one of the few amusements that gained in popularity among the working class during times of economic hardship. There was usually only a minimal charge or none at all to join a public library or to borrow books. When the Elberfeld town council raised the price of a lending card in the municipal library from a minimal 10 pfennigs to 30 pfennigs, 1,400 readers were lost. The number of workers using the library was halved. Those libraries with reading rooms were more of an attraction to workers as they offered not only reading material, including the daily newspapers, but warmth and peace for free.

Having established that only a minority of the working class in any particular location took advantage of the new borrowing facilities, library records reveal that not even this group could fulfil the hopes of the reformers in their choice of reading material. In Düsseldorf, for instance, fiction far outnumbered any other category of literature borrowed in the period of 1899 to 1904, accounting for 77 per cent of all books lent in 1903–4.[69] To some extent the popularity of fiction and light reading did reflect the composition of libraries' stocks, but this category was borrowed at a higher rate than others: around ten times per year, per book, compared to an average of 5.6 times for all other categories. Even in the Krupp factory library in Essen, bearing in mind the ideological basis of the Krupp welfare programme and management's recognition of the importance of training and education to the success of the company, the number of fictional books borrowed in 1903–4 far outnumbered all other categories put together.[70]

All the signs point to a fairly independent attitude on the part of the workers in their selection of reading materials, whether they borrowed from the public library or from one run by the SPD, trade union or employer, all of whom censored the materials available. In 1895, in an article published in *Die Neue Zeit* entitled 'What does the German Worker Read?', a breakdown of categories of books borrowed by members of a Berlin trade union between 1891 and 1894 shows that although the library held more materials under the economics and technical literature section, novels were still the most frequently borrowed, 26 times per book on average compared with 15 for economics and 7.5 for technical literature.[71] Furthermore, socialist and trade union libraries such as those in Leipzig around the turn of the century show a similar pattern. Organized workers too were attracted more to light reading than more serious political material. Indeed, Hans-Josef Steinberg dispels all notions that SPD and trade-union members were keen to read party and socialist literature borrowed from their own libraries. He concludes by saying, 'the majority of socialist workers were absolutely alien to socialist theory and had little interest in theoretical party literature.' Only a small minority of educated workers borrowed books from the party literature shelves.[72]

The effect of the public library system on working-class reading habits is difficult to assess. Bearing in mind that the evidence presented above suggests that only a minority of members of public libraries were working-class, that the number of books borrowed per year, per person rarely reached double figures and even then with no guarantee that the book had been read, it is not difficult to agree with Ronald Fullerton that libraries had a negligible short-term effect, particularly in view of the continuing popularity of 'trash literature' and pamphlet fiction which never entirely succumbed to the 'good literature' campaign. In Fullerton's words, 'commercial pamphlet series remained the recreational reading choice for a large part of the German population'.[73]

Lungs of the city

'Good examples engender good manners' wrote Bochum's Mayor Lange in 1881, referring to the benefits to be accrued from the town's public park and striking a tone made familiar by those with a social conscience in this period.

This public park is not only used by the better situated classes but day in, day out, numerous members of working-class families are to be seen walking there. And in this way, because the different classes can pass the time and take exercise in this public town park, it follows that a dam and a barrier will be set up against the brutality and unruliness of morally depraved persons. This can only be beneficial with regard to moral improvement.[74]

In fact the Bochum town council had decided as early as 1869 that a park was an 'irrefutable necessity', in view of the rapid increase of the population of the town. Plans were drawn up, the plan was costed and by 1876 Bochum had the first municipally financed public park in the Ruhr. All this was two decades before widespread concern with public health and lower-class recreation in the 1890s brought about the creation of public parks throughout Germany.

However, Bochum was not typical; rather, its experience was more representative of the new industrial towns which lacked central open spaces and thus required positive planning measures. Older cities were proud of their promenades, walks, squares and parks, embellished with trees, shrubs and flowers. In Düsseldorf, which prided itself as a garden town, a green belt consisting of parks and avenues had been incorporated into the overall town plan in the eighteenth century, and provision was made for further green areas if the town expanded.[75] Yet the significance and function of such open spaces cannot be understood purely in recreational terms. These promenades and parks were planned and purpose-built for the urban, provincial upper classes. They were aesthetically pleasing but socially exclusive spaces used by elites to display, compete for and confirm their status. Common recreational space, that which had previously functioned as common land for festivals and games, began to disappear or be enclosed, either officially when land was privatized, or unofficially when certain spaces became class-bound.[76] If the lower classes were not physically barred from entering designated promenades and parks, or made to pay an entrance fee, they were excluded in less tangible ways.

The combination of a reduction in the amount of open, public space in urban centres, the intensification of industrial growth and the rapid increase of the urban population who were forced to lived in cramped, insanitary housing, more or less thrust the issue of park provision onto the local political agenda in the final third of the nineteenth century. Parks began to occupy an important place in the rhetoric of social reformers and rational recreation campaigners. Like a number of the panaceas recommended by these groups, public parks were seen as having almost limitless potential. Initially the liberal bourgeoisie concentrated on the health advantages to be gained from public access to open spaces; a similar argument was put forward by those who advocated gardens for colony housing schemes, and later allotments, of which it has been said that they 'provided the perfect complement to emerging German social thought that emphasized physical fitness and nutrition, as well as spiritual cleanliness.'[77] Parks were seen as oases in the midst of the dirt and noise of the city. 'An ugly town, full of noise which has grown too quickly, lying on one dreary level, over which storms rage in winter and the dust flies in summer, has little to offer the worker', was how Marie Bernays described Mönchengladbach in 1910; but, of course, she added, 'in the town there is the public park, attractively laid out, and which is suitable for walks.'[78] 'To the worker, a rich man was not he who ate and drank well but he who went walking' – true in the case of factory workers who rarely saw daylight at all during the winter months.[79] Parks, and presumably also the fresh air therein, were also judged to be beneficial in the control and treatment of diseases and illnesses like tuberculosis. New York's Central Park was once described as the 'lungs of the city'.[80] It had long been regarded as beneficial for children to have access to fresh air; now adults were to be the recipients of a similar initiative.

Of more importance in the eyes of the social reformers, however, was the diversionary potential inherent in the notion of a public park. Just as it was hoped that libraries would divert the working class away from sinful pleasures like drinking in pubs and reading trash literature, so the parks were seen as agents in the same process. Germany was not alone in ascribing this function to parks and open spaces. In Britain middle-class reformers realized that by denying the working class access to public spaces they were forcing them into public houses.[81] In the United States too the public park movement was similarly inspired. One of the most influential landscape architects of the period, F. L. Olmstead (the architect of New York's Central Park), believed that parks were capable of diverting people 'from unwholesome, vicious, destructive methods and habits of seeking recreation'.[82] The fact that Bochum's mayor believed in the importance of 'good examples' places him in the mainstream of this line of thought which stressed the desirability of contact between the classes and the consequent filtration of manners from the top down.

Municipal authorities certainly would not have entered so wholeheartedly into the public park movement had they not been motivated by financial considerations. The adornment of Düsseldorf was carried out with the attraction of business and visitors firmly in mind, and although the

Bochum authorities acknowledged the recreational function of a proposed animal reserve in 1913, the potential income it would generate, along with the increased number of visitors which would indirectly benefit the business community, were equally persuasive arguments.[83] The British experience of public park provision, in spite of the General Enclosure Act of 1836 and the supply of considerable sums of money by the government, tended to be inspired by private philanthropy and local pressure. In Germany, however, central and local government were directly responsible for the provision of public spaces, with some support from local businesses. We have already seen how the Bochum town council set up a commission to look into the problem. This incidentally committed the town to an annual bill of around 14,000 marks.[84] In Düsseldorf the municipal authorities took their duties regarding the maintenance of Düsseldorf's reputation as a garden town very seriously indeed, to the extent that a Parks Department managed the city's open spaces. This is not to say that public pressure groups did not exert influence in the area. A great number of nature protection associations were formed towards the end of the century and, if Bochum and Düsseldorf are at all typical, residents and newspapers maintained a steady interest in the provision and unkeep of parks and gardens.[85] Certainly, when the Bochum authorities decided to erect an animal reserve adjoining the park in 1913, interest in the project from the bourgeois and business community was quite considerable, resulting in a generous display of public philanthropy.[86]

In spite of the fairly emphatic arguments in favour of the creation of parks, the majority, at least in the early years of the movement, were not designed or located with the working class in mind. Municipal authorities were more concerned with the aesthetic appearance of their parks and with the contribution that such amenities would make to the civic standing of their towns. So local government departments put themselves in the hands of landscape architects who designed parks in accordance with their own philosophies rather than the specific interests of the community.

The architect Strauss of Cologne drew up the plans for Bochum's public park. He initially envisaged it being put to a variety of uses, so he incorporated flower beds, two pools and a waterfall, rest areas, a games area for children and a restaurant. The park was criss-crossed with paths, encouraging visitors to walk or 'promenade', since Bochum had no other formal promenades where this social activity could take place. Moreover, the park was situated on the site of former common land to the northeast of the town, some distance away from working-class districts. The streets bordering the park were lined with middle-class residences, and its restaurant soon became a meeting place for those on an afternoon stroll. Indeed, one historian of Bochum has noted that the 1890s saw the emergence of a town park quarter serving the economic and social life of the town's elite. The erection of a Bismarck tower in the centre of the park in 1909 really consolidated its character.[87] Furthermore, the behaviour of visitors was regulated by a set of park bylaws laid down in 1877, enforced by the park wardens and, in the final instance, backed by the police. Visitors were forbidden, among other things, to walk on the grass, to pick flowers, to collect fallen leaves, to bring dogs into the park, to make excessive noise, to run or to throw stones. Unaccompanied children under the age of 12 were not permitted and in 1884, when the rules were revised, persons who were 'not orderely and decently dressed' were not allowed in the park.[88] By the 1880s the park was already too small to accomodate the ever-increasing number of visitors. In August 1895 the *Märkischer Sprecher* noted that 'during good weather all types of seat are continually occupied between three and seven in the afternoon.'[89] On weekdays the park was frequented by the upper and middle classes and by children with their governesses, but on Sundays 'the masses' were said to stroll there. Going for a walk was one of the most popular pastimes for workers and their familes. In 1912 a study commissioned by the *Verein für Sozialpolitik* found that almost two thirds of the 173 workers in the sample went walking for their main form of relaxation.[90]

Bochum was proud of its park and it was often compared favourably with those of other towns in the region. Notwithstanding this achievement, to the elites of nearby Düsseldorf Bochum was just another dirty industrial town like any other in the Ruhr, not to be compared with 'the quiet streets, beautiful gardens and shady parks' of Düsseldorf.[91] In 1900, however, the *Düsseldorf General Anzeiger* proclaimed, 'Düsseldorf has become a real garden town.'[92] The occasion was the creation of a public park on the southeast side of the city in Oberbilk, an industrial, working-class suburb. In 1893, in the wake of a more general *Volksgarten* movement that had seen Düsseldorf's nearest rival create a public park a few years earlier, a competition was announced to design the park, which was to be created on 11 hectares of land previously parcelled out to a great number of individuals and which had to be purchased by the city. The cost was assessed at 15 million marks.[93] Most striking were the guidelines laid down for the architects of this *Volkspark*. The park was clearly conceived as a public amenity and the winning design took into account the needs of local residents, with wide paths, seats and spacious playing fields.[94] The *General Anzeiger* described it as a 'real place of amusement'; phraseology that denoted a distinct swing away from traditional notions of the park as a bourgeois promenade.[95] Certainly this type of park was the exception rather than the rule in Germany before the First World War. Only towns and cities with an international outlook or a strong Social Democratic Party pressing for such an amenity for the inhabitants of industrial areas had such a recreational space.[96]

The use of open spaces never ceased to be a class issue. Unofficial appropriation of public space by the urban bourgeoisie did not stop with the introduction of urban planning. An examination of the complaints submitted to the Parks Department and the police illustrates the continuing problem of access to and control of public land. An example from Düsseldorf illustrates both aspects of the situation well. In 1909 a resident of one of the middle-class houses surrounding the Lessingplatz in Ober-bilk, the architect Erich Badermann, complained to the police about the tremendous nuisance on 'weekdays as well as evenings [caused] by drunkards or else workshy scoundrels like adolescent lads [who] occupy [the benches] and pass round the schnapps bottles.' In view of the fact that the residents of the Lessingplatz, consisting of the 'better public' including 'clerks, pensioners and good bourgeois families', paid high rents for 'airy apartments with beautiful, open views' [over the square], Badermann argued that they should be able to use their open space in peace.[97] It is his attitude towards property and land that makes Badermann's complaint so interesting – and familiar. On the one hand, the residents were afraid the value of their property would fall as a result of the goings-on in the square, and on the other they regarded the public space as their own personal property, to which they applied their own standards of behaviour. The reply Badermann received from the police may not have satisfied him, but it was encouraging as far as the provision of open spaces for the use of the public was concerned: 'There is no doubt that public places are not only created for the inhabitants of fine houses but are also for the use of the working-class population.' Furthermore, the police added that disturbances in the Lessingplatz were no more frequent than in any other public space in the city.[98]

Most parks and open spaces in Düsseldorf appear to have been the subject of conflict and complaint at one time or another. Late-night revellers, drunkards, idlers, prostitutes, vandals and high-spirited adolescents were, by all accounts, to be found in public parks and squares along with more minor nuisances like football players and children playing games. In these circumstances there was a danger that those who had been convinced of the necessity of open spaces for the use of the working class would be forced to eat their words. It seemed that parks were increasingly becoming the focus for all the working-class excesses they were meant to prevent. Take the celebrated Düsseldorf *Volksgarten*. Within a few years of its creation a catalogue of misdemeanours and complaints had been compiled by visitors and park staff. They varied from the relatively innocuous case of two factory girls caught one evening carving initials into a bench, to the more serious incident one afternoon where several persons were observed capturing birds.[99] Fights were also common. Of much greater concern were the regular complaints about prostitutes plying their trade in the park. The head gardener called attention to the problem in 1898, but nothing had changed two years later when a chalet in the park served as a focus for 'the coarsest and commonest outrages' perpetrated by the pimps and their charges, 'so that no upright person can pass this part of the park.'[100]

Incidents such as these, although undoubtedly involving a minority, gave the working class as a whole a bad name and may have convinced some that any further provision of facilities in the name of rational recreation would be ill-advised. In 1910 a rumour spread among the inhabitants of Düsseldorf's Platanenstrasse, a working-class district of the city, that the Parks Department had decided to cease the construction of landscaped areas in working-class quarters. This was strongly denied.[101] Although it would be wrong to suggest that incidents like those quoted above were by any means typical of working-class behaviour in public parks, it would also be misleading to create the impression that members of the working class immediately abandoned their popular culture or everyday patterns of behaviour upon entering a park. Parks did not eradicate or even reform deeply embedded attitudes. Just as the public libraries could not alter working-class reading preferences overnight, so the parks too could not function as agents of social control. For instance, the consumption of alcohol and the noise that almost invariably accompanied it was one of the most frequent causes for complaint, but, as Chapter 3 has illustrated, drinking was an integral part of working-class leisure culture so perhaps it is not surprising that alcohol found its way into parks, especially when double standards were openly practised. Alcohol was sold in the Bochum park restaurant, but the price and social exclusivity of that establishment most likely prohibited consumption there by the working class. If the water fountains were not sufficient to quench their thirst (a rather naive suggestion of Mayor Lange's), then the workers probably brought their own beer into the park instead.[102]

Despite the creation of a number of public parks towards the end of the century there remained a lack of space in urban areas for lower-class recreations. Although the Düsseldorf city council was proud of the Kaiser-Wilhelm Park on the banks of the Rhine, this was planned to serve the sporty Düsseldorf elite with its tennis courts and yachting and rowing facilities. It was not until the Weimar Republic that the Social Democrats initiated a national park development programme.[103] Children and young people were continually admonished for playing 'wild games', or football, and for making a nuisance of themselves on public open spaces.[104] Playgrounds and sports facilities were urgently required. In 1904 the Britannia football club in Düsseldorf requested the provision of a grassy area to play on, noting that facilities for the game in the city fell far short of those in many smaller towns. Amenities for the working class only improved when the middle classes began to alter their attitudes towards physical exercise and outdoor actitivites. The middle-class movement away from decorous behaviour towards sport and active recreation, which manifested itself in the formation of numerous sports clubs, had the side effect of creating playgrounds for children and playing fields, tennis courts and the like for the adult public. In Germany the strength of the Social Democratic Party and its sponsorship of active recreational pursuits contributed equally to the provision of such facilities, but this only became universal after the First World War. By 1921 Düsseldorf alone had 120 gymnastic and sports clubs with around 15,000 members who had the use of approximately 132,500 square metres of recreational space, including a playing field and football pitch in the *Volksgarten* in Oberbilk and almost 60,000 square metres of space in the Kaiser-Wilhelm Park.[105]

Unlike their counterparts, the libraries and public entertainment evenings, parks were difficult to maintain as bastions of middle-class behaviour and culture, simply because of the relative freedom permitted there. The ability of parks to transcend class barriers manifestly failed, giving way to a struggle between the middle-class values and standards considered appropriate in a public park, backed up by official enforcement, and working-class notions of what public spaces should be used for. Indeed, the public park movement appears to have accentuated the class segregation of leisure in the short term, not only within specific parks but in the context of public space provision as a whole.

Social reform or social control?

The bourgeois-liberal reformers had hoped for mass working-class acceptance of the middle-class values preached to them via the ideology of rational recreation. After the overwhelmingly negative stance adopted by the middle class in the 1860s and 1870s, expressed through criticism and suppression of those working-class recreational pursuits perceived as coarse and uncivilized, the new generations who formed the socially concerned *Bildungsbürgertum* might have anticipated a more favourable response to their positive attempts to improve the amusements of the working class. Few could have been satisifed with the response their ideas engendered. Only a small minority of workers and their families forsook the working-class pubs, clubs and urban entertainments for the morally uplifting and improving recreations advocated and organized by middle-class voluntary associations. Moreover, it is likely that those who did attend the entertainment evenings or borrowed books from the public libraries belonged to the skilled working class. This was the group which, as Chapter 5 illustrated, was most likely to engage in organized, cooperative ventures. It was already beginning to adopt bourgeois models of social organization and sociability by forming voluntary assocations and was probably already some distance from 'immoral' amusements. Some had helped form their own self-help organizations, while others were active in promoting moral causes like temperance. They were unlikely to have caused a drunken disturbance in a public park. It was but a small step for these workers to engage in recreational activities that were organized by bourgeois reformers and indeed imbued with the rational recreation message. On the other hand, popular entertainment in the music and dance halls was reaching a peak in this period, as was the consumption of popular fiction, and there was no shortage of consumers for either.

A combination of ideology and practical obstacles goes some way towards explaining the failure of the rational recreation initiative in reaching a larger proportion of the working class. Bourgeois-liberal reform was always somewhat double edged; it combined genuine social concern at the material and social conditions of the working class with a more selfish desire to shape society to meet its own ends: the familiar tension between social reform and social control. Social reform in the industrial arena, for instance, was often tempered by the desire to create a more efficient workforce to ensure economic success. The factory paternalists were the most obvious proponents of this philosophy. Temperance reform too was peddled by a movement more concerned with social discipline than with the health advantages to be achieved by abstinence. Likewise, it was hoped that the reform of workers' recreation would have more long-term social, economic and political consequences: the combat of Social Democracy, the *disziplinierung* of the working class in public and the creation of a 'play discipline' to complement the capitalist, industrial work discipline.

Middle-class ideology refused to compromise with working-class taste. The socially harmonious utopia envisaged by the reformers was jeopardized by their insistence on inter-class activity and cooperation on bourgeois terms. This was true not only of the entertainment evenings whose programmes rarely strayed very far from patriotic and moral themes, but also of the public libraries, where the reading material pandered to middle-class taste, and of the parks too, where park wardens were ever vigilant against working-class indiscretions. The rhetoric of social harmony belied the failure to regard members of the working class as equals. Its members would only attain equality with the middle class in the cultural arena when they had been 'elevated' and educated to accept bourgeois norms and values without question. Finally, in spite of the reformers' recognition of 'labour' and their early efforts to work with the trade unions, an important element in the rationale behind rational recreation remained the provision of a counter-attraction to Social Democratic activities. For those committed party or trade-union members, bourgeois recreation provision and its vision of the future was the antithesis of that advocated by the Social Democrats. The majority of the working class, then, were ideologically alienated from middle-class recreation initiatives.

In practical terms, workers' failure to patronize the public libraries and entertainment evenings in large numbers was not a financial question, as the costs involved were negligible. Rather, as Gareth Stedman Jones has argued, 'the necessity to obtain work, to remain fit enough for work, and to make ends meet is far more important than any packaged consumerist ideology which succeeds in intruding upon the workers' weekly or nightly period of rest and recuperation.'[106] Leisure was still secondary to work in the working-class experience. The length of the working day, the distance travelled between home and workplace, and the intensity of the work itself all contributed to the inability of workers to take advantage of the new recreational amenities on offer. Only the public parks found almost wholesale acceptance on account of their accessibility, flexible opening hours and opportunities for comparative freedom of movement.

In failing to compromise the ideology of recreational reform, and by imposing practical obstacles in the path of more broadly based working-class participation, the middle-class reformers succeeded in appropriating many of the new leisure facilities for themselves. Calls for rational recreation fell on deaf ears within the working class (whose needs had not been correctly defined) and among many of the middle-class public too, who persisted in their old practice of commandeering spaces and amenities for their exclusive use. Bourgeois–liberal attempts to reform the leisure pursuits of the working class should not, however, be assessed in entirely negative terms. Their ideology was just one element of a broader trend towards controlled and sanitized amusement which was also advocated by confessional groups and the Social Democratic Party. The latter could even be described as unwilling allies of the advocates of rational recreation: both stressed the need for self-control and self-improvement in social, educational and cultural spheres, and both fabricated divisions between the 'rough' and 'respectable' elements of the working class. 'Conventicles of respectability' were not only to be found within the ranks of the skilled working class.

It would have been naive of the reformers to have expected large-scale acceptance of their ideology, but it is equally naive of historians to interpret their actions within a framework of social control. Social control, in the modern usage of the term, implies the imposition of a set of values by the dominant class in order to effect the integration of the working class into its social order. But, as many have argued recently, this blanket acceptance of the effectiveness of social control ignores the reality, which is that attempts at cultural imposition involve struggle and conflict, and rarely is the transition completed. 'The working class was eminently capable of generating its own cultural evolution and development in response to aspirations and needs experienced by different groups within it', writes F. M. L. Thompson.[107] The fact that workers did not, for the most part, subscribe to rational recreation ideology (by continuing to read mass fiction, by idling around in parks, by playing football in open spaces and by continuing to patronize, in enormous numbers, the pub, the music hall and the ballroom) in the face of police supervision, employers' paternalism and state repression, demonstrates the degree of vitality and independence achieved by working-class leisure culture by the turn of the century.

The reformers of the 1880s and 1890s did of course render some service to urban inhabitants: they directed attention towards the lack of recreational facilities in urban areas, they provided amenities themselves and, most important, they implanted the notion that the provision of recreational amenities was the responsibility of external agencies, especially municipal authorities. Until then these bodies had been more concerned with the suppression and control of popular amusements. Now town councils began to plan for leisure; budgets were drawn up and spaces given over to recreational amenities in prime city centre locations. Local government officials began to realize that commercial and municipal recreation provision could coexist; indeed, the taxes gathered from the former helped to pay for the latter.

Yet in the final analysis, commercialization did more than middle-class reform to transform the leisure activities of the working class. The entertainment entrepreneurs were far more sensitive to the needs and tastes of urban inhabitants than the arbiters of public taste and decency were. While there is little evidence to suggest a popular demand for uplifting amusements, libraries and other cultural institutions, the numbers attending the speciality theatres, cinemas and funfairs suggest that the mainstream recreational trend was proceeding in a different direction from that proposed by the reformers. By the First World War social harmony through leisure, the dream of the recreation reformers, was on the way to being achieved – but in circumstances which would not have received their approval.

Notes

1 Roberts, *Drink, Temperance and the Working Class*, pp. 73–7.
2 W. Köllmann, *Sozialgeschichte der Stadt Barmen im 19. Jahrhundert* (Tübingen: Mohr, 1960), p. 158. On the early history of the ZWAK see J. Reulecke, *Soziale Friede durch Soziale Reform. Der Centralverein für das Wohl der arbeitenden Klassen in der Frühindustrialisierung* (Wuppertal; Hammer, 1983).
3 Bochum industrialists certainly believed in self-help and the moral improvement of the poor – see Crew, *Town in the Ruhr*, pp. 123–7.
4 D. Fricke, 'Zentralverein für das Wohl der arbeitenden Klassen', in Fricke (ed.), *Die Bürgerlichen Parteien in Deutschland 1830–1945*, vol. 2 (Leipzig: Bibliographisches Institut, 1970), p. 874.
5 Fricke, *Die Bürgerlichen Parteien*, p. 874.
6 On the Gesellschaft für Soziale Reform see D. Krüger, 'Ein "Morgenrot wirklicher Sozialreform". Die Gesellschaft für Soziale Reform und die Entwicklung der Arbeiterbeziehungen im Ersten Weltkrieg', in G. Mai (ed.), *Arbeiterschaft in Deutschland 1914–18* (Düsseldorf: Droste, 1985), pp. 29–76; G. Müller, 'Bürgerliche Sozialreformbestrebungen nach den Reichstagswahlen von 1907. Zur Konzeption und Wirksamkeit der Gesellschaft für Soziale Reform', in

Zeitschrift für Geschichtswissenschaft, vol. 35 (1987), pp. 308–19; K. Saul, *Staat, Industrie, Arbeiterbewegung im Kaiserreich* (Düsseldorf: Bertelsmann, 1974), especially p. 26; Fricke, 'Verein für Sozialpolitik', in Fricke (ed.), *Die Bürgerlichen Parteien*, pp. 735–42. On the *Bildungsbürgertum* in general see W. Conze and J. Kocka (eds), *Bildungsbürgertum im 19. Jahrhundert* (Stuttgart: Klett Cotta, 1985).

7 Köllmann, *Sozialgeschichte*, p. 161.
8 Ibid., p. 165.
9 E. I. Kouri, *Der Deutsche Protestantismus und die Soziale Frage 1870–1919. Zur Sozialpolitik im Bildungsbürgertum* (Berlin: Walter de Gruyter, 1984), p. 165.
10 Hickey, *Workers in Imperial Germany*, p. 54; Seeling, *Geschichte der Gerresheimer Glashütte*, p. 46. Cf. E. McCreary, 'Social Welfare and Business: The Krupp Welfare Program, 1864–1914', in *Business History Review*, vol. 42 (1968), pp. 24–49.
11 Nolan, *Social Democracy and Society*, p. 107.
12 E. G. Spencer, *Management and Labor in Imperial Germany. Ruhr Industrialists as Employers, 1896–1914* (Brunswick, NJ: Rutgers University Press, 1984), pp. 74–5.
13 A. Lees, 'Critics of Urban Society in Germany, 1854–1914', in *Journal of the History of Ideas*, vol. 40 (1979), pp. 61–83.
14 Roberts, *Drink, Temperance and the Working Class*, p. 130.
15 On the missionary mentality of the church see Köllmann, *Sozialgeschichte*, p. 155, and D. Mühlberg, *Arbeiterleben um 1900* (Berlin: Dietz, 1983), p. 166. On the Protestant church see Kouri, *Der Deutsche Protestantismus*, p. 67.
16 Kouri, *Der Deutsche Protestantismus*, p. 89.
17 HStAD, RK 7676: Die Volksunterhaltung: Zeitschrift für die gesamten Bestrebungen auf dem Gebiete der Volksunterhaltung (Berlin, 1898).
18 J. Reulecke, '"Veredelung der Volkserholung" und "edle Geselligkeit". Sozialreformische Bestrebungen zur Gestaltung der arbeitsfreien Zeit im Kaiserreich', in Huck (ed.), *Sozialgeschichte der Freizeit*, p. 142; Roberts, *Drink, Temperance and the Working Class*, p. 130. Similar fears had been expressed in Britain when the Ten Hours Bill was introduced – see R. Storch, 'The Problem of Working-Class Leisure. Some Roots of Middle Class Moral Reform in the Industrial North, 1825–50', in A. P. Donajgrodzki (ed.), *Social Control in Nineteenth Century Britain* (London: Croom Helm, 1977), p. 145.
19 Reulecke, 'Veredelung der Volkserholung', p. 146.
20 Ibid., p. 147.
21 See Roberts, *Drink, Temperance and the Working Class*, on the German temperance movement.
22 Reulecke, 'Veredelung der Volkserholung', p. 147.
23 Ibid., p. 148.
24 HStAD, RK 7676: Die Volksunterhaltung (Berlin, 1898).
25 Bailey, *Leisure and Class*, p. 171 and P. Bailey, '"A Mingled Mass of Perfectly Legitimate Pleasures." The Victorian Middle Class and the Problem of Leisure', in *Victorian Studies*, vol. 21 (1977–8), pp. 7–28. On the cross-fertilization of ideas on social reform see J. Reulecke, 'English Social Policy around the Middle of the 19th Century as seen by German Social Reformers', in W. Mommsen (ed.), *The Emergence of the Welfare State* (London: Croom Helm, 1981), pp. 32–49.
26 StAB, LA 1179: RPA, 12 October 1900.
27 HStAD, RD 10816: Volksunterhaltungsabende Düsseldorf, 12 April 1892.
28 MS, 24 February 1900.
29 E. Schmidt, 'Die Entwicklung der deutschen Volksbibliotheken', in *Der Arbeiterfreund*, vol. 50 (1912), p. 461.

30 R. Schenda, *Volk ohne Buch. Studien zur Sozialgeschichte der Populären Lesestoffe 1770–1910* (Munich: dtv, 1977), p. 443.

31 Ibid., p. 56.

32 R. Braun, *Soziale und kultureller Wandel* (Stuttgart and Zurich: Rentsch, 1965), cited in Schenda, *Volk ohne Buch*, p. 57.

33 Schenda, *Volk ohne Buch*, pp. 441–5, 446–7.

34 R. Fullerton, 'Creating a Mass Book Market in Germany. The Story of the Colporteur Novel 1870–1890', in *Journal of Social History*, vol. 10 (1977), p. 265.

35 M. Bromme, *Lebensgeschichte eines modernen Fabrikarbeiters* (Jena: Diederichs, 1905) and see Schenda, *Volk ohne Buch*, p. 455, for a breakdown of the working-class family's budget and the place within this for reading materials.

36 Fullerton, 'Creating a Mass Book Market', p. 268; R. Fullerton, 'Toward a Commercial Popular Culture in Germany: the Development of Pamphlet Fiction, 1871–1914', in *Journal of Social History*, vol. 12 (1979), p. 490.

37 See Fullerton, 'Toward a Commercial Popular Culture', p. 496; on the content of the new commercial fiction see Fullerton, 'Creating a Mass Book Market', pp. 269–74 and 'Toward a Commercial Popular Culture', pp. 498–9; for a more detailed analysis see Schenda, *Volk ohne Buch*, pp. 334–436.

38 Fullerton, 'Toward a Commercial Popular Culture', p. 499.

39 Ibid., p. 500.

40 Schenda, *Volk ohne Buch*, p. 477.

41 Ibid., p. 487; see also R. Lenman, 'Mass Culture and the State in Germany, 1900–26', in R. J. Bullen, H. Pogge von Strandmann and A. B. Polonsky (eds), *Ideas into Politics: Aspects of European History 1880–1950* (London: Croom Helm, 1984), p. 53. A survey carried out at the end of the Weimar Republic refuted the alleged connection between cinema and everyday life and crime – see D. Peukert, *Jugend Zwischen Krieg und Krise. Lebenswelten von Arbeiterjungen in der Weimarer Republic* (Cologne: Bund, 1987), p. 219.

42 On the Lex Heinze and the more general 'moral panic' of the 1890s see Lenman, 'Mass Culture and the State in Germany' and Lenman, 'Art, Society and the Law in Wilhelmine Germany'.

43 HStAD, RD 10821: Volksbibliothek in Kempen, 22 February 1903.

44 D. Langewiesche and K. Schönhoven, 'Arbeiterbibliotheken und Arbeiterlektüre in Wilhelminischen Deutschland', in *Archiv für Sozialgeschichte*, vol. 16 (1976), p. 152.

45 R. Engelsing, *Analphabetentum und Lektüre. Zur Sozialgeschichte des Lesens in Deutschland* (Stuttgart: Metzler, 1973), p. 135.

46 Ibid., p. 129. However, in spite of the impressive number of libraries set up by the public education associations in the 1870s, only around one tenth of these still existed ten years later.

47 These were the library in the Evangelical Association house in Herne with 1,000 volumes and the Catholic Community library in Altenbochum with 700; StAB, KrA 283: Nachweisung der im Landkreise Bochum vorhandenen Bibliotheken, 1902.

48 The Libraries Bill was passed in Britain in 1850 'to promote the establishment and extension of public libraries'. See T. Kelly, *A History of Public Libraries in Great Britain 1845–1965* (London: Library Association, 1973).

49 HStAD, RD 33004: Denkschrift betreffend Organisation des Volksbibliothekenswesens im Regierungsbezirks Düsseldorf, 24 October 1903.

50 MS, 13 January 1900.

51 HStAD, RD 33004: Nachweisung über die Verwendung der für Einrichtung

und Erweiterung von Volksbibliotheken im Regierungsbezirks Düsseldorf durch Erlass von 22. November 1904, No. 24546.

52 Langewiesche and Schönhoven, 'Arbeiterbibliotheken', p. 151. Schenda notes that in 1895 only one third of a book per head per year was borrowed from a public library in German cities, *Volk ohne Buch*, p. 451.

53 HStAD, RD 10817: Christlicher Zeitschriftenverein, Berlin, 19 November 1896.

54 Langewiesche and Schönhoven, 'Arbeiterbibliotheken', p. 152.

55 StAB, KrA 283: 1907; Fullerton, 'Toward a Commercial Popular Culture', p. 502.

56 E. Mehlich, cited in Lidtke, *The Alternative Culture*, p. 182.

57 Lidtke, *The Alternative Culture*, p. 184.

58 HStAD, RD 33004: Jahres-Bericht über die städtische Lesehalle und 3 städtischen Volksbibliotheken der Stadt Düsseldorf, 1903–4.

59 Langewiesche and Schönhoven, 'Arbeiterbibliotheken', pp. 200–4, tables 23 and 24. In the library of the Leipzig Workers' Association, for instance, no less than 615 out of a total of 1599 volumes were fiction, while history and biography totalled 428 volumes, – see K. Haenisch, 'Was Lesen die Arbeiter?', in *Die Neue Zeit*, vol. 8 (1900), pp. 691–6. Even in the Krupp factory library the greatest number of books held were fiction: 13,566 out of a total of 34,422 in 1903, HStAD, RD 10822: Bericht der Kruppschen Bücherhalle 1902–4.

60 HStAD, RD 33004: Düsseldorf Volksbibliotheken und Beihülfe, 2 May 1905.

61 Engelsing, *Analphabetentum*, pp. 124–5. Langewiesche and Schönhoven, 'Arbeiterbibliotheken', in a more detailed breakdown of the social stratification of public library usage, illustrate similarly wide variations.

62 The presence of trade-union and SPD libraries may well have influenced the relatively low figure of 6 per cent working-class members in Leipzig public libraries – see Haenisch, 'Was Lesen die Arbeiter?', pp. 691–6.

63 Schenda, *Volk ohne Buch*, p. 450.

64 HStAD, RD 10822: Bericht der Kruppschen Bücherhalle 1902–4.

65 Engelsing, *Analphabetentum*, p. 138; see also Lidtke, *The Alternative Culture*, p. 227, table 7, Appendix C.

66 Engelsing, *Analphabetentum*, p. 138.

67 Haenisch, 'Was Lesen die Arbeiter?', pp. 694–5.

68 HStAD, RD 10821: Elberfeld, 12 March 1904.

69 HStAD, RD 10819: Düsseldorf Jahres-Bericht – städtische Lesehalle und Volksbibliothek; RD 33004: Jahres-Bericht über die städtische Lesehalle und 3 städtische Volksbibliotheken der Stadt Düsseldorf 1903–4.

70 HStAD, RD 10821: Kruppschen Bücherhalle 1903–4.

71 Advocatus, 'Was liest der deutsche Arbeiter?', in *Die Neue Zeit* vol. 13 (1894–5), pp. 814–17.

72 Steinberg, 'Workers' Libraries in Imperial Germany', pp. 171–6; Lidtke, *The Alternative Culture*, pp. 187–8 on workers' reading tastes.

73 Fullerton, 'Toward a Commercial Popular Culture', p. 502.

74 C. Lange, 'Die Wohnungsverhältnisse der ärmeren Volksklassen in Bochum', in *Schriften des Vereins für Sozialpolitik*, vol. 30 (1886), p. 99.

75 E. Spohr, *Düsseldorf – Stadt und Festung* (Düsseldorf: Schwann, 1979), p. 373.

76 On the privatization of formally public space by the middle class in Britain see Cunningham, *Leisure in the Industrial Revolution*, pp. 76–97; P. Borsay, 'The Rise of the Promenade: the Social and Cultural use of Space in the English Provincial Town, c. 1660–1800', in *British Journal for Eighteenth Century Studies*, vol. 9 (1986), pp. 125–38.

77 G. K. Lewis, 'The Kleingarten: Evolution of an Urban Retreat', *Landscape*, vol.

23 (1979), p. 35. For the development of allotments in Bochum see StAB, B 94: Bochum Schrebergartenverein Ehrenfeld, and B 102: Bochumer Schrebergartenverein 'Erholung am Stadtpark e.V'.

78 Bernays, 'Auslese und Anpassung der Arbeiterschaft', p. 237.

79 Ibid.

80 On New York's Central Park see C. Stone, 'Vandalism: Property, Gentility, and the Rhetoric of Crime in New York City 1890–1920', in *Radical History Review*, vol. 26 (1982), p. 17.

81 In Britain the Select Committee on Drunkenness, when it met in 1834, heard evidence from Edwin Chadwick, who said that if urban populations had public amenities like parks, zoos, museums and theatres, the consumption of liquor might fall – see G. Chadwick, *The Park and the Town. Public Landscape in the 19th and 20th Centuries* (London: Architectural Press, 1966).

82 F. L. Olmstead, cited in R. Rosenzweig, 'Middle-Class Parks and Working-Class Play: The Struggle over Recreational Space in Worcester, Massachusetts, 1870–1910', in *Radical History Review*, vol. 21 (1979), p. 33. For the park movement in the USA in general see G. Cranz, 'Changing Roles of Urban Parks. From Pleasure Garden to Open Space', in *Landscape*, vol. 22 (1978), pp. 9–14.

83 StAB, B 800: Erläuterungsbericht zu dem Projekten eines Tierschutzparkes zu Bochum, 1 December 1913.

84 StAB, B 796: 1891; Lange, 'Die Wohnungsverhältnisse', p. 99.

85 The Nature Protection Movement was closely associated with bourgeois-liberal reformers. Their concern was not so much environmental but rather with the complementary relationship between nature and social harmony. In 1910 Konrad Günther wrote in the movement's journal, *Die Naturschutz*: 'Only in fresh nature can a man relax after work and find strength for new activity, only under green trees and in clear air can the ordinary person find peace and happiness.'

86 For example, the *Bochumer Anzeiger* donated 400 marks, the Automobilgesellschaft Lueg promised 500 marks and a number of individuals donated animals, StAB, B 800: letter from August Hackert to Bochum Oberbürgermeister, 20 May 1914. In Düsseldorf the relationship between the business community and the provision of municipal facilities was strengthened by the decision to hold the 1880 Business Exhibition in the grounds of the zoological gardens. Weidenhaupt notes, however, that in spite of the pretensions of the Düsseldorf elite commercial interests were always given priority, which effectively restricted the provision of open spaces for the working class – see H. Weidenhaupt, *Kleine Geschichte der Stadt Düsseldorf* (Düsseldorf: Schwann, 1983), pp. 130–1.

87 On Bochum's early urban development see Croon, 'Studien zur Sozial- und Siedlungsgeschichte der Stadt Bochum'.

88 Bochum Polizeiverordnungen 1884; E. Schmidt, 'Zierde, Vergnügen, gesunde Luft und gute Lehren. Zur Geschichte der Stadtparks in Bochum und anderswo', in H. H. Hanke (ed.), *Bochum: Wandel in Arkitektur und Stadtgestalt* (Bochum: Studienverlag Brockmeyer, 1985), p. 115. For regulations in Düsseldorf city parks, see StAD, II 1441: Die Oeffentlichen Luftanlagen und die Singvögel 1823–98.

89 MS, 3 August 1895.

90 F. Schumann, 'Auslese und Anpassung der Arbeiterschaft in der Automobilindustrie und einer Wiener Maschinenfabrik: Die Arbeiter der Daimler-Motoren-Gesellschaft Stuttgart Untertürkheim', in *Schriften des Vereins für Sozialpolitik*, vol. 135 (1911), p. 107.

91 E. von Hesse Wartegg, in *Zeitschrift für Kommunalwirtschaft und Kommunalpolitik*, vol. 3–4 (1911).
92 *Düsseldorf General Anzeiger*, 23 May 1900.
93 StAD, III 3304: Volksgarten, 20 November 1893.
94 Baron W. von Engelhardt, Direktor des städtischen Gartenamte, 'Düsseldorfs Grünanlagen', in Lux (ed.), *Düsseldorf*, p. 63.
95 *Düsseldorf General Anzeiger*, 23 May 1900.
96 W. Schmidt (ed.), *Von 'Abwasser' bis 'Wandern'. Ein Wegweiser zur Umweltgeschichte* (Hamburg: Körber-Stiftung, 1986), p. 140.
97 StAD, III 3327: Correspondence between Erich Badermann and Düsseldorf Parks Department, 29 March 1909 and 17 September 1909.
98 Ibid.: Düsseldorf Polizeiverwaltung, 14 October 1909.
99 StAD, III 3305: Volksgarten, park warden's report, 22 May 1897. StAD, III 3306: Volksgarten, head gardener's report, 30 December 1901.
100 StAD, III 3305: Volksgarten, head gardener's report, 1 June 1898; III 3306: Mißstände im Volksgarten, November 1900.
101 StAD, III 3327: Platanenstrasse resident to Düsseldorf Oberbürgermeister, 12 March 1910.
102 Lange, 'Die Wohnungsverhältnisse', p. 99.
103 Schmidt, *Von 'Abwasser' bis 'Wandern'*, p. 40.
104 Street football had been regarded as a problem in Britain too. It was made illegal there in the early nineteenth century but the issue reoccurred in the 1930s, and the imprisonment of boys in Glasgow for the alleged 'crime' led to a public outcry – see S. G. Jones 'State Intervention in Sport and Leisure in Britain between the Wars', in *Journal of Contemporary History*, vol. 22 (1987), pp. 163–82.
105 StAD, III 3749: Düsseldorf Leibesübungen, Umfrage 1921.
106 Stedman Jones, 'Class Expression versus Social Control?', p. 109.
107 F. M. L. Thompson, 'Social Control in Victorian Britain', in *Economic History Review*, 2nd series, vol. 34 (1981), p. 196.

7

From control to commercialization

Entertaining the masses

The previous chapters have shown that until the turn of the century the active leisure of the urban working-class consisted of visits to pubs, clubs, music and dance halls and the occasional festive occasion supplemented by walking, gardening, reading and other less commercial pastimes. These still tended to be based in the neighbourhood and served to maintain and sometimes strengthen residual cultural loyalties and identities. The first decade of the twentieth century, however, signalled a turning point in people's perception and experience of leisure and entertainment in Germany. In the years immediately before the First World War urban leisure activities began to embrace a more dynamic, exciting dimension which not only provided a real alternative to the organized and sanitized recreations sponsored by bourgeois-liberal reformers, but also cut across the hitherto separatist nature of working-class leisure. The cinema spearheaded this entertainment explosion, which was characterized by large-scale, mass amusements appealing to broader sections of the urban populace. It incorporated many other areas of recreational experience too, including sport, funfairs, day trips and the mass media. At first sight this development appears rather incongruous against the backdrop of widespread moral disapprobation and ideas of rational recreation in the 1880s and 1890s. In reality, however, the supposedly new entertainments on offer were both a continuation of more established popular recreations, revamped and publicized by astute entrepreneurs, and an extension of the increasingly public amusements enjoyed by the middle classes. It was the urban bourgeoisie who, while decrying the drinking and dancing of the lower classes, began to take its own recreations into the public arena, visiting theatres, playing sport, strolling in the parks and zoological gardens, and commandeering trains to escape from the cities. Simultaneously, municipal councils and the larger employers began to legitimize leisure for the working class by providing new facilities expressly for non-work pleasures. While the vast majority of the working class never accepted the organization of leisure on middle-class terms, they did not reject the concept of public leisure altogether. In a perverse way, the rational

169

recreation efforts of bourgeois reformers gave an impetus to the leisure industry by identifying a market and beginning to break down some of the barriers that had hitherto confined working-class leisure activities to restricted areas and hindered the emergence of a mass, broad-based, public leisure industry.

What is striking about modern leisure provision is the relatively sudden proliferation of new recreational pleasures. The cinema of course is the most celebrated example of the new phenomenon, but the moving pictures were just one element of a larger movement towards the provision of entertainment that would appeal to growing numbers of people from a variety of backgrounds. Funfairs, for example, became increasingly popular after the Great War; sport underwent a transformation, with the numbers of spectators outnumbering the participants; and with the advent of a cheap and efficient public transport system the day excursion finally became a reality for working-class families. In addition, the mass media not only became a part of this new leisure experience but also contributed to its popularization; cinema and radio became the prime media for the communication and establishment of trends and fashions in music, dances, fashion and even language.

The preconditions for the development of a mass entertainment and leisure industry were all present in Germany from the end of the 1890s.[1] The presence of a large and concentrated urban population provided the necessary supply of punters. Düsseldorf was officially a *Großstadt* in 1892 when its population reached 100,000 and by 1900 it was a city of some 213,000 people. Bochum had over 65,000 inhabitants in that year. The rise in the real income of a large proportion of the working class was a further prerequisite of the emergence of a mass leisure industry. The ability to purchase non-necessary items increased as real wages, on average, rose steadily between 1871 and 1914. From the 1890s on, a more rapid increase was experienced than previously as wages rose by around 13 per cent between 1900 and 1913.[2] Moreover, average family size decreased more rapidly after the war and an increasing number of married women took outside employment. The amount of leisure time available to the industrial labour force also slowly increased with the decisive breakthrough, the eight-hour day, achieved in 1918. Although widespread abuse of this law meant that after the war, many workers were still labouring for long hours the mere suggestion that the working class would now have more time on its hands prompted local councils to plan for the anticipated rise in demand for recreation facilities, even if this concern was still tempered by the social control ideology. Thus a meeting of the Bochum town council in March 1919 discussed the provision of sports fields 'so that young people upon the introduction of the eight-hour day do not dispose of their free time in the cinemas and pubs'.[3] After the war football began to attract larger numbers of working-class players and supporters, having previously been dominated by middle-class sportsmen, largely as a consequence of more free time and a reduction in admission charges.

The construction of an efficient local urban transport system was a further impetus for the emerging commercial leisure sector, making it feasible for people to travel out of their neighbourhoods for their entertainment and facilitating a reduction in the time and energy taken by workers to travel to and from work, leaving them with surplus energy for active leisure pursuits. It also enabled entertainment acts to reach more towns, thereby creating national and international stars. Meanwhile, technological innovation had reached Germany from Britain and the United States. The motion picture camera and kinetoscope had the most obvious impact in the early development of the leisure sector, but later the gramophone and the radio were also to transform people's leisure time. So too, in less dramatic terms, did the invention of the pneumatic tyre and the application of rubber to sport (for the bladder inside leather footballs, for example). Even the humble *Bierkneipe* was transformed by technological innovation: the small bars of Düsseldorf, it was said, were energized by electronic pianos and 'shrieking gramophones'. Demand was tremendous, prompting the *Märkischer Sprecher* to remark in 1900 that 'people want to amuse themselves at any price'.[4] Finally, although difficult to quantify, it seems likely that the experience of war intensified people's demand for amusements once it was over and may even have hastened the movement towards more class-transcending leisure activities.

As the managers of the old entertainment establishments responded to this demand by updating their decor and introducing modern attractions, new facilities were built on a large scale. Public halls were gradually provided in the town centres to house all manner of amusements and purpose-built premises increasingly dominated the entertainment profile of a town, able to accommodate hundreds and sometimes thousands of spectators. On the eve of the First World War it is estimated that there were around 2,500 cinemas in Germany with an average capacity of 200 seats.[5] The larger theatres were able to house up to 1,000 people at once. Düsseldorf's Apollo was attended by over 600,000 people in 1922–3.[6] About two million people were said to visit the cinema every day by this date.

Sporting events began to attract similar numbers of participants and spectators. Football only truly became a mass spectator sport after the war. At the end of 1905 the German Foootball Association had 433 affiliated clubs with almost 25,000 members. By 1920 membership had reached a million, a trend reflected at the local level. The famous Gelsenkirchen club, FC Schalke 04, had a mere 16 members at its foundation in 1904. Ten years later this figure had increased to around 90 and after the war and the expansion of the club to include boxing, athletics and handball sections as well as football, over 1,000 people belonged to FC Schalke.[7] The most

171

important games attracted thousands of spectators, with fans travelling long distances to attend. The German cup final in 1923, played between two local rivals, 1. FC Nürnberg and SpVgg Fürth, was watched by around 30,000 people.[8] Spectator sports such as cycle racing and boxing also gained in popularity, aided by the construction of huge arenas and commercial marketing strategies. Düsseldorf's new multi–purpose sports stadium, built after the war, seated 40,000 spectators around the main arena and another 20,000 around the cycling track, catering to the hordes of cycling fans, many of whom belonged to clubs. By 1924 the combined membership of the workers' cycling associations, Solidarität and Freiheit, totalled 304,500.[9] And although this period saw the growth of the Workers' Sport Movement, eventually achieving a membership of over one million by the 1920s, a majority of members of bourgeois sports clubs were still workers.

Crowds of people converged on transport networks, particularly at holiday times. As early as 1905 it was estimated that over 100,000 people used the trams to reach the Düsseldorf fair in July, while Bochum's tram and railway stations were frequently crowded, especially at Easter and Whitsuntide, with people aiming to get into the countryside. Some 41,000 marks were spent on tickets at Bochum's railway station on Whit Sunday in 1900.[10] Static amusement parks thronged with people, especially during the summer. On one Sunday in August 1919 almost 30,000 people visited the Lunapark in Wattenscheid near Bochum.[11]

Apart from the sheer numbers of people involved, in what sense were the leisure activities enjoyed by millions in the decades preceding and following the First World War different from earlier recreational pursuits? Can the difference be seen in terms of the transmission of universal values, as some have suggested, or was it the alleged class-transcending nature of the new amusements that marked a break with the past? Did mass commercial entertainment displace the sectional cultures within the working class, and were hitherto 'sharp cultural class barriers' washed away by the new means of mass communication?[12] This chapter will attempt to answer these questions by looking in particular at the most modern form of mass commercial entertainment before 1914, the cinema.

The rise of the cinema

Mass, commercial entertainment was no sudden invention of the twentieth century. A similar strategy had been pioneered by the pamphlet fiction publishers and distributors of the 1870s and 1880s. Their product was cheap, accessible, cleverly marketed and widely distributed. It succeeded in reaching millions of readers. Their success lay in an astute interpretation of the market and an ability to adapt to and meet its demands and vicissitudes.[13]

Reading remained the most frequent everyday leisure activity well into the Weimar Republic, particularly among young people, who were to become the most important market for the new recreational products. Immediately before the outbreak of war in 1914 the cinema emerged as a dynamic accompaniment (not rival) to this already well developed and ingrained popular leisure culture. 'In many ways', wrote an early historian of the film industry, 'cinema was simply a filming of those pulp-fiction pamphlets, a pictorial recitation of their contents, but one that was far more effective because the actions and adventures were actually portrayed visually.'[14] Indeed, many regarded this new medium as little more than trash literature in moving pictures.[15]

The comparisons between these two successful manifestations of commercial culture are numerous. The roots of popular fiction were to be found in the popular culture peddled by the army of itinerants earlier in the nineteenth century. Similarly, moving pictures were first popularized by travelling entertainers eager to outdo their competitors by introducing a new attraction. The late 1890s was the age of the travelling cinema or *Wanderkino*, accompanying the mechanical gimmicks and amusements that turned up at fairs, in public houses and in variety shows all over the country. Just as entertainers had been forced to go on the road with their acts, continually in search of new audiences, the early cinemas also had to be itinerant; films were expensive to purchase and could not be shown too often in the same place. Only when film companies began to lease films for hire were the first static cinemas established around 1904–5.[16] Initially these were fairly humble affairs, usually an empty shop hired for the purpose or the back room of a pub, the windows blacked out with paper and adorned with a few posters and handwritten programmes.[17] In some of the smallest 'cinemas', or *Kintopps* as they were known, the screen was set up in the middle of the room, so those seated behind it saw the film back to front. By 1912 there were around 1,500 of these early cinemas in Germany, mostly in densely populated industrial areas and ports as these could furnish a regular audience.[18] Düsseldorf had ten cinemas by this date; some of the first films were shown at the Apollo Theatre as early as 1900. The first cinema built specifically for the purpose of showing films, the *Welt-Kinematograph* on Graf-Adolf Strasse, opened in 1906. For its size, however, Düsseldorf was not particularly well provided; in 1910 Essen had no less than 21 cinemas, while Hamburg had 40, and Berlin residents could visit any one of 139 cinemas.[19] Nevertheless, more than 6,000 seats were available in Düsseldorf's 12 cinemas in 1921.

In some places the demand for cinemas was such that venues previously used for other forms of entertainment, like classical theatres and the circus, were converted into cinemas. By the war, entrepreneurs in the entertainment business had recognized the full potential of moving pictures and were willing to invest considerable sums in the new venture. This investment provided almost 2,500 cinemas by 1914, with a further 1,000 being opened between 1914 and 1920. The high point was not reached until 1925, when almost one and a half million seats were available in 3,878 cinemas around the country.[20] By then moving pictures were big business. Cinema owners organized themselves into the Verein Deutscher Kinematographen-theaterbesitzer (Association of German Cinema Owners) to protect their interests against what they saw as the insidious entertainment tax imposed on receipts by municipal authorities and the volatile policies of government. The major German film company, Universum Film Aktiengesellschaft (UFA), had been formed in 1917. A number of journals devoted to films and the cinema, like *Der Kinematograph*, were published. And probably the most obvious signs that the cinema had become a mass recreational pursuit were the negative reaction it elicited from moral watchdogs and the implementation of censorship.

The cinema certainly emerged as the most popular form of entertainment in the urban centres. It was even said to rival the public house in the affections of the working class, threatening the existence of many drinking places as well as the variety theatres and circuses. A visit to the cinema was a relatively cheap form of entertainment: between 10 and 30 pfennigs gained entry to the early silent films, cheaper than standing room in the theatre. When purpose-built cinemas were erected, seating even became quite comfortable and cinema owners often adopted an open-all-hours policy, running film reels continually so people could just call in when they had some spare time.

There was also an element of fascination with the living pictures that attracted so many sections of the population to the cinema. The novelty value of the silver screen caused great excitement, especially among young people and members of the working class. These groups seem to have formed the vast majority of cinema audiences, at least until the 1920s when movie-going became more respectable. Within the ranks of the working class women and children were particularly keen cinema-goers. Women found the local cinema the ideal place to spend their infrequent leisure time. Working-class women might call in during the day, often with children in tow, while working girls visited the cinema after work. But it was the youth of Germany, both girls and boys, more than any other group, who were the most enthusiastic supporters of the cinema. The group who had wholeheartedly adopted the commercial cultural and leisure pursuits of the prewar years, pulp fiction and dance halls in particular, universally accepted the cinema with little sexual or class demarcation. In spite of the numerous alternatives on offer, by the end of the Weimar Republic the majority of young people were attending the cinema: 50 per cent of boys and 62 per cent of girls went at some time or another.[21] For some, the chance to pursue a leisure activity in the company of friends rather than family (most went with friends of their own sex), to escape parental supervision, or to pursue a relationship in the relative privacy of the darkened cinema was just as much an attraction as the films were.[22] Briggs' statement that 'the cinema did not so much divert an older audience from other kinds of entertainment as create an enormous new one' rings as true for Germany as it does for Britain.[23]

Yet, in spite of the convenience of the cinema as a leisure venue for numerous groups, in the final analysis it was the films themselves that drew people. The quest for excitement, sensation and, it must be said, a good laugh on the part of the masses was satisfied by the content of the most popular types of films, the so-called dramas, allegedly full of 'crass representations of human emotions, death scenes from criminal life and so on, all shown in a sensational way.'[24] In Düsseldorf the police commented upon the 'desire for sensation by the masses . . . which the multiple murder, suicide, adultery and other crimes [provide] at present in increasingly crass forms.'[25] This apparent need for excitement was neither new nor restricted to the cinema, however. In theatres variety acts were becoming more and more daredevil and popular reading material reflected the same trend. Neither was this sensationalism a mere gimmick invented by the film industry. Film-makers seemed to be responding to a real demand from the punters. The suggestion that a municipal cinema be opened in Mülheim/Ruhr was rejected on the grounds that the educational films it was proposed to show were not financially viable, the implication being that only sensational films could fill the seats.[26] This sentiment was echoed by the authorities in Duisburg who noted:

> The visitors to the local 'cinemas' are recruited mainly from the working class and it is with this group that the producers have to reckon in the main and the performances are on the whole limited to its taste. A cinema which only showed technical, scientific and also humorous films to the exclusion of dramatic productions must suffer from a shortage of customers and in financial terms it could not compete with the other cinemas.[27]

Critics were correct in equating these films with popular commercial fiction; cinema was said to 'bring the sensational pictures to life'. They stood on more shaky ground, however, when positing a link between trash literature, sensational films and urban crime, especially juvenile crime. Films portraying criminal acts were said to encourage imitation. The loose morals allegedly held by young people were partially blamed on the erotic content of popular dramas. Youth and working-class people alike were credited with few powers of distinction between fiction and reality. Any critical analysis was thought to be suppressed by the emotions engendered by the films. 'The extent to which trash literature and the cinema are responsible for corrupting the character of our young people is shown by the rising number of police investigations into the criminal actions of young people', remarked the Solingen authorities in 1909,[28] followed by a similar assertion by the Düsseldorf police a year later: 'it is also of course clear from the court proceedings in recent years that the punishable activities of young people, which multiply from one day to the next, can be blamed on frequent attendance at cinema performances.'[29] Censorship was thus deemed to be the most effective method of sanitizing film content.

Cinema censorship was first introduced in Berlin in 1906, after considerable lobbying by pressure groups like the Kinoreformbewegung (Cinema Reform Movement), which later became the Kinematographische Reformpartei (Cinema Reform Party). By 1910 the police in the Düsseldorf administrative district were applying their own censorship code to all films shown, although not equally, one may add.[30] Censorship was more severe in industrial towns like Essen, where the cinemas were said to be frequented by the 'uneducated' members of the working class, 'given to brutality and violence'. It was less harsh in towns like Düsseldorf whose cinema-goers consisted of a larger proportion of supposedly more discriminating, better educated inhabitants.[31] In 1912 the Düsseldorf police announced that they would censor all 'films with immoral content'; all those containing 'frightening scenes' which might strain the nerves of the audience or harm young people; all those which contained 'crimes, particularly murder, attempted murder, robbery, theft, forgery, fraud, prostitution, suicide, torture of animals'; and all those in which the establishment, people in authority and those wearing uniform were ridiculed. There was also a number of extra provisions for children's films.[32] Some films were simply edited, others were banned completely – like *Das Chloroform*, which included a scene of two women being robbed on a train while sedated with the eponymous substance, presumably banned for fear of imitation.[33]

During the war special censorship measures were introduced, banning the trashy, sensationalist films that were regarded as incompatible with the gravity of the situation, as well as all foreign films. The latter action seriously diminished the quantity of films released for public screening since between 80 and 90 per cent of all films shown before the war had been produced abroad.[34] At the same time it was a filip to the domestic film industry, especially the newly formed newsreel companies.[35] After the war, however, for a brief period before the implementation of the Weimar constitution, a wave of films were produced in the sexual enlightenment genre, the so-called *Aufklärungsfilme*; *Hyenas of Lust*, *From Brothel to Marriage* and *Vows of Chastity* were just a few. The latter incidentally caused an anti-semitic street riot by the generally orderly bourgeois cinema-goers of Düsseldorf.[36] While the Weimar constitution did include a commitment to freedom of art and expression, a compromise between the Social Democrats, Liberals and the Centre Party produced a qualifying clause that reserved the right to introduce censorship in certain conditions and specific circumstances. Such a provision within the constitution was partly a reflection of conservative policy towards youth and the control of popular culture, but it also suited the Social Democrats to retain the right to suppress manifestations of a culture they regarded as neither worthy nor genuine.[37] Moreover, under the 1920 *Reichlichtspielgesetz* a film could be banned if it threatened public order, or was blasphemous in any way, or damaged national security, with the rider that 'permission is not to be refused for political, social, religious, ethical or ideological reasons as such'.[38] However, only 90 films failed to gain the censor's approval between 1924 and 1929, just over 1 per cent of all films reviewed, and the same number as before 1920.[39]

The key point here is not the number of films stopped by the censor but the extent of interference in and control over the production and consumption of a popular cultural form. In his seminal paper on mass entertainment Asa Briggs is correct to highlight

the way in which massive market interests have come to dominate an area of life which until recently was dominated by individuals themselves with the intermittent help of showmen and the more regular help of . . . innkeepers and bookmakers. The massiveness of the control is certainly more revealing than the often dubious statements made by the controllers about the character of the 'masses' whose wants they claim they are satisfying.[40]

Certainly Social Democrats regarded the commercial cinema as an agent of bourgeois propaganda, controlled from above, targeted to render the working class totally passive. A contributor to the leading socialist journal, *Die Neue Zeit*, wrote of the hypnotic effect of the events on the screen on working-class audiences who were too tired after a day's work to examine the contents critically.[41] Few on the left credited the cinema with any positive influence. Emilie Altenloh was an exception. In 1914 she wrote, 'rest from work should not place any new demands on the individual . . . the average person needs something which is effortless', citing the cinema as a good example.[42] For the majority of SPD leaders, however, effortless meant dangerous; cinema had replaced religion as the opiate of the masses. Its popularity implied the anonymity of a mass culture that had the ability to undermine the workers' culture painstakingly shaped by the party, a danger which became more imminent in the Weimar Republic. To what extent did the new commercial mass culture undermine and then supersede the specific proletarian culture(s) of the *Kaiserreich*? How far were residual expressions of working-class culture eroded and replaced by a homogeneous Weimar leisure culture based on the mass consumption of national precepts?

Commercial culture versus working-class culture

While the cinema and other new forms of amusement were certainly attracting vast numbers of people it would not be wise to extrapolate from this that local cultural values were being eroded. However, a number of related factors conspired to create, in appearance at least, a more universal, homogeneous leisure culture in urban centres. The transformation of this urban leisure culture, while appearing to accelerate from the turn of the century on, has to be judged against a history of several decades of attempts by the state to superimpose a national culture on the German people, to break down the local, religious and ethnic cultural divisions which were seen as threatening to the stability of the new Germany. Thus, attempts were made to repress local and regional customs and traditions like the parish fair, and particular religious and ethnic cultural forms like the Polish associational movement were encouraged to integrate into a fictional all-embracing German culture. Simultaneously, cultural forms were imposed from above, like the Sedan Day celebrations and events revering the monarchy.

Independently of this movement inspired and guided from above, forms of popular culture gradually receded from local control. The disintegration of the close-knit community was often the cause of the disappearance of community-based recreations such as animal-baiting, while the acquisition of former common land by local authorities signalled the demise of some neighbourhood festivals. As urban populations increased and the demand for entertainment grew from the 1890s onwards, local entertainment entrepreneurs, notably those publicans who had become concert- or dance-hall proprietors, failed to keep pace with the changes. Leisure and entertainment moved into the hands of big business; the owners of large theatres, halls and cinemas operated on a far larger scale, with greater profit margins. They no longer relied on special occasions to boost their incomes in order to break even. 'Time is money' was their motto – and they stayed open all hours to attract enough custom to maximize their profits.

Moreover, most of the large entertainment establishments where the newest films were shown, or the most famous variety acts appeared, or the most exciting sporting events took place, were located in the city centres. This drew people away from the comparatively less exciting and more familiar entertainment on offer in their own neighbourhoods. So leisure and entertainment not only became concentrated in the hands of relatively few wealthy entrepreneurs, it became geographically centralized as well. This had the effect of squeezing local entertainment provision at both ends. Centrally located entertainment also benefited from the demand for more sophisticated amusements from rural inhabitants. While they already received watered-down versions of the new commercial culture on their doorsteps – such as the popular press, serialized and pamphlet fiction and travelling cinemas – the advent of cheap transport enabled them to swell the ranks of urban revellers. It was often easier for countryfolk to reach the town centre than the suburbs. Previous forms of entertainment had confirmed and perpetuated the rural–urban divide and at the same time had emphasized religious, gender, ethnic and occupational divisions within the working class. Some of the new amusements, while not eliminating these divisions, certainly papered over the cracks. In purely practical terms such differences were no longer recognized or important in the huge, anonymous auditoria and stadia and darkened cinemas. Even the seating allowed the mingling of different groups who could avoid any real social contact with one another.

The key to success in this highly competitive era was not necessarily innovation, as it had been in the past. Competition within the industry was conducted along the lines of excellence, fame and an ability to read the market while maintaining the broadest popular appeal. National and international artistes of the highest calibre were preferred to local amateurs, films were imported from abroad, mainly from the United States, and even sporting events drew the largest crowds when nationally or internationally famous players were involved. In 1911 a film of a world championship boxing match between the Americans Jeffries and Johnson drew enormous crowds in Germany wherever it was shown, although or perhaps because it had already gained notoriety by sparking off race riots in the United States when the black Johnson won, prompting the Essen police to ban the film, fearing the worst.[43]

Localism, regionalism and the representation of religious, ethnic or other interests, did not fill seats in huge cinemas, auditoria and stadia as readily as did universal values with an appeal to all groups, although one might add that partisan sentiments were often expressed through the medium of what appeared to be genuine national obsessions (like football). The producers of commercial culture tried to avoid any reflection of 'real life' which would have meant tackling social divisions and antagonisms. One of the prime, indeed defining characteristics of mass commercial entertainment was its homogeneity. The silent films were the forerunners of this trend. They were easily accessible and understood by Germans and non-Germans, literate and illiterate alike. In terms of content, in spite of their sensationalist nature, films remained fairly neutral. 'There can be little arguing', writes Paul Monaco, 'that feature films only rarely addressed [themselves] directly to contemporary social problems. Instead, movies find their relationship to society in oblique symbolism . . . One of the most striking characteristics of film is its kinship to the dream.'[44] And of course the more foreign films were imported to be shown to German audiences, especially from Hollywood, the less likely they were to relate directly to their viewers' experience.

Homogeneity or universalism was to be found on the sports field too. Although teams built up considerable local followings, they began to compete against one another in regional, national and international competitions, necessitating formal, uniform rules, organization and discipline, eventually promoting a wider identification with one's country on the part of both players and supporters. However, although the relationship between sport and nationalism has been widely acknowledged – the obsession with healthy bodies, rippling muscles and thus national preparedness for military conflict, all part of the national revival, on the part of a German and French bourgeois gymnasts – after the turn of the century sport became part of the more general commercialization of leisure emphasizing self-enjoyment and individual diversion.[45] The determination to win and the forming of friendships within the team, suggests a prominent historian of sport in Germany, were more important than class-consciousness.[46] The Olympic Games were revived in 1896 and by the 1920s national and international sports displays and competitions organized by the Workers' Sport Movement were regular events; they also held their alternative Workers' Olympiad.[47] In non-socialist sport competition and victory became the focus of interest of most players and supporters. The players with one of the most famous football teams in the Ruhr, FC Schalke 04, were typical when they said, 'We want to play football. We want nothing to do with anything else . . . Politics and religion have no role to play in our association.'[48]

Universal values were fostered and promoted in a far more sophisticated, direct and far-reaching way than ever before, by means of the mass media. Film and, later, radio did far more than simply advertise what was on offer. They contributed to the emergence of a mass culture by transmitting the same message to readers, viewers and listeners belonging to all classes, nationalities, religions and regions. The press, film and radio were able to create a mass market for products and services by dictating taste and fashion in areas like music, dancing and clothing.

Young people were particularly important as receivers and transmitters of the new cultural values. They were avid cinema-goers and easily influenced by the associated fashions, music and stars.[49] The sports movement was especially popular among young people, particularly boys. By 1926 there were 76 national youth associations in Germany, with almost four and a half million members under the age of 21. In fact, 43 per cent of 14 to 21 year olds belonged to one or more youth organization, the majority in sports clubs (46.8 per cent of boys and 17.7 per cent of girls).[50] The inclination of young people towards sectionally biased organizations, like religious youth associations or the youth branches of the labour movement, was less remarkable than their growing membership of non-affiliated groups. Young, single people came increasingly to represent a new force in consumer demand, moving away from their parents' loyalties, creating, perhaps for the first time, a clear generation gap and embracing the new commercial mass leisure culture instead.

The gradual encroachment of a commercial entertainment culture into the hitherto sectional cultures that existed in urban working-class communities could never have happened to such an extent in the 1920s without tapping a new consumerist ideology in a working class that was undergoing change in terms of its structure, geographical distribution, level of integration and political loyalty. The religious, ethnic and other loyalties that continued to divide the working class in Bochum and Düsseldorf until the First War were losing their sharpness. This was the result of secular trends, the 'Germanization' of foreign immigrants and more general improvements in housing and education which tended to contribute to the alleviation of the physical and psychological ghettoization both of the working class as a whole and of groups within it. Divisions were also reduced by the greater spending power of all groups, the growing ability to make choices about how to spend one's leisure time and exposure to cultural influences which were not obviously attempts at social control (compared with, say, the rational recreation initiative of the 1890s).[51] All of this caused the Social Democrats much frustration. As they saw it, the working class was stuck on the first step of the evolutionary relationship to bourgeois culture. 'They are proud of the fact that they can imitate everything bourgeois', complained one SPD functionary; 'for the most part, they have petit bourgeois ideals: drinking, trashy literature, jazz, boxing and so forth.'[52]

The early years of the Weimar Republic are famous as the heyday of the socialist cultural initiative, expressed through a dense network of educational, recreational and sporting associations affiliated to the SPD and the Communist Party (KPD), transcending residual divisions within the working class and bringing about vast improvements in the conditions for the implementation of this policy. In Germany as a whole the SPD had almost 500 trade union hostels and meeting rooms, 77 trade union houses, 581 libraries and 98 reading rooms, 429 education committees and 451 youth commissions in 1914.[53] On the other hand, success in this department was tempered by a failure to come to terms with and successfully compete against the commercial leisure industry. The problem lay in the SPD's refusal to accept cultural forms which they regarded as the 'poison of civilization'; alcohol, the pub, cinema and trashy literature were regarded as the antitheses of educational improvement.[54] These forms of amusement were escapist and superficial and therefore could only distract the attention of the worker away from the values of the labour movement. Of course, this rejection of proletarian culture, the culture of everyday life, had been a constant feature of socialist cultural policy throughout the *Kaiserreich*, but only now did this attitude appear incongruous in the context of the new republic. Possibly comforted or even protected by the apparent increase in membership of the party and its associated clubs and organizations – the workers' sports associations boasted over a million members by the late 1920s – the SPD refused to acknowledge the sheer scale of the working-class embrace of commercial pleasures.

The cinema was an obvious medium for the labour movement to use, as an agent of both propaganda and education, a fact acknowledged by a few in the movement as early as 1914. Writing in *Die Neue Zeit*, Franz Förster commented that 'the cinema has become a strength to be reckoned with by publicists, politicians, legislators and, particularly, the Social Democratic education initiative.' Förster recommended that the SPD purchase its own equipment and establish its own cinemas, making use of the numerous trade-union premises, and employ travelling cinemas to reach smaller towns. He also proposed the publication of film reviews and critiques in the party press.[55] Although practical impediments to these suggestions (mainly the high cost of equipment and the need to adhere to official fire regulations) hindered any large-scale exploitation of the cinema, one cannot escape the conclusion that an absence of political will within the party leadership was equally to blame for the SPD's failure to tap this important market. In 1924 in the SPD's cultural organ, *Kulturwille*, Heinrich Geissler challenged the party to give the cinema a 'proletarian character'.[56] Yet the full implications of the advantages of film were only realized by the SPD the following year when a propaganda film was shown in all cinemas promoting the candidacy of Hindenberg in the forthcoming presidential elections.[57] The cinema had been a popular means of entertainment and communication at least since the end of the war in 1918, but it was not until the late 1920s that the SPD took full advantage of its benefits and then only for politically expedient reasons. The socialists used cinema seriously for the first time in the 1928 election, showing party propaganda films in its mobile cinemas. Even then, the labour movement always had difficulty in raising the finance to produce its own films – it could cost upwards of 300,000 marks – and it had limited success in founding its own cinemas.[58] The KPD overcame the financial hurdle by buying in films like Eisenstein's *Battleship Potemkin* from the Soviet Union and eventually both parties restricted themselves to propaganda films. Neither ever discarded its distaste for the medium that they both described as 'the most important capitalist means for controlling people'.[59]

The split in the labour movement after 1919 intensified the problems facing the socialist cultural initiative. The SPD's policy was less clearly articulated than before the war, while the KPD adopted an increasingly hardline position that subjected all cultural activity to the service of the proletarian struggle and that was manifested in attempts to convert members of SPD clubs to the Communist movement. As long as the socialist leadership stuck to its definition and practice of culture it alienated workers who were increasingly able to participate in a leisure culture previously beyond their grasp. When added to improved living and working conditions, this could only widen the gap that already existed between the everyday experiences of the working class and the horizons of political culture. There were certainly areas of cross-fertilization but these tended to work in one direction, with elements of popular workers' culture finding acceptance within the socialist cultural movement rather than vice versa. Workers' libraries, for instance, were eventually pressurized into stocking the books their members wanted to read; the workers' sport movement was forced to compromise its radical and somewhat unpopular policy of cooperation and team performance in favour of competition and the reward of excellence.[60] Peukert's assertion that '"Workers culture" as labour movement culture and the everyday popular culture of the lower classes [were still] mutually exclusive' would appear to need little qualification.[61]

The triumph of commercial culture?

None of the new mass commercial leisure forms was the sole province of the working class in general or of any group within it. The cinemas, sports arenas and funfairs became spaces where the classes, religions, ethnic groups and sexes could mix. Thus some degree of social harmony in leisure was achieved, a dream that had existed only as a utopian vision in the minds of liberal reformers several decades earlier. Indeed, the transcendant nature of commercial leisure was its strength, coupled with its ability to communicate to all groups, irrespective of individual loyalties. Some historians have interpreted this as the democratization of leisure, and even of culture. As Heinrich August Winkler writes:

> Cultural goods (*Bildungsgüter*), which had hitherto been status symbols of a narrow upper class, were made available to the broadest groups in the population via records, film, radio and paperbacks . . . On the other hand, popular entertainment products, from jazz and the pop song to the comedy film, penetrated the higher milieu.[62]

It is this degree of widespread acceptance of products of the commercial leisure sector (and note the waning of criticism of the cinema in particular after the 1914–18 war), and the extent to which goods and services filtered both upwards and downwards, that distinguished leisure in the 1920s from that of the prewar period. To quote Winkler once again: '"mass culture" . . . was distinguishable not only from traditional workers' culture, but also from conventional bourgeois culture', forming what he calls a 'type of bourgeois-proletarian mixture'.[63]

However, the triumph of commercial leisure did not necessarily signal the disappearance of older, traditional forms and expressions of working-class culture. Most, if not all, of the leisure activities enjoyed by the working class – festivals, drinking, dancing and associational life – persisted into the 1920s, some less vibrant or reformed, others revitalized or adapted to changing circumstances. Similarly, the middle classes, while enjoying the cinema later, and the radio and gramophone in the privacy of their own homes, continued to patronize the classical theatre, opera, cafés and restaurants and formed the vanguard of modernism in Weimar Germany.[64] Commercial culture, then, was an arena where the two groups could meet on neutral ground while not excluding the simultaneous enjoyment of some more class-bound activities. The working class began to lose its marginal position in urban society, becoming more integrated into the mainstream, and the mainstream shifted so that it was no longer the creation and provenance of the bourgeoisie.

In the Weimar Republic, cultural socialism lost its sense of direction in the leisure sphere, although, as Dieter Langewiesche has rightly pointed out, it did have successes in education and influenced other aspects of everyday life, like child-rearing, family life, even housing and furniture design.[65] While the expansion of the socialist associational movement continued apace the sheer size of some of its branches, notably the Deutsche Arbeitersängerbund (Federation of Workers' Choral Societies) and the Arbeiter Turn und Sport Bund, (the sports movement) meant that some of the original aims were compromised and it was difficult to distinguish committed socialist members from those of their comrades who merely joined in order to have access to the facilities. Moreover, as the ideology and practice of the SPD's cultural socialism was diluted so the Communists became increasingly uncompromising, creating an unbridgeable gulf between the two.[66] One institution, however, retained its place and importance in the political (and still predominantly male) culture of the working class – the tavern. Ethnic, occupational and religious differences which had fostered an intense localism around tavern life gave way, particularly in the cities, to political affiliations. This process is vividly illustrated by Anthony McElligott's study of political street violence in Hamburg in the early 1930s, a phenomenon that centred upon taverns dominated by the SPD, KPD and National Socialists.[67]

Those involved in overt political activity such as the 1918–19 revolution and the battles on the streets at the end of the Weimar Republic were doubtless a minority. Was political passivity the consequence of the masses' embrace of the commercial sector? Mass entertainment was certainly escapist and diversionary and the dominant values transmitted by this culture, while not overtly bourgeois and conventional, were not alternative or oppositional either. Did audiences transfer their hopes and dreams onto the stars of stage, screen and football field? Certainly some film stars and football players were idolized but it is unlikely that they became proxies for the displaced desires of the working class. Did the new consumer ideology, the ability of many to buy what had previously been regarded as luxuries, cushion the later effects of economic stagnation and depression? The severity of the economic crisis would suggest that such an interpretation is dangerously naive, but the later success of National Socialists in tapping the mass media does seem to indicate that commercialization had succeeded in creating an individualist mentality and diverted energy from seeking fundamental change through collective action. There is little evidence to support the alternative hypothesis, that working–class exposure to mass commercial culture created a feeling of frustration at not being able to achieve what they saw on the screen or were urged to buy by newspaper and film advertising.

The early years of the twentieth century did witness some positive developments in the realm of popular leisure and social life. For the first time women were found to be participating in the recreations their husbands' brothers and fathers had enjoyed for years (although men managed to create a new male-dominated leisure sphere: football).[68] The reasons for this were both practical and psychological. More practical clothing for women, particularly shorter skirts, enabled them to enjoy sport and active leisure pursuits. Many young, single women gained greater independence than their mothers had experienced by working in clerical positions or as store assistants. With their wages they could afford to frequent the cinemas and dance halls and purchase the latest fashions, make-up and, later, records and magazines. In the wake of these new-found freedoms attitudes towards the role of women in society began to change, if slowly. The majority of working-class men accepted the relative independence gained by women, up to certain limits. Young people, too, emerged as an identifiable group, particularly after the war. Children now became 'teenagers' before they were deemed adults and meeting their demands for amusement helped shape the leisure market probably more than any other factor.

By the 1920s commercialization had virtually created a new popular culture of the masses, a process that had little to do with control from above. Government attempts to impose a homogeneous national culture on a heterogeneous German nation since the 1870s came to nothing. Rather, the new culture was more the result of a supply and demand curve determined by a new group of consumers and entrepreneurs. The working class now regarded leisure as a right not a luxury, and it was its consumer power that stimulated the production of new forms of entertainment to transport it away from reality to a world dominated by excitement, sensation and collective fervour.

Notes

1 A. Briggs, 'Mass Entertainment: The Origins of a Modern Industry', Joseph Fisher Lecture in Commerce, Adelaide, 1960.

2 Bry, *Wages in Germany*, p. 54.
3 MS: 22 March 1919.
4 Ibid.: 6 June 1900.
5 By comparison, there were around 3,500 cinemas in Britain in 1914.
6 StAD, III 8950: Düsseldorf Stadttheater 1922–3.
7 *Statistisches Jahrbuch für das Deutsche Reich*, vol. 28 (1907); R. A. Woeltz, 'Sport, Culture and Society in Late Imperial and Weimar Germany: Some Suggestions for Future Research', in *British Journal of Sports History*, vol. 4 (1977), pp. 304–5. Note the parallel developments in Britain and France – see S. G. Jones, 'Work, Leisure and Unemployment between the Wars', in *British Journal of Sports History*, vol. 3 (1986), pp. 55–80, and on France R. Holt, *Sport and Society in Modern France* (London: Macmillan, 1981). On FC Schalke 04 see S. Gehrmann, 'Fußball in einer Industrieregion. Das Beispiel FC Schalke 04', in Reulecke and Weber (eds), *Fabrik, Familie, Feierabend*, p. 385. Studies of football teams in Germany are few and far between. On football in the Ruhr see R. Lindner and H. T. Breuer, *'Sind doch nicht alles Beckenbauers'. Zur Sozialgeschichte des Fußballs im Ruhrgebiet* (Frankfurt am Main: Suhrkamp, 1982). However, there is nothing as comprehensive as T. Mason's *Association Football and English Society 1863–1915* (Brighton: Harvester, 1980). It should also be noted here that not all teams were as unpartisan as FC Schalke appeared to be. Note the strong local identification with 1 FC Nürnberg in Bavaria; in other European countries football teams were strongly associated with local religious (Glasgow Rangers and Celtic; Liverpool and Everton) and political (FC Barcelona, associated with Catalan nationalism) affiliations, T. Mason, 'The Blues and the Reds', *Transactions of the Historic Society of Lancashire and Cheshire*, vol. 134 (1984), pp. 107–28.
8 M. L. Müller, 'Sozialgeschichte des Fussballsports in Raum Frankfurt am Main 1890–1933' (Dissertation, Universität Frankfurt am Main, 1989), p. 91.
9 H. Haeffs, 'Sport und Turnen', in Lux (ed.), *Düsseldorf*, pp. 301–3. *Statistisches Jahrbuch für das Deutsche Reich* (1926).
10 *Düsseldorfer Volkszeitung*, 25 July 1905; MS, 5 June 1900.
11 *Bochumer Volksblatt*, 15 August 1919.
12 H. A. Winkler, *Der Schein der Normalität, Arbeiter und Arbeiterbewegung in der Weimarer Republik 1924 bis 1930* (Berlin/Bonn: Dietz, 1985), p. 122.
13 D. Peukert, *Jugend Zwischen Krieg und Krise* (Cologne: Bund, 1987), p. 216.
14 W. Panofsky, *Die Geburt des Films* (1944) cited in G. Stark, 'Cinema, Society and the State: Policing the Film Industry in Imperial Germany', in G. Stark and B. K. Lackner (eds), *Essays on Culture and Society in Modern Germany* (Texas: MUP, 1982), p. 130, n. 24.
15 B. Zeller (ed.), *Hätte Ich Das Kino* (Stuttgart: Sonderausstellungen des Schiller-Nationalmuseums, 1976), p. 67.
16 On the development of the early cinema in Germany see F. von Zglinicki, *Der Weg des Films* (Hildesheim: Olms, 1979) and Stark, 'Cinema, Society and the State.'
17 Zeller, *Hätte Ich Das Kino*, p. 57.
18 von Zglinicki, *Der Weg des Films*, p. 319.
19 Ibid.
20 Ibid.
21 Peukert, *Jugend Zwischen Krieg und Krise*, p. 218.
22 In 1933, 53.1 per cent of boys went to the cinema with another male, 20.2 per cent with a girl; 42.8 per cent of girls went with a girlfriend and 26.5 per cent with a boyfriend – see Peukert, *Jugend Zwischen Krieg und Krise*, p. 218.

23 Briggs, 'Mass Entertainment', p. 18. See also D. Mühlberg, 'Kulturgeschichte der Arbeiterklasse und Kino – Ueberlegungen zu einem möglichen Forschungsansatz', in *Filmwissenschaftliche Beiträge*, vol. 2 (1981), pp. 13–14.

24 HStAD, RD 9004: Polizei-Verfügung, Zensur der Kino-Vorführungen, Essen, 2 June 1910.

25 Ibid.: Düsseldorf Polizei-Verwaltung, Erlass einer Polizeiverordnung über die Kino-Zensur, 24 January 1910.

26 HStAD, RD 30483: Mülheim/Ruhr, 30 April 1912.

27 Ibid.: Duisburg 7 May 1912.

28 HStAD, RD 9004: Schundliteratur und Kinotheater, Solingen 3 March 1909.

29 Ibid.: Düsseldorf Polizei-Verwaltung, 24 January 1910.

30 See Stark, 'Cinema, State and Society' for a comprehensive account of censorship of the film industry in Germany.

31 HStAD, RD 46077: Filmzensure, Essen, 26 September 1915; cf. HStAD, RD 30483: Krefeld – Vereinheitlichung der Censur der Kino-theater, 11 March 1912. It was argued by the Krefeld authorities that a common censor system could not be applied, since Krefeld had a majority of women over men in its population.

32 HStAD, RD 46077: Conference of Düsseldorf police inspectors on the censorship of public cinema performances, 17 January 1912.

33 HStAD, RD 30480: Verbotene Kinematographen-Bilder, Berlin 4 November 1911.

34 T. J. Saunders, 'Comedy as Redemption: American Slapstick in Weimar Culture?', in *Journal of European Studies*, vol. 17 (1987), p. 254.

35 On the development of the German film and newsreel industry during the war see D. Welch, 'Cinema and Society in Imperial Germany, 1905–1918', in *German History*, vol. 8 (1990), pp. 28–45.

36 On the so-called *Aufklärungsfilme* see P. Monaco, *Cinema and Society. France and Germany during the Twenties* (New York: Elsevier, 1976), pp. 52–3.

37 For SPD policy towards commercial culture see D. Peukert, *Grenzen der Sozialdisziplinierung. Aufstieg und Krise der deutschen Jugendfürsorge 1878 bis 1932* (Cologne: Bund, 1986), pp. 181–4.

38 Reichlichtspielgesetz, 12 May 1920.

39 Monaco, *Cinema and Society*, p. 56.

40 Briggs, 'Mass Entertainment', pp. 28–9.

41 S. Drucker, 'Das Kinoproblem und unsere politischen Gegner', in *Die Neue Zeit*, vol. 32 (1914), p. 868.

42 E. Altenloh, *Zur Soziologie des Kino* (Jena: Diederichs, 1914).

43 HStAD, RD 46077: newspaper cutting from Gelsenkirchen (unidentified), 18 March 1911.

44 Monaco, *Cinema and Society*, p. 7.

45 Woeltz, 'Sport, Culture and Society'; E. Weber, 'Gymnastics and Sports in Fin-de-Siècle France: Opium of the Classes?', in *American Historical Review*, vol. 76 (1971), pp. 70–98.

46 H. Ueberhorst, *Frisch, Frei, Stark und Treu. Die Arbeitersportbewegung in Deutschland, 1893–1933* (Düsseldorf: Droste, 1973), p. 281. Cf. P. Friedemann, 'Der Krise der Deutschen Arbeitersportbewegung am Ende der Weimarer Republik', in F. Boll (ed.), *Arbeiterkulturen zwischen Alltag und Politik: Beiträge zum Europäischen Vergleich in der Zwischenkriegzeit* (Düsseldorf: Europaverlag, 1986), pp. 229–40.

47 R. Wheeler, 'Organised Sport and Organised Labour: The Workers' Sport Movement', in *Journal of Contemporary History*, vol. 13 (1978), pp. 191–210.

48 Gehrmann, 'Fußball in einer Industrieregion', p. 398.
49 Peukert, *Jugend Zwischen Krieg und Krise*, p. 219.
50 Ibid., pp. 220–1.
51 For general details regarding the working class's spending power, leisure time, social and geographical mobilization and so on in the Weimar Republic see Winkler, *Der Schein der Normalität*, especially ch. 1, pp. 13–176.
52 K. Heilbut, cited in van der Will and Burns, *Arbeiterkulturbewegung in der Weimarer Republik*, p. 187.
53 H. Groschopp, *Zwischen Bierabend und Bildungsverein. Zur Kulturarbeit in der Deutschen Arbeiterbewegung vor 1914*, (Berlin: Dietz, 1985), p. 115.
54 For the labour movement's attitude not only to the cinema but also to other forms of proletarian amusement see Mühlberg, 'Kulturgeschichte der Arbeiterklasse und Kino', pp. 19–22.
55 F. Förster, 'Das Kinoproblem und die Arbeiter', in *Die Neue Zeit*, vol. 32 (1914), pp. 483–7.
56 H. Geissler in *Kulturwille*, cited in F. Heidenreich, *Arbeiterbildung und Kulturpolitik. Kontroversen in der sozialdemokratischen Zeitschrift 'Kulturwille' 1924–1933*, (Berlin: Argument 1983), p. 93.
57 Heidenreich, *Arbeiterbildung und Kulturpolitik* p. 93.
58 On the response of the SPD to the rise of cinema see D. Langewiesche, 'Working-Class Culture and Working-Class Politics in the Weimar Republic', in R. Fletcher (ed.), *Bernstein to Brandt: A Short History of German Social Democracy* (London: Edward Arnold, 1987), pp. 110–15; Guttsman, *Workers' Culture in Weimar Germany*, pp. 254–74.
59 Langewiesche, 'Working-Class Culture', p. 113.
60 See Guttsman, *Workers' Culture in Weimar Germany*, especially pp. 11–13.
61 Peukert, *Grenzen der Sozialdisziplinierung*, p. 188.
62 Winkler, *Der Schein der Normalität*, p. 145. The interpretation of Weimar culture as a democratic one is not new. See, for example, J. Hermand and F. Trommler, *Die Kultur der Weimarer Republik* (Munich: Nymphenburger, 1978), pp. 69–74.
63 Winkler, *Der Schein der Normalität* pp. 144–5.
64 M. Eksteins, *The Rites of Spring: The Great War of the Twentieth Century* (London: Bantam Press, 1989).
65 Langewiesche, 'Working-Class Culture', p. 109. On proletarian lifestyle and *Wohnkultur* see also Guttsman, *Workers' Culture in Weimar Germany*, pp. 182–4.
66 Guttsman, *Workers Culture in Weimar Germany*, chs 5, 6.
67 McElligott, 'Street Politics in Hamburg', pp. 83–90.
68 Müller, 'Sozialgeschichte des Fussballsports', p. 93.

8

Conclusions: a working-class leisure culture?

In little less than 50 years the leisure activities of the German working class had undergone a massive transformation. They had become less bloody and more disciplined, less sacred and more secular, less spontaneous and more organized, culminating in the modern entertainment and leisure culture of the twentieth century. Both the quantity and quality of amusements improved. Not only was there more choice of leisure activities after the First World War, the amusements on offer were generally of a higher standard: seats in cinemas instead of standing room only in low-grade music halls; football pitches in place of the street; and libraries stocked with novels rather than flimsy pamphlets. These improvements were a result of the acknowledgement of leisure as a universal right, and of rising living standards including greater free time and disposable income.

This work has shown that the emergence of modern leisure was strongly determined by the structures and functions of industrial society. It would be impossible to isolate it from the prevailing political, economic and social relations which in turn derived from the victory of industrial capitalism. In early modern Europe, according to Peter Burke, the essential changes in popular culture were brought about by philosophical and religious movements – the Renaissance, Reformation and Counter-Reformation. However, around 1800, he argues, 'the growth of towns, the spread of schools and the development of the railways, among other factors, made rapid change in popular culture possible, indeed inevitable.'[1] The present study took as its starting point precisely such a watershed period, which in Germany was around the middle of the nineteenth century, and found a strong current of continuity in the cultural process. Many forms of street and itinerant entertainment had their roots in the tradition of spectacle and the grotesque. The pageantry and ritual of the festivals did not disappear; rather, these elements were appropriated by new groups seeking to establish for themselves a cultural identity. 'Traditional' popular culture did not vanish in the nineteenth century, as Burke suggests, but was adapted to conform to the demands of urban industrial society. The triumph of industrial capitalism, as E. P. Thompson has shown, involved no less of a cultural transformation than that which occurred in early modern Europe. The new philosophy of the Industrial Revolution – time equals money –

imposed new values on society.[2] Customs and beliefs associated with the pre-industrial economy formed a locus of resistance to modern industrial work practices. Irregular festivals and undisciplined amusements were not compatible with the capitalist work ethic. The popular culture of industrial society became riven by class divisions. By the final quarter of the nineteenth century the culture of the working-class was clearly distinct from that of the *Mittelstand* and the bourgeoisie.

The demarcation of working-class culture was effected by a twofold process: the withdrawal of the bourgeoisie from erstwhile popular events and activities, and the formation of new class-specific recreations. The middle class withdrew from the parish fair during the process of its transformation from a local religious festival to an urban funfair, character-ized by crass entertainment and bare-faced commercialism. In compensa-tion the urban middle class commandeered the carnival, infused its official elements with bourgeois pretension and relegated the working class to the side-lines. It also invented tradition by reincarnating local civic festivals in order to bolster its power and status as a group *vis à vis* the working class and the state.[3] Henceforward, any attempts by the state to foster a national festival culture foundered in the face of already fairly entrenched segrega-tion. Other popular forms of leisure activity exhibited the same class-exclusiveness: temperance never made decisive inroads into working-class drinking behaviour; working-class clubs maintained a discreet distance from their bourgeois counterparts; even in dance halls the fashionable dances of the period were never seriously threatened by middle-class obsessions with decorum and respectability. The leisure activities of the German working class were thus part of a new, distinctly urban culture fashioned by workers both from the remnants of values and customs held dear in an earlier social system, and from the requirements of conforming to a social structure in which their role was well defined and yet subservient to the needs of others.

It was suggested in the introduction to this study that workers' leisure activities were influenced, if not determined, by the kind of work they were employed in and the meaning they derived from this work. It is clear that in purely instrumental and material terms work was a major influence on choice of leisure activity. In addition to the obvious constraints of time and money the experience of the work process was of paramount import-ance. Few miners, for instance, were keen to participate in gymnastics at the end of an exhausting shift underground. Pigeon fancying was more appealing. Certainly the additional money and energy enjoyed by skilled workers allowed them more choice and discretion in their pursuit of leisure, but in addition their level of identification and satisfaction with the final product of their labours may have encouraged them to seek similar satisfaction in their leisure interests. Skilled men were more prominent in clubs and associations, especially those affiliated to the labour movement, and they were generally more enthusiastic supporters of rational recreations and self-improvement. Only further mechanization and the eight-hour day signalled greater equality of leisure opportunities. However, choice of leisure activity was just as likely to be determined by age, sex or marital status. Young, single men dominated the leisure market until the turn of the century while women, married couples and the elderly were given a limited choice. Young, single women only made their presence felt with the appearance of the dance halls and cinemas.

Workers' leisure was far more resilient and flexible than we have been led to believe. Indeed, one of the most striking conclusions of this study is the positive, even assertive role played by the working class in the face of pressure to reform and sanitize popular recreational pursuits. So-called cruel and barbarous amusements disappeared because working people stopped enjoying them, not in response to the zeal of humane reformers; many parish fairs survived following pressure from a tacit alliance between the working class and the local *Mittelstand*; music-hall entertainment was tailored to the demands of audiences who clapped and accompanied songs they knew and loved. Blatant attempts to suppress amusements seen as threatening the social equilibrium rarely succeeded unless reinforced by government legislation. What is perhaps surprising in this period of alleged all-pervasive state control was the reluctance of central government to interfere with the pursuit of pleasure unless the activity could be perceived as a threat to the still-fragile national unity. Central and local government did provide financial and moral support to bourgeois reform organizations at the end of the nineteenth century, which could be judged as a positive attempt to secure social consensus (the bread and circuses approach), but the desired effect was rarely achieved. New recreational facilities were, to a limited extent, taken advantage of while the message they were intended to convey was ignored. Thus the working class borrowed fiction from public libraries and played football and drank beer in public parks. When a social consensus was finally achieved in the cultural sphere in the 1920s it happened in spite of middle-class manipulation rather than because of it.

This assertiveness was, I would suggest, a rational expression of political and economic impotence. It is a truism to spell out the innately weak position of the working class in a society run by strong central government serviced by an elite-dominated bureaucracy, military and judiciary, an undemocratic electoral system and a police system with considerable powers to make its own laws and make its presence felt. In addition the SPD adopted a policy of non-participation in government and fostered the creation of a culture that was essentially isolated from the society around it. In these circumstances the working class was forced to fall back on its own resources, creating its own recreations and amusements, formulating a radical response to the failure of society at large to recognize and meet its recreational needs. Workers frequently acted independently, often in defiance of socialist policy. Evidence of the existence of a vision of a future society will not be found, but the *Schnapskasinos*, the voluntary associations and even the music and dance halls provided scope for the collective affirmation of a common predicament. The 'culture of poverty', which encompassed not merely cheap amusements and recreations tailored to working-class everyday realities but also housing and family life, attitudes towards sexuality and respectability and household budget management, was a sober consequence of hardship and insecurity.[4] The alternative culture of a future utopian society envisaged by leading Social Democrats only made sense to a few educated workers. Saving, adult education, cultural edification: such concepts did not enter the vocabulary of the majority of the working class before the First World War.

In terms of their electoral support the socialists could justifiably claim to be the party of labour by the turn of the century, but their attempts to politicize the working class by means of sponsoring social and cultural initiatives foundered largely as a result of the leadership's inability or unwillingness to come to terms with the rough side of working-class everyday life. Certainly in both Bochum and Düsseldorf the Social Democrats gained support from the multi-cultural working class (both towns sent SPD deputies to the Reichstag in 1911), and pockets of an alternative socialist subculture did exist, notably the voluntary associations, the education initiatives and the trade unions. But this was a respectable labour movement consisting of mainly skilled workers, whose pronouncements on working-class leisure activities were often reminiscent of those of their middle-class opponents. Contemporary socialists created and perpetuated the myth of two mutually exclusive subcultures by reaffirming the dichotomy between the respectable culture of the labour movement and the culture of the uneducated, unorganized lumpenproletariat. Social Democrats failed to realize, or refused to acknowledge, that the culture of improvement had little relevance to the daily lives of the majority of workers. This culture of poverty spawned a radical response to the failure of society and the SPD to recognize and meet workers' recreational needs. Institutions like the *Schnapskasinos* and the fledgling voluntary associations, beyond satisfying material requirements, provided an arena for the creation of a collective identity; they aided workers' adaptation to industrial life and gave them practice in organizational and political skills. *Arbeiterkultur* was not, therefore, the same as *Arbeiterbewegungskultur* but it was just as important in towns with a weak socialist movement in fostering an alternative workers' culture to that being foisted upon them by the bourgeoisie, the churches and the state.

Much has been made in this book of the absence of a clear class-consciousness among German workers in this region before 1914, as evidenced by their strong cultural loyalty to their confessional or ethnic identities. Yet these divisions were not necessarily a sign of weakness and in certain cases were a definite focus of strength and opposition to the dominant culture. For instance, it was impossible to recruit Catholics to participate in national festivals in commemoration of Bismarck, the Kaiser and victory over the French at Sedan, owing to the Chancellor's diminution of Catholics to a minority in the Reich and the subsequent suppression of their rights during the *Kulturkampf*. Similarly, attempts to force the pace of Polish integration, such as the law requiring Polish associations to converse in German, strengthened the resolve of ethnic Poles to maintain their separate identity. While the separate religious, ethnic and occupational leisure cultures perpetuated one another's isolation, however, they all progressed along identical paths. Each group criticized the others but they failed to address the more fundamental problem: how to provide an alternative to the commercially inspired amusements which they feared would engulf their sectional interests, and which eventually did. So while they frustrated state attempts to homogenize and sanitize working–class culture and partially hindered the efforts of the SPD to fashion a socialist culture that would traverse indigenous loyalties, these groups succumbed to the power of economic interests disguised as mass entertainment.

In the Weimar Republic the SPD, now virtually part of the establishment and for whom a vote was no longer considered a protest, gradually abandoned its antipathy to popular culture and slowly incorporated some elements into the party operation. The party met the working-class rank and file half way. By the 1920s the German working class had undergone a process of stabilization and class formation that had reached maturity. Worker mobility into and between major industrial centres remained at an extremely high and fairly constant level until 1914. After the war, owing to a combination of diminishing population pressure (the result of a decrease in the birth rate and the loss of many young men in the war) and economic stabilization, mobility rates across city boundaries dramatically decreased for both individuals and families, simultaneously reducing work-force fluctuation in the factories.[5] As the flow of migrants from the east dried up Germans began to migrate overseas, to the United States in particular until 1925, and from this date on the population in the provinces of the Rhineland and Westphalia increased only in line with the average demographic growth in the Reich as a whole.[6] Poles, the most numerous minority before the war, began to move back to the new Poland in the 1920s; others migrated to northern France in the search for work, and in 1924 the rationalization of the mining industry occasioned the break-up of many Polish ghettos. 'Towards the end of the Weimar Republic', writes Kristoph Klessmann, 'the Polish minority was reduced to about one-third of its pre-war strength: it was socially integrated though not completely assimilated.'[7]

The working class had become more homogeneous. It began to lose its divisive features and consequently became more receptive to the introduction of what has been called standardization, from the manufacture and retailing of consumer goods to the emergence of the commercial leisure industry with its universal values.[8] For its part, the new leisure industry also helped to reduce the divisions within the working class. The cinemas were relatively inexpensive and open at all times at everyone's convenience. Sport, especially football, was easily translated from the local to the national level. The press, and later the radio, enabled all supporters to follow their team's progress. Indeed, it was the mass media above all that unified the working class into an identifiable target group, to the advantage not just of commercial entertainment entrepreneurs but of political parties too.

Yet the emergence of a commercial culture did not imply complete uniformity. Theories like Hobsbawm's 'standardization' obscure the diversity that still characterized working-class life. Religious and ethnic divisions may have become less important, but the constraint of poverty still restricted the access of many working-class families to so-called popular, mass leisure activities. Moreover, it led to the formation of new divisions within the working class. Politically the labour movement split two ways, reflecting dissatisfaction and frustration with the policies of the majority Social Democrats and greater political consciousness among the working class. The 1920s also witnessed a hitherto less distinct division, between those in work and the unemployed. The jobless were only temporarily excluded from commercial culture, however, and, unless their political stance dictated otherwise, retained the ambition to return to it. Similarly the SPD, and then the KPD, avoided outright condemnation of the popular manifestations of the new culture, preferring to adapt and use the new forms of communication within the newly defined boundaries. Thus the KPD's enthusiasm for the cinema as a propaganda tool kept it in touch with popular culture. The SPD's predilection for mass sporting occasions likewise placed it within the mainstream trend. Both the SPD and the KPD benefited from the popular obsession with the products of commercial enterprise by turning some aspects of it to their own advantage, a policy that promised greater success than earlier attempts to reject manifestations of popular street culture out of hand.

Workers' culture was not an invention of industrial society but it was a response to it. The consequences of industrialization, urbanization and technological social change, did not destroy all vestiges of popular culture practised by the working class. Yet workers' culture was not a creation of the labour movement either. Rather, it was a rough amalgam of the myriad cultures imported into the urban environment in the second half of the nineteenth century, it was shaped by the ideologies that governed that society and it adapted to objective changes in the structure of society and the subjective needs of the workers themselves. Workers' culture in Imperial Germany was not a received culture, it was dynamic and assertive, and by the outbreak of war in 1914 the German working class had established for itself a set of rules and forms of behaviour that were quite distinct from those of the bourgeoisie and the Social Democratic Party.

Notes

1 Burke, *Popular Culture in Early Modern Europe*, pp. 244–81. See also P. Burke, 'Popular Culture between History and Ethnology', in *Ethnologia Europaea*, vol. 14 (1984), pp. 5–12, for his assigning of cultural change to distinct periods. This interpretation has been criticized by W. Brückner, 'Popular Culture: Konstrukt, Interpretament, Realität', in *Ethnologia Europaea*, vol. 14 (1984), pp. 14–24.
2 Thompson, 'Time, Work Discipline and Industrial Capitalism', p. 80.
3 E. Hobsbawm and T. Ranger (eds), *The Invention of Tradition* (Cambridge: Cambridge University Press, 1983).
4 Grüttner, 'Die Kultur der Armut', pp. 12–32.
5 D. Langewiesche and F. Lenger, 'Internal Migration: Persistence and Mobility', in K. Bade (ed.), *Population, Labour and Migration in 19th and 20th Century Germany* (Leamington Spa: Berg, 1987), pp. 87–100.
6 Winkler, *Der Schein der Normalität*, pp. 115–16.
7 K. Klessmann, 'Long Distance Migration, Integration and Segregation of an Ethnic Minority in Industrial Germany: the Case of the "Ruhr Poles"', in Bade (ed.), *Population, Labour and Migration*, p. 112.
8 E. Hobsbawm, 'The Making of the Working Class 1870–1914', in his *Worlds of Labour* (London: Weidenfeld & Nicolson, 1984), pp. 194–213, especially p. 204 where he points to 'A single, fairly standardized, national pattern of working-class life [in Britain]: and at the same time one increasingly specific to the working class.'

Bibliography

Unpublished Sources

Hauptstaatsarchiv Düsseldorf
  Regierung Aachen
  Regierung Düsseldorf
  Regierung Köln

Stadtarchiv Bochum
  Amt Kreisausschuß
  Amt Landratsamt
  Amt Langendreer
  Amt Linden–Dahlhausen
  Amt Stadt Bochum
  Amt Weitmar
  Amt Werne
  Nachlass Küppers

Stadtarchiv Düsseldorf
  II: Akten der Stadt Düsseldorf
  III: Akten der ehemaligen städtischen Polizeiverwaltung
  XX: Vereinsakten

Newspapers

Bochumer Volksblatt
Märkischer Sprecher
Düsseldorf Anzeiger
Düsseldorf General Anzeiger
Düsseldorfer Volkszeitung
Niederrheinische Volkstribune
Düsseldorfer Volksblatt
Düsseldorfer Zeitung
Kölnische Zeitung

Books and Articles

Abrams, L. Prostitutes in Imperial Germany 1870–1918: Working Girls or Social Outcasts? In R. J. Evans (ed.), *The German Underworld*, pp. 189–209. London: Routledge, 1988.

Advocatus, Was liest der deutsche Arbeiter? *Die Neue Zeit*, vol. 13 (1894–5), pp. 814–17.

Altenloh, E. *Zur Soziologie des Kino*. Jena: Diederichs, 1914.

Altick, R. *The Shows of London*. Cambridge, MA: Belknap, 1978.

Aron, R. On Leisure in Industrial Societies. In J. Brooks (ed.), *The One and the Many: the Individual in the Modern World*, pp. 157–72. New York: Harper and Row, 1962.

Bächthold-Stäubli, H. (ed.) *Handwörterbuch des Deutschen Aberglaubens*, 9 vols. Berlin & Leipzig: Walter de Gruyter & Co., 1927–42.

Bacon, A. W. Leisure and the Alienated Worker. A Critical Reassessment of Three Radical Theories of Work and Leisure'. *Journal of Leisure Research*, vol. 7 (1975), pp. 179–90.

Bailey, P. *Leisure and Class in Victorian England. Rational Recreation and the Contest for Control*. London: Routledge 1978.

Bailey, P. 'A Mingled Mass of Perfectly Legitimate Pleasures.' The Victorian Middle Class and the Problem of Leisure. *Victorian Studies*, vol. 21 (1977–8), pp. 7–28.

Bajohr, S. Illegitimacy and the Working Class. Illegitimate Mothers in Brunswick 1900–1933. In R. J. Evans (ed.), *The German Working Class*, pp. 142–73. London: Croom Helm, 1982.

Bajohr, S. *Vom bitteren Los der kleinen Leute: Protokolle über den Alltag Braunschweiger Arbeiterinnen und Arbeiter 1900 bis 1933*. Cologne: Bund, 1984.

Bakhtin, M. *Rabelais and his World*. 1965, repr. Bloomington, Ind.: Indiana University Press, 1984.

Bernays, M. Auslese und Anpassung der Arbeiterschaft der geschlossenen Grossindustrie. Dargestellt an den Verhältnissen der Gladbacher Spinnerei und Weberei. *Schriften des Vereins für Sozialpolitik*, vol. 133 (1910), pp. 1–417.

Bishop, J. and Hoggett, P. *Organising around Enthusiasms. Patterns of Mutual Aid in Leisure*. London: Comedia, 1986.

Blackbourn, D. and Eley, G. *Peculiarities of German History*. Oxford: Oxford University Press, 1984.

Blessing, W. The Cult of the Monarchy. Political Loyalty and the Workers' Movement in Imperial Germany. *Journal of Contemporary History*, vol. 13 (1978), pp. 357–75.

Blessing, W. *Staat und Kirche in der Gesellschaft. Institutionelle Autorität und Mentaler Wandel in Bayern während des 19. Jahrunderts*. Göttingen: Vandenhoek & Ruprecht, 1982.

Blessing, W. Fest und Vergnügen der kleinen Leute: Wandlungen vom 18. bis 20. Jahrhundert. In R. van Dülmen and N. Schindler (eds), *Volkskultur: zur Wiederentdeckung des vergessen Alltags (16.–20. Jahrhundert)*, pp. 352–79. Frankfurt am Main: Fischer, 1984.

Borsay, P. The Rise of the Promenade: the Social and Cultural Use of Space in the English Provincial Town, c.1660–1800. *British Journal for Eighteenth Century Studies*, vol. 9 (1986), pp. 125–38.

Bose, G. and Brinkmann, E. *Circus: Geschichte und Aesthetik einer niederen Kunst* Berlin: Wagenbeck, 1978.

Brakelmann, G. Die Anfänge der Evangelischen Arbeitervereinbewegung in Gelsenkirchen 1882–1890. In K. Düwell and W. Köllman (eds), *Rheinland-Westfalen im Industriezeitalter*, vol. 3, pp. 40–55. Wuppertal: Hammer, 1983.

Bibliography

Brand, H-J. Kirchliches Vereinswesen und Freizeitgestaltung in einer Arbeitergemeinde 1872–1933: das Beispiel Schalke. In Huck (ed.), *Sozialgeschichte der
Freizeit*, pp. 207–22.

Brepohl, W. *Industrievolk im Wandel von der Agraren zur Industriellen Daseinsformen
dargestellt am Ruhrgebiet*. Tübingen: Mohr, 1957.

Briggs, A. Mass Entertainment: The Origins of A Modern Industry. Joseph Fisher
Lecture in Commerce, Adelaide, 1960.

Bromme, M. T. W. *Lebensgeschichte eines modernen Fabrikarbeiters*. Jena: Diederichs,
1905.

Brückner, W. Popular Culture: Konstrukt, Interpretament, Realität. *Ethnologia
Europaea*, vol. 14 (1984), pp. 14–24.

Brüggemeier, F-J. *Leben vor Ort: Ruhrbergleute und Ruhrbergbau 1889–1919*. Munich:
C. H. Beck, 1983.

Brüggemeier, F-J. and Niethammer, L. Wie Wohnten Arbeiter im Kaiserreich?
Archiv für Sozialgeschichte, vol. 16 (1976), pp. 61–134.

Brüggemeier, F-J. and Niethammer, L. Schlafgänger, Schnapskasinos und Schwerindustrielle Kolonie. Aspekte der Arbeiterwohnungsfrage im Ruhrgebiet vor
dem Ersten Weltkrieg. In J. Reulecke and W. Weber (eds), *Fabrik, Familie,
Feierabend*, pp. 135–76. Wuppertal: Hammer, 1978.

Bry, G. *Wages in Germany 1871–1945*. Princeton NJ: Princeton University Press,
1960.

Burke, P. *Popular Culture in Early Modern Europe*. London: Temple Smith, 1978.

Burke, P. Popular Culture Between History and Ethnology. *Ethnologia Europaea*,
vol. 14 (1984), pp. 5–12.

Chadwick, G. *The Park and the Town. Public Landscape in the 19th and 20th Centuries*.
London: Architectural Press, 1966.

Clarke, J., Critcher, C. and Johnson, R. (eds) *Working Class Culture: Studies in
History and Theory*. London: Hutchinson, 1979.

Clarke, P. *The English Alehouse c. 1200–1830*. London: Longman, 1983.

Conze, W. and Kocka, J. (eds) *Bildungsbürgertum im 19. Jahrhundert*. Stuttgart: Klett-
Cotta, 1985.

Cranz, G. Changing Roles of Urban Parks. From Pleasure Garden to Open Space.
Landscape, vol. 22 (1978), pp. 9–14.

Crew, D. F. *Town in the Ruhr: A Social History of Bochum 1860–1914*. New York:
Columbia University Press, 1979.

Crew, D. F. Steel Sabotage and Socialism: the Strike at the Dortmund Union
Steelworks in 1911. In R. J. Evans (ed.), *The German Working Class*, pp. 108–14.
London: Croom Helm, 1982.

Crew, D. F. The Constitution of 'Working-Class Culture' as a Historical Object,
Britain and Germany 1870–1914. Unpublished paper, 1983.

Croon, H. Die Stadtvertretungen in Krefeld und Bochum im 19. Jahrhundert. In
R. Dietrich and G. Oestrich (eds), *Forschungen zu Staat und Verfassung-Festgabe für
Fritz Hartung*, pp. 289–306. Berlin: Humboldt, 1958.

Croon, H. Bürgertum und Verwaltung in den Städten des Ruhrgebiets im 19.
Jahrhundert. *Tradition*, vol. 9 (1964), pp. 23–41.

Croon, H. Studien zur Sozial und Siedlungsgeschichte der Stadt Bochum. In P.
Busch, H. Croon, C. Hahne (eds), *Bochum und das mittlere Ruhrgebiet*, pp. 85–114.
Paderborn: Gesellschaft für Geographie und Geologie Bochum e.v. 1965.

Cunningham, H. *Leisure in the Industrial Revolution*. London: Croom Helm, 1980.

Dann, O. Die Anfänge politischer Vereinsbildung in Deutschland. In U. Engelhardt (ed.), *Soziale Bewegung und Politische Verfassung*. Stuttgart: Klett Cotta,
pp. 197–232.

Davies, A. Leisure and Poverty in Salford. Unpublished paper, Anglo-German conference on Working-Class Culture, Lancaster University, 1988.

De Grazia, S. *Of Time, Work and Leisure.* New York: Anchor Books, 1962.

Debus, C. *Arbeiterwohnungswesen im Rheinisch-Westfälisch Industriebezirk.* Zur Sozial und Gewerbepolitik der Gegenwart, 1890.

Diefendorf, J. M. *Businessmen and Politics in the Rhineland 1789–1834.* Princeton, NJ: Princeton University Press, 1980.

Dingle, A. E. Drink and Working-Class Living Standards in Britain, 1870–1914. *Economic History Review,* 2nd series, vol. 25 (1972), pp. 608–22.

Dingwerth, L. *Mit dem Zeichenstift durch Bochum.* Bochum: Studienverlag Brockmeyer, 1984.

Dowe, D. The Working Men's Choral Movement in Germany before the First World War. *Journal of Contemporary History,* vol. 13 (1978), p. 269–96.

Dröge, F. and Krämer-Badoni, T. *Die Kneipe.* Frankfurt: Suhrkamp, 1987.

Drucker, S. Das Kinoproblem und unsere politischen Gegner. *Die Neue Zeit,* vol. 32 (1914), pp. 867–72.

Duisburg Autorenkollektiv. *'Und vor Allen Dingen das is' Wahr!' Eindrücke und Erfahrungen aus der Filmarbeit mit alten Menschen im Ruhrgebiet.* Duisburg: 1979.

Dumazedier, J. *Toward a Society of Leisure.* Paris: The Free Press, 1967.

Ehalt, H. C. *Geschichte von Unten. Fragestellungen, Methoden u. Projeckte einer Geschichte des Alltags.* Vienna: Böhlau, 1984.

Eksteins, M. *Rites of Spring. The Great War in the Twentieth Century.* London: Bantam Press, 1989.

Eley, G. Joining Two Histories: The SPD and the German Working Class, 1860–1914. In G. Eley (ed.), *From Unification to Nazism: Reinterpreting the German Past,* pp. 171–99. London: Allen and Unwin, 1986.

Engelhardt, U., Sellin, V., Stuke, H. *Soziale Bewegung und Politische Verfassung.* Stuttgart: Klett Cotta, 1976.

Engelsing, R. *Analphabetentum und Lektüre. Zur Sozialgeschichte des Lesens in Deutschland.* Stuttgart: Metzler, 1973.

Erenberg, L. A. *Steppin' Out. New York Nightlife and the Transformation of American Culture 1890–1930.* London: Greenwood, 1981.

Evans, R. J. Prostitution, State and Society in Imperial Germany. *Past and Present,* vol. 70 (1976), pp. 106–29.

Evans, R. J. (ed.) *Society and Politics in Wilhelmine Germany.* London: Croom Helm, 1978.

Evans, R. J. Politics and the Family: Social Democracy and the Working-Class Family in Theory and Practice before 1914. In R. J. Evans and W. R. Lee (eds), *The German Family,* pp. 256–88. London: Croom Helm, 1981.

Evans, R. J. The Sociological Interpretation of German Labour History. In R. J. Evans, *The German Working Class,* pp. 15–53. London: Croom Helm, 1982.

Evans, R. J. Religion and Society in Modern Germany. *European Studies Review,* vol. 12 (1982), pp. 249–88.

Evans, R. J. *Death in Hamburg.* Oxford: Clarendon, 1987.

Evans, R. J. *Kneipengespräche im Kaiserreich. Stimmungsberichte der Hamburger Politischen Polizei 1892–1914.* Hamburg: Rowohlt, 1989.

Fletcher, R. (ed.) *Bernstein to Brandt: A Short History of German Social Democracy.* London: Edward Arnold, 1987.

Förster, F. Das Kinoproblem und die Arbeiter. *Die Neue Zeit,* vol. 32 (1914), pp. 483–7.

Fout, J. C. The Woman's Role in the Working-Class Family in the 1890s from the

Bibliography

Perspective of Women's Autobiographies. In J. C. Fout. (ed.), *German Women in the Nineteenth Century* pp. 295–319. London: Holmes and Meier, 1984.

Fricke, D. (ed.) *Die Bürgerlichen Parteien in Deutschland 1830–1945*, 2 vols. Leipzig: Bibliographiches Institut, 1970.

Friedemann, P. Feste und Feiern in Rheinisch-westfälischen Industriegebiet. In Huck (ed.), *Sozialgeschichte der Freizeit*, pp. 161–85.

Friedemann, P. Anspruch und Wirklichkeit der Arbeiterkultur 1891–1933. In D. Petzina (ed.), *Fahne, Fäuste, Korper: Symbolik und Kultur der Arbeiterbewegung*, pp. 101–12. Essen: Klartext, 1986.

Friedemann, P. Der Krise der Deutschen Arbeitersportbewegung am Ende der Weimarer Republik. In F. Boll (ed.), *Arbeiterkulturen zwischen Alltag und Politik: Beiträge zum Europäschen Vergleich in der Zwischenkriegzeit*, pp. 229–40. Düsseldorf: Europaverlag, 1986.

Fullerton, R. Creating a Mass Book Market in Germany. The Story of the Colporteur Novel 1870–1890. *Journal of Social History*, vol. 10 (1977), pp. 265–83.

Fullerton, R. Toward a Commercial Popular Culture in Germany: the Development of Pamphlet Fiction, 1871–1914. *Journal of Social History*, vol. 12 (1979), pp. 489–512.

Gailus, M. Berliner Strassengeschichten. In H. C. H. Ehalt (ed.), *Geschichte von Unten. Fragestellungen, Methoden und Projeckte einer Geschichte des Alltags*. Vienna: Böhlau, 1984.

Gainsborough Commission. *Life and Labour in Germany*. London: Simpkin, Marshall, Hamilton, Kent & Co., Ltd, 1906.

Geary, D. Arbeiterkultur in Deutschland und Großbritannien im Vergleich. In D. Petzina (ed.), *Fahne, Fäuste, Korper: Symbolik und Kultur der Arbeiterbewegung*, pp. 91–100. Essen: Klartext, 1986.

Gehrmann, S. Fußball in einer Industrieregion. Das Beispiel FC Schalke 04. In J. Reulecke and W. Weber (eds), *Fabrik, Familie, Feierabend*, pp. 377–98. Wuppertal: Hammer, 1978.

Gerlach, P. Die Arbeiterbewegung. In Lux (ed.), *Düsseldorf*, pp. 131–5.

Giegler, H. *Dimensionen und Determinanten der Freizeit*. Opladen: Westdeutscherverlag, 1982.

Glaser, H. (ed.) *Von der Kultur der Leute*. Berlin: Ullstein, 1983.

Gobbers, E. *Artisten. Zirkus und Varieté in Alter und Neuer Zeit*. Düsseldorf: Droste, 1949.

Göhre, P. *Three Months in a Workshop*. (tr. A. B. Carr) London: Swan Sonnenschein & Co., 1895.

Grän, M. *Erinnerungen aus einer Bergarbeiterkolonie im Ruhrgebiet*. Münster: F. Coppenrath, 1983.

Groschopp, H. Bürgerliches Vereinswesen und Lebensreformbewegung vor 1914. *Weimarer Beiträge*, vol. 30 (1984), p. 1852–69.

Groschopp, H. *Zwischen Bierabend und Bildungsverein, Zur Kulturarbeit in der Deutschen Arbeiterbewegung vor 1914*. Berlin: Dietz, 1985.

Grosshennrich, F-J. *Die Mainzer Fastnachtvereine. Geschichte, Funktion, Organisation und Mitgliederstruktur*. Wiesbaden: Franz Steiner, 1980.

Grüttner, M. Working-Class Crime and the Labour Movement. Pilfering in the Hamburg Docks 1888–1923. In R. J. Evans (ed.), *The German Working Class*, pp. 54–79. London: Croom Helm, 1982.

Grüttner, M. *Arbeitswelt an der Wasserkante: Sozialgeschichte der Hamburger Hafenarbeiter 1886–1914*. Göttingen: Vandenhoek & Ruprecht, 1984.

Grüttner, M. Alkoholkonsum der Arbeiterschaft 1871–1939. In T. Pierenkemper (ed.), *Haushalt und Verbrauch in Historischer Perspektive*, pp. 229–73. Sonderdruck: Scripta mercaturae, 1987.

Grüttner, M. Die Kultur der Armut. In H. G. Haupt, A. Jost, G. Leithäuser, V. Mückenberger, Ch. Riechers, H. J. Steinberg (eds), *Soziale Bewegungen: Geschichte und Theorie*, pp. 12–32. Frankfurt am Main: Campus, 1987.

Günter, R. u. a. Eisenheim: Die Erfahrung einer Arbeiterkolonie. In L. Niethammer (ed.), *Wohnen im Wandel*, pp. 188–210.

Gutman, H. *Work, Culture and Society in Industrialising America*. New York: Blackwell, 1978.

Guttsman, W. L. *Workers' Culture in Weimer Germany: Between Tradition and Commitment*. Oxford: Berg, 1990.

Haenisch, W. Was Lesen die Arbeiter? *Die Neue Zeit*, vol. 18 (1900), pp. 691–6.

Hammerich, K. Skizzen zur Genese der Freizeit als eines Sozialen Problem. *Kölner Zeitschrift für Sociologie und Sozialpsychologie*, vol. 26 (1974), pp. 267–81.

Hanke, H. H. (ed.) *Bochum: Wandel in Architektur und Stadtgestalt*. Bochum: 1985.

Harrison, B. *Drink and the Victorians: The Temperance Question in England 1815–72*. London: Faber, 1971.

Harrison, B. Animals and the State in Nineteenth Century England. *English Historical Review*, vol. 88 (1973), pp. 786–820.

Haspel, J. and Reuss, K. H. Alltagskultur in Ulmer Arbeiterquartieren während der Industrialisierung. In H. E. Specker (ed.), *Stadt und Kultur*. Sigmaringen: Thorbecke, 1983.

Heidenreich, F. *Arbeiterbildung und Kulturpolitik. Kontroversen in der sozialdemokratischen Zeitschrift 'Kulturwille' 1924–1933*. Berlin: Argument, 1983.

Henning, F-W. *Düsseldorf und seine Wirtschaft: Zur Geschichte einer Region. Bd.1: Von den Anfängen bis 1860. Bd.2: Von 1860 bis zur Gegenwart*. Düsseldorf: Droste, 1981.

Hermand, J. and Trommler, F. *Die Kultur der Weimarer Republik*. Munich: Nymphenburger, 1978.

Hickey, S. H. F. Class Conflict and Class Consciousness: Coal Miners in the Bochum Area of the Ruhr 1870–1914. PhD thesis, University of Oxford, 1976.

Hickey, S. H. F. The Shaping of the German Labour Movement: Miners in the Ruhr. In Evans (ed.), *Society and Politics in Wilhelmine Germany*, pp. 215–40.

Hickey, S. H. F. *Workers in Imperial Germany: The Miners of the Ruhr*. Oxford: Clarendon, 1985.

Hobsbawm, E. *Worlds of Labour: Further Studies in the History of Labour*. London: Weidenfeld & Nicolson, 1984.

Hobsbawm, E. and Ranger, T. (eds) *The Invention of Tradition*. Cambridge: Cambridge University Press, 1983.

Holt, R. *Sport and Society in Modern France*. London: Macmillan, 1981.

Hoyer, F. A. Die Vereinsdeutsche – Karikatur oder Wirklichkeit? *Deutsche Rundschau*, vol. 90 (1964), pp. 16–21.

Hübner, M. *Zwischen Alkohol und Abstinenz. Trinksitten und Alkoholfrage im deutschen Proletariat bis 1914*. Berlin: Dietz, 1988.

Huck, G. (ed.) *Sozialgeschichte der Freizeit. Untersuchungen zum Wandel der Alltagskultur in Deutschland*. Wuppertal: Hammer, 1980.

Hunley, J. D. The Working Classes, Religion and Social Democracy in the Düsseldorf Area. *Societas*, vol. 4 (1974), pp. 131–49.

Hüttenberger, P. Die Entwicklung zur Großstadt bis zur Jahrhundertwende (1856–1900). In H. Weidenhaupt (ed.), *Düsseldorf: Geschichte von den Ursprüngen bis ins 20. Jahrhundert*, vol. 2, pp. 481–662. Düsseldorf: Schwann, 1988.

Iggers, G. The Political Theory of Voluntary Associations in Early Nineteenth Century German Liberal Thought. In D. B. Robertson (ed.), *Voluntary Associations. A Study of Groups in Free Societies*. Richmond, Va: John Knox Press: 1966.

Bibliography

Irsigler, F. and Lassota, A. *Bettler und Gaukler, Dirnen und Henker. Außenseiter in einer mittelalterlichen Stadt.* Cologne: dtv, 1989.

Jacoby, A. P. and Babchuk, N. Instrumental and Expressive Voluntary Associations. *Sociology and Social Research*, vol. 47 (1963), pp. 461–71.

Jagusch, A. Die Entwicklung des V. f. L. Bochum 1848 e. V. unter besonderer Berücksichtigung der Fußballabteilung. Dissertation Ruhr-Universität Bochum, 1975.

Jasper, K. *Der Urbanisierungsprozess dargestellt am Beispiel der Stadt Köln.* Cologne: Rheinisch-Westfälischen Wirtschaftsarchiv zu Köln e.v., 1977.

Jeggle, U. Alkohol und Industrialisierung. In H. Cancik (ed.), *Rausch-Ekstase – Mystik. Grenzformen religiöser Erfahrung*, pp. 78–94. Düsseldorf: Patmos, 1978.

Jones, S. G. Work, Leisure and Unemployment between the Wars. *British Journal of Sports History*, vol. 3 (1986), pp. 55–80.

Jones, S. G. *Workers at Play: A Social and Economic History of Leisure, 1918–1939.* London: Routledge, 1986.

Jones, S. G. State Intervention in Sport and Leisure in Britain between the Wars. *Journal of Contemporary History*, vol. 22 (1987), pp. 163–82.

Kautsky, K. Der Alkoholismus und seiner Bekämpfung. *Die Neue Zeit*, vol. 9 (1891), pp. 1–8, 46–55, 77–89, 105–16.

Kehm, B. *Der 1. Mai im Spiegel der Bochumer Presse 1927–55.* Bochum: D. G. B., 1986.

Kelly, T. *A History of Public Libraries in Great Britain 1845–1965.* London: Library Association, 1973.

Klessmann, K. *Polnische Bergarbeiter im Ruhrgebiet 1870–1914.* Göttingen: Vandenhoek & Ruprecht, 1978.

Klessmann, K. Kaiser Wilhelms Gastarbeiter. Polen als Bergarbeiter im Ruhrgebiet. In L. Niethammer, B. Hombach, T. Fichter, U. Borsdorf (eds), *Die Menschen machen ihre Geschichte nicht als freien Stücken*, pp. 105–7. Berlin/Bonn: Dietz, 1984.

Klessmann, K. Long-Distance Migration, Integration and Segregation of an Ethnic Minority in Industrial Germany: the Case of the 'Ruhr Poles'. In K. Bade (ed.), *Population, Labour and Migration in 19th and 20th Century Germany*, pp. 101–14. Leamington Spa: Berg, 1987.

Knopp, G. *Die Preussische Verwaltung des Regierungsbezirks Düsseldorf 1899–1919.* Cologne: Gröte, 1974.

Koch, R. Die Entwicklung des VfL Bochum auf dem Hintergrund der Deutschen Turn und Sportbewegung des 19. und 20. Jahrhundert. Dissertation, Ruhr-Universität Bochum, 1977.

Koch, W. H. *Bochum Dazumal.* Düsseldorf: Droste, 1974.

Kocka, J. Arbeiterkultur als Forschungsthema. *Geschichte und Gesellschaft*, vol. 5 (1979), pp. 5–11.

Köllmann, W. *Sozialgeschichte der Stadt Barmen in 19. Jahrhundert.* Tübingen: Mohr, 1960.

Königstein, H. *Die Schiller-Oper in Altona.* Frankfurt am Main: Suhrkamp, 1983.

Korff, G. 'Heraus zum 1 Mai': Maibrauch zwischen Volkskultur, bürgerlicher Folklore und Arbeiterbewegung. In van Dülman and Schindler (eds), *Volkskultur*, pp. 246–81.

Kosok, E. Arbeiterfreizeit und Arbeiterkultur im Ruhrgebiet. Eine Untersuchung ihrer Erscheinungsformen und Wandlungsprozesse 1850–1914. Doctoral dissertation, Ruhr-Universität Bochum, 1989.

Kouri, E. I. *Der Deutsche Protestantismus und die Soziale Frage 1870–1919. Zur Sozialpolitik im Bildungsbürgertum.* Berlin: Walter de Gruyter, 1984.

Kramer, D. *Freizeit und Reproduktion der Arbeitskraft.* Giessen: Pahl-Rugenstein, 1975.

Bibliography

Kraus, A. Gemeindeleben und Industrialisierung. Das Beispiel des evangelischen Kirchenkreises Bochum. In J. Reulecke and W. Weber (eds), *Fabrik, Familie, Feierabend*, pp. 273–96. Wuppertal: Hammer, 1978.

Krüger, D. Ein 'Morgenrot wirklicher Sozialreform'. Die Gesellschaft für Soziale Reform und die Entwicklung der Arbeiterbeziehungen im Ersten Weltkrieg. In G. Mai (ed.), *Arbeiterschaft in Deutschland, 1914–1918*, pp. 29–76. Düsseldorf: Droste, 1985.

Kuczynski, J. *Die Geschichte der Lage der Arbeiter under dem Kapitalismus*, 20 vols. Berlin: Akademie, 1960–9.

Küther, C. *Menschen auf der Straße: Vagierende Unterschichten in Bayern, Franken und Schwaben in der zweiten Hälfte des 18. Jahrhunderts*. Göttingen: Vandenhoek & Ruprecht, 1983.

Lange, C. Die Wohnungsverhältnisse der ärmeren Volksklassen in Bochum. *Schriften des Vereins für Sozialpolitik*, vol. 30 (1886), pp. 73–105.

Langewiesche, D. *Zur Freizeit des Arbeiters. Bildungsbestrebungen und Freizeitgestaltung österreichischer Arbeiter im Kaiserreich und in der Ersten Republik*. Stuttgart: Klett Cotta, 1980.

Langewiesche, D. Politik – Gesellschaft – Kultur. Zur Problematik von Arbeiterkultur und kulturellen Arbeiterorganisationen in Deutschland nach dem 1. Weltkrieg. *Archiv für Sozialgeschichte*, vol. 22 (1982), pp. 359–402.

Langewiesche, D. The Impact of the German Labour Movement on Workers' Culture. *Journal of Modern History*, vol. 59 (1987), pp. 506–23.

Langewiesche, D. Working-Class Culture and Working-Class Politics in the Weimar Republic. In Fletcher (ed.), *From Bernstein to Brandt*, pp. 103–14.

Langewiesche, D. and Lenger, F. Internal Migration: Persistence and Mobility. In K. Bade (ed.), *Population, Labour and Migration in 19th and 20th Century Germany*, pp. 87–100. Leamington Spa: Berg, 1987.

Langewiesche, D. and Schönhoven, K. Arbeiterbibliotheken und Arbeiterlektüre in Wilhelminische Deutschland. *Archiv für Sozialgeschichte*, vol. 16 (1976), pp. 135–204.

Lees, A. Debates about the Big City in Germany 1854–1914. *Societas*, vol. 5 (1975), pp. 31–48.

Lees, A. Critics of Urban Society in Germany, 1854–1914. *Journal of the History of Ideas*, vol. 40 (1979), pp. 61–83.

Lenman, R. Art, Society and the Law in Wilhelmine Germany: the Lex Heinze. *Oxford German Studies*, vol. 8 (1973), pp. 86–113.

Lenman, R. Mass Culture and the State in Germany, 1900–26. In R. J. Bullen, H. Pogge von Strandmann and A. P. Polonsky (eds), *Ideas into Politics: Aspects of European History 1880–1950*, pp. 51–59. London: Croom Helm, 1984.

Levenstein, A. *Die Arbeiterfrage*. Munich: E. Reinhardt, 1912.

Lewis, G. K. The Kleingärten: Evolution of an Urban Retreat. *Landscape*, vol. 23 (1979), pp. 33–7.

Lidtke, V. Social Class and Secularisation in Imperial Germany. The Working Classes. *Leo Baeck Institute Yearbook*, vol. 25 (1980), pp. 21–40.

Lidtke, V. *The Alternative Culture: Socialist Labor in Imperial Germany*. New York: Oxford University Press, 1985.

Lindner, R. and Breuer, H. T. *Sind doch nicht Alles Beckenbauers. Zur Sozialgeschichte des Fußballs im Ruhrgebiet*. Frankfurt am Main: Suhrkamp, 1982.

Lucas, E. *Arbeiterradikalismus: Zwei Formen von Radikalismus in der deutschen Arbeiterbewegung*. Frankfurt am Main: Roter Stern, 1976.

Lüdtke, A. Arbeitsbeginn, Arbeitspausen, Arbeitsende. Bedürfnisfriedigung und Industriearbeit im 19. und frühen 20. Jahrhundert. In Huck (ed.), *Sozialgeschichte der Freizeit*, pp. 95–122.

Bibliography

Lux, H. A. (ed.) *Düsseldorf*. Düsseldorf: Weidlich, 1925.

Machtan, L. and Ott, R. 'Batzebier!' Ueberlegungen zur sozialer Protestbewegung in den Jahren nach der Reichsgründung am Beispiel der süddeutschen Bierkrawalle von Frühjahr 1873. In H. Volkmann and J. Bergmann (eds), *Sozialer Protest*, pp. 128–66. Opladen: Westdeutscher Verlag, 1984.

Malcolmson, R. *Popular Recreations in English Society 1700–1850*. Cambridge: Cambridge University Press, 1973.

Mallman, K-M. Saufkasinos und Konsumvereine. *Der Anschnitt*, vol. 32 (1980), pp. 200–6.

Malvache, J-L. *Arbeitersport in Bochum*. Bochum: DGB, 1984.

Marrus, M. Modernisation and Dancing in Rural France: From 'La Bourreé' to 'Le Fox-Trot'. In J. Beauroy (ed.), *The Wolf and the Lamb. Popular Culture in France, from the old Regime to the Twentieth Century*, pp. 141–160. Saratoga, Ca: Anma Libri, 1976.

Martius, W. *Der Kampf gegen den Alkoholmissbrauch. Mit besonderer Berucksichtigung des Deutschen Vereins gegen den Missbrauch geistiger Getränke*. Halle: 1884.

Mason, T. *Association Football and English Society 1863–1915*. Brighton: Harvester, 1980.

Mason, T. The Blues and the Reds. A History of the Liverpool and Everton Football Clubs. *Transactions of the Historic Society of Lancashire and Cheshire*, vol. 134 (1984), pp. 107–28.

Matull, W. *Der Freiheit einer Gasse. Geschichte der Düsseldorfer Arbeiterbewegung*. Düsseldorf: Schwann, 1979.

McCreary, E. Social Welfare and Business: The Krupp Welfare Program, 1864–1914. *Business History Review*, vol. 42 (1968), pp. 24–49.

McElligott, A. Street Politics in Hamburg. *History Workshop*, vol. 16 (1983), pp. 83–90.

McLeod, H. *Religion and the People of Western Euorpe 1789–1970*. Oxford: Oxford University Press, 1981.

McLeod, H. Protestantism and Workers in Imperial Germany. *European Studies Review*, vol. 12 (1982), pp. 323–43.

Meyer-Renschhausen, E. *Weibliche Kultur and Soziale Arbeit. Eine Geschichte der Frauenbewegung am Beispiel Bremens 1810–1927*. Frankfurt am Main: Böhlau, 1990.

Monaco, P. *Cinema and Society, France and Germany during the Twenties*. New York: Elsevier, 1976.

Mooser, J. *Arbeiterleben in Deutschland 1900–1970*. Frankfurt am Main: Suhrkamp, 1984.

Morf, R. *Die Verkürzung der täglichen Arbeitszeit*. Zurich: 1898.

Mosse, G. *The Nationalization of the Masses*. New York: Fertig, 1975.

Mott, J. Miners, Weavers and Pigeon Racing. In M. A. Smith, S. Parker and C. S. Smith (eds), *Leisure and Society in Britain*, pp. 88–96. London: Allen Lane, 1973.

Muchembled, R. *Popular Culture and Elite Culture in France 1400–1750*. Trans. L. Cochrane, Baton Rouge, La.: Louisiana University Press, 1985.

Mühlberg, D. Kulturgeschichte der Arbeiterklasse und Kino – Ueberlegungen zu einem möglichen Forschungsansatz. *Filmwissenschaftliche Beiträge*, vol. 2 (1981), pp. 6–27.

Mühlberg, D. *Arbeiterleben um 1900*. Berlin: Dietz, 1983.

Müller, G. Bürgerliche Sozialreformbestrebungen nach den Reichstagswahlen von 1907. Zur Konzeption und Wirksamkeit der Gesellschaft für Soziale Reform. *Zeitschrift für Geschichtswissenschaft*, vol. 35 (1987), pp. 308–19.

Müller, M. L. Sozialgeschichte des Fußballsports in Raum Frankfurt an Main 1890–1933. Dissertation, Universität Frankfurt am Main 1989.

204

Bibliography

Müller-Schlosser, H. *Die Stadt an der Düssel.* Düsseldorf: Droste, 1949.

Murphy, R. *Guestworkers in the German Reich. A Polish Community in Wilhelmine Germany.* New York: Columbia University Press, 1983.

Nahrstedt, W. Freizeit und Aufklärung. Zum Funktionswandel der Feiertage seit dem 18. Jahrhundert in Hamburg (1743–1860). *Vierteljahrschrift zur Sozial-und Wirtschaftsgeschichte*, vol. 57 (1970), pp. 46–92.

Nahrstedt, W. Die Entstehung des Freiheitsbegriffs der Freizeit. Zur Genese einer grundlegenden Kategorie der modernen Industriegesellschaften (1755–1826). *Vierteljahrschrift zur Sozial-und Wirtschaftsgeschichte*, vol. 60 (1973), pp. 311–42.

Neuhausen, J. *Damals in Düsseldorf.* Düsseldorf: Hoch, 1964.

Niess, W. Von Arbeitervereinslokalen zu den Volkshäusern (1848–1933). *Hessische Blätter für Volks-und Kulturforschung*, vol. 16 (1984), pp. 141–56.

Niethammer, L. (ed.) *Wohnen im Wandel. Beiträge zur Geschichte des Alltags in der Bürgerlichen Gesellschaft.* Wuppertal: Hammer, 1979.

Nipperdey, T. *Gesellschaft, Kultur, Theorie. Gesammelte Aufsätze zur Neueren Geschichte.* Göttingen: Vandenhoek & Ruprecht, 1976.

Nipperdey, T. Verein als Soziale Struktur in Deutschland im späten und frühen 19. Jahrhundert. In Nipperdey, *Gesellschaft, Kultur, Theorie*, pp. 174–205.

Nolan, M. *Social Democracy and Society: Working Class Radicalism in Düsseldorf 1890–1920.* Cambridge: Cambridge University Press, 1981.

Nye, R. B. Saturday Night at the Paradise Ballroom: or Dance Halls in the Twenties. *Journal of Popular Culture*, vol. 7 (1973), pp. 14–22.

Opaschowski, H. W. *Pädigogik der Freizeit.* Bad Heilbronn: Klinkhardt, 1976.

Ostwald, H. *Großstadt Dokumente.* Berlin: H. Seemann, 1905–8.

Otto, K. A. Arbeitszeit: Erfahrungen und Erwartungen der Kampf um die Arbeitszeit im Kaiserreich. *Geschichtsdidaktik*, vol. 10 (1985), pp. 374–96.

Parker, S. *The Future of Work and Leisure.* London: MacGibbon & Kee, 1971.

Parker, S. *Sociology of Leisure.* London: Allen & Unwin, 1976.

Parker, S. *Leisure and Work.* London: Allen & Unwin, 1983.

Pechartscheck, K. Die Veränderung der Lebenshaltung und ihrer Kosten bei Deutschen Bergarbeiterfamilien in den Jahren 1876–1912. Dissertation, University of Freiburg, 1933.

Pelzer, J. Satire oder Unterhaltung? Wirkungskonzepte im Deutschen Kabarett zwischen Bohemerevolte und antifaschistischer Opposition. *German Studies Review*, vol. 9 (1986), pp. 45–65.

Perry, E. 'The General Motherhood of the Commonwealth.' Dance Hall Reform in the Progressive Era. *American Quarterly*, vol. 37 (1985), pp. 719–33.

Petzoldt, L. *Volkstümliche Feste. Ein Führer zu Volksfesten, Märkten und Messen in Deutschland.* Munich: C. H. Beck, 1983.

Peukert, D. Arbeiteralltag: Mode oder Methode? In H. Haumann (ed.), *Arbeiteralltag in Stadt und Land: Neue Wege der Geschichtsschreibung*, pp. 8–39. Berlin: Argument, 1982.

Peukert, D. *Grenzen der Sozialdisziplinierung. Aufstieg und Krise der deutschen Jugendfürsorge 1878 bis 1932.* Cologne: Bund, 1986.

Peukert, D. *Jugend Zwischen Krieg und Krise. Lebenswelten von Arbeiterjungen in der Weimarer Republik.* Cologne: Bund, 1987.

Phayer, J. M. *Sexual Liberation and Religion in Nineteenth Century Europe.* London: Croom Helm, 1977.

Pieper, L. *Die Lage der Bergarbeiter im Ruhrgebiet.* Stuttgart and Berlin: Studien, 1903.

Poole, R. Lancashire Wakes Week. *History Today*, vol. 34 (August 1984), pp. 22–9.

Prahl, H-W. *Freizeit-Soziologie.* Munich: Kösch, 1977.

Bibliography

Reck, S. *Arbeiter nach der Arbeit; Sozialhistorische Studien zu den Wandlungen des Arbeiteralltags.* Giessen: Focus, 1977.

Reid, D. The Decline of Saint Monday. Working-Class Leisure in Birmingham 1760–1875. Unpublished paper, Society for the Study of Labour History Conference, University of Sussex, 1975.

Reulecke, J. Vom Blauen Montag zum Arbeiterurlaub. Vorgeschichte und Entstehung des Erholungsurlaubs für Arbeiter vor dem Ersten Weltkrieg. *Archiv für Sozialgeschichte,* vol. 16 (1976), pp. 205–48.

Reulecke, J. English Social Policy around the Middle of the 19th Century as seen by German Social Reformers. In W. Mommsen (ed.), *The Emergence of the Welfare State,* pp. 32–49. London: Croom Helm, 1981.

Reulecke, J. 'Veredelung der Volkserholung' und 'edle Geselligkeit'. Sozialreformische Bestrebungen zur Gestaltung der arbeitsfreien Zeit im Kaiserreich. In Huck (ed.), *Sozialgeschichte der Freizeit,* pp. 141–160.

Reulecke, J. *Sozialer Friede durch Soziale Reform. Der Centralverein für das Wohl der arbeitenden Klassen in der Frühindustrialisierung.* Wuppertal: Hammer, 1983.

Ritter, G. A. Workers' Culture in Imperial Germany: Problems and Points of Departure for Research. *Journal of Contemporary History,* vol. 13 (1978), pp. 165–89.

Roberts, E. *A Woman's Place. An Oral History of Working-Class Women, 1890–1940.* Oxford: Blackwell, 1984.

Roberts, J. Der Alkoholkonsum deutscher Arbeiter im 19. Jahrhundert. *Geschichte und Gesellschaft,* vol. 6 (1980), pp. 220–42.

Roberts, J. Drink and Industrial Work Discipline in Nineteenth Century Germany. *Journal of Social History,* vol. 15 (1981–2), pp. 25–38.

Roberts, J. Drink and Working-Class Living Standards in Late Nineteenth Century Germany. In W. Conze and U. Engelhardt (eds), *Arbeiterexistenz im 19. Jahrhundert: Lebenstandard and Lebengestalting deutscher Arbeiter and Hardwerker,* pp. 74–91. Stuttgart: Klett Cotta, 1981.

Roberts, J. Drink and the Labour Movement: The Schnapps Boycott of 1909. In R. J. Evans (ed.), *The German Working Class,* pp. 80–107. London: Croom Helm 1982.

Roberts, J. Wirtshaus und Politik in der Deutschen Arbeiterbewegung. In Huck (ed.), *Sozialgeschichte der Freizeit,* pp. 123–40.

Roberts, J. *Drink, Temperance and the Working Class in Nineteenth Century Germany.* London: Allen & Unwin, 1984.

Rosenhaft, E. *Beating the Fascists? The German Communists and Political Violence 1929–1933.* Cambridge: Cambridge University Press, 1983.

Rosenzweig, R. Middle-Class Parks and Working-Class Play: The Struggle over Recreational Space in Worcester, Massachusetts, 1870–1910. *Radical History Review,* vol. 21 (1979), pp. 31–46.

Rosenzweig, R. *Eight Hours for What We Will. Workers and Leisure in an Industrial City 1870–1920.* Cambridge: Cambridge University Press, 1983.

Ross, E. Survival Networks: Women's Neighbourhood Sharing in London before World War One. *History Workshop,* vol. 15 (1983), pp. 4–27.

Roth, G. *The Social Democrats in Imperial Germany: A Study in Working-Class Isolation and Negative Integration.* Totowa, NJ: Bedminster Press, 1963.

Rühle, O. *Kultur und Sittengeschichte des Proletariats,* 2 vols. Berlin: 1930, Giessen: Focus, 1976.

Rürup, R. *Deutschland im 19. Jahrhundert, 1815–71.* Göttingen: Vandenhoek & Ruprecht, 1984.

Saul, K. *Staat, Industrie, Arbeiterbewegung im Kaiserreich.* Düsseldorf: Bertelsmann, 1974.

Saul, K, Flemming J., Stegmann, D., Witt, P. C., (eds) *Arbeiterfamilien im Kaiserreich: Materiellen zur Sozialgeschichte in Deutschland 1871–1914*. Düsseldorf: Droste, 1982.

Saunders, T. J. Comedy as Redemption: American Slapstick in Weimar Culture? *Journal of European Studies*, vol. 17 (1987), pp. 253–77.

Scharfe, M. Distances between the Lower Classes and Official Religion: Examples from Eighteenth Century Württemburg Protestantism. In K. von Greyerz (ed.), *Religion and Society in Early Modern Europe 1500–1800*, pp. 157–74. London: Allen & Unwin, 1984.

Schenda, R. *Volk ohne Buch. Studien zur Sozialgeschichte der Populären Lesestoffe 1770–1910*. Munich: dtv, 1977.

Scheuch, E. Soziologie der Freizeit. In R. König (ed.), *Handbuch der Empirischen Sozialforschung 2*. Stuttgart: Anke, 1977.

Schieder, W. Kirche und Revolution. Sozialgeschichtliche Aspekte der Trierer Wallfahrt von 1844. *Archiv für Sozialgeschichte*, vol. 14 (1974), pp. 419–54.

Schindler, N. Karneval, Kirche und die Verkehrte Welt. Zur Funktion der Lachkultur im 16. Jahrhundert. *Jahrbuch für Volkskunde*, vol. 7 (1984), pp. 9–57.

Schivelbusch, W. *Das Paradies, der Geschmack und die Vernunft. Eine Geschichte der Genussmittel*. Munich & Vienna: Ullstein, 1980.

Schlossmacher, N. *Düsseldorf im Bismarckreich: Politik und Wahlen, Parteien und Vereine*. Düsseldorf: Schwann, 1985.

Schmidt, E. Die Entwicklung der deutschen Volksbibliotheken. *Der Arbeiterfreund*, vol. 50 (1912), p. 461.

Schmidt, E. Zierde, Vergnügen, gesunde Luft and gute Lehren. Zur Geschichte des Stadtparks in Bochum und anderswo. In Hanke (ed.), *Bochum*, pp. 109–21.

Schmidt, W. (ed.) *Von 'Abwasser' bis 'Wandern'. Ein Wegweiser zur Umweltgeschichte*. Hamburg: Körber-Stiftung, 1986.

Schulte, R. *Sperrbezirke. Tugendhaftigkeit und Prostitution in der bürgerlichen Welt*. Frankfurt am Main: Syndikat, 1979.

Schumann, F. Auslese und Anpassung der Arbeiterschaft in der Automobilindustrie und einer Wiener Maschinenfabrik: Die Arbeiter der Daimler-Motoren-Gesellschaft Stuttgart-Untertürkheim. *Schriften des Vereins für Sozialpolitik*, vol. 135 (1911).

Scott, J. C. Membership and Participation in Voluntary Associations. *American Sociological Review*, vol. 22 (1957), pp. 315–26.

Scribner, R. Reformation, Karneval and the World turned Upside-Down. *Social History*, vol. 3 (1978), pp. 303–29.

Scribner, R. Cosmic Order and Daily Life: Sacred and Secular in Pre-Industrial German Society. In K. von Greyerz (ed.), *Religion and Society in Early Modern Europe 1500–1800*, pp. 17–32. London: Allen & Unwin, 1984.

Seeling, H. *Geschichte der Gerresheimer Glashütte – Ursprung und Entwicklung 1864–1908*. Studien zur Düsseldorfer Witschaftsgeschichte, vol. 1. Düsseldorf: Lintz, 1964.

Seippel, M. *Das Maiabendfest in Bochum*. Bochum: Rheinisch-Westfälische Verlags-Anstalt, 1881.

Seippel, M. *Bochum Einst und Jetzt. Ein Rück-und Rundblick bei der Wende des Jahrhundert 1901*. Bochum: Rheinisch-Westfälische Verlags-Anstalt, 1901.

Senelick, L. Politics as Entertainment: Victorian Music-Hall Songs. *Victorian Studies*, vol. 19 (1975–6), pp. 149–80.

Society for the Study of Labour History, The Working Class and Leisure: Class Expression and/or Social Control. Unpublished conference papers, University of Sussex, 1975.

Bibliography

Sodor, M. *Hausarbeit und Stammtischsozialismus. Arbeiterfamilie und Alltag im Deutschen Kaiserreich*. Giessen: Focus, 1980.

Spencer, E. G. *Management and Labour in Imperial Germany. Ruhr Industrialists as Employers, 1896–1914*. Brunswick, NJ: Rutgers University Press, 1984.

Spencer, E. G. State Power and Local Interests in Prussian Cities: Police in the Düsseldorf District 1848–1914. *Central European History*, vol. 19 (1986), pp. 293–313.

Spencer, E. G. Policing Popular Amusements in German Cities. The Case of the Prussian Rhine Province 1815–1914. *Journal of Urban History*, vol. 16 (1990), pp. 366–85.

Sperber, J. The Transformation of Catholic Associations in the Northern Rhineland and Westphalia 1830–70. *Journal of Social History*, vol. 15 (1981), pp. 253–63.

Sperber, J. Roman Catholic Religious Identity in Rhineland-Westphalia 1800–70: Quantitative Examples and some Political Implications. *Social History*, vol. 7 (1982), pp. 305–18.

Sperber, J. *Popular Catholicism in Nineteenth Century Germany*. Princeton, NJ: Princeton University Press, 1984.

Spohr, E. *Düsseldorf – Stadt und Festung*. Düsseldorf: Schwann, 1979.

Stark, G. Cinema, Society and the State: Policing the Film Industry in Imperial Germany. In G. Stark and B. K. Lackner (eds), *Essays on Culture and Society in Modern Germany*, pp. 122–66. Texas: M.U.P., 1982.

Statistisches Jahrbuch für das Deutsche Reich

Stearns, P. *Lives of Labour*. London: Croom Helm, 1975.

Stearns, P. The Effort at Continuity in Working-Class Culture. *Journal of Modern History*, vol. 52 (1980), pp. 626–55.

Stedman Jones, G. Working-Class Culture and Working-Class Politics in London 1870–1900. *Journal of Social History*, vol. 7 (1973–4), pp. 460–501.

Stedman Jones, G. Class Expression versus Social Control? A Critique of Recent Trends in the Social History of Leisure. *History Workshop*, vol. 4 (1977), pp. 162–70.

Steinberg, H-J. Workers' Libraries in Imperial Germany. *History Workshop*, vol. 1 (1976), pp. 166–80.

Stone, C. Vandalism: Property, Gentility, and the Rhetoric of Crime in New York City 1890–1920. *Radical History Review*, vol. 26 (1982), pp. 13–34.

Storch, R. The Problem of Working-Class Leisure. Some Roots of Middle Class Moral Reform in the Industrial North, 1825–50. In A. P. Donajgrodzki (ed.), *Social Control in Nineteenth Century Britain*, pp. 138–62. London: Croom Helm, 1977.

Tenfelde, K. *Sozialgeschichte der Bergarbeiterschaft an der Ruhr im 19. Jahrhundert (1815–1889)*. Bonn/Bad Godesberg: Neue Gesellschaft, 1977.

Tenfelde, K. Bergmännisches Vereinswesen im Ruhrgebiet während die Industrialisierung. In J. Reulecke and W. Weber (eds), *Fabrik, Familie, Feierabend*, pp. 315–44. Wuppertal: Hammer, 1978.

Tenfelde, K. Mining Festivals in the Nineteenth Century. *Journal of Contemporary History*, vol. 13 (1978), pp. 377–403.

Thomas, K. Work and Leisure in Pre-Industrial Society. *Past and Present*, vol. 29 (1964), pp. 50–62.

Thomas, K. *Man and the Natural World*. London: Allen Lane, 1983.

Thompson, E. P. Time, Work Discipline and Industrial Capitalism. *Past and Present*, vol. 38 (1967), pp. 58–97.

Thompson, F. M. L. Social Control in Victorian Britain. *Economic History Review*, 2nd series, vol. 34 (1981), pp. 189–208.

Bibliography

Tillmann, H. Das Sozialistengesetz in Düsseldorf bis 1887: Reaktionen der Oeffentlichkeit und Unterdrückung der Arbeiterbewegung. Dissertation, Universität Düsseldorf, 1980.

Tobin, E. War and the Working Class: The Case of Düsseldorf 1914–18. *Central European History*, vol. 18 (1985), pp. 257–98.

Turk, E. The Great Berlin Beer Boycott of 1894. *Central European History*, vol. 15 (1982), pp. 377–97.

Ueberhorst, H. *Frisch, Frei Stark and Treu. Die Arbeitersportbewegung in Deutschland, 1893–1933.* Düsseldorf: Droste, 1973.

Van der Will, W. and Burns, R. *Arbeiterkulturbewegung in der Weimarer Republik: Vol. 1, Eine historische-theoretische Analyse der kulturellen Bestrebungen der sozialdemokratisch organisierten Arbeiterschaft. Vol. 2, Texte – Dokumente – Bilder.* Frankfurt am Main: Ullstein, 1982.

Van Dülman, R. and Schindler, N. (eds) *Volkskultur. Zur Wiederentdeckung des Vergessenen Alltags (16.–20. Jahrhundert).* Frankfurt am Main: Fischer, 1984.

Veblen, T. *The Theory of the Leisure Class.* New York: Macmillan, 1912.

Vogt, I. Einige Fragen zum Alkoholkonsum der Arbeiter. Kommentar zu J. S. Roberts 'Der Alkoholkonsum Deutscher Arbeiter im 19. Jahrhundert'. *Geschichte und Gesellschaft*, vol. 8 (1982), pp. 134–40.

Von Zglinicki, F. *Der Weg des Films.* Hildesheim: Olms, 1979.

Wagner, J. V. *Hakenkreuz über Bochum. Machtergreifung und Nationalsozialistischer Alltag in einer Revierstadt.* Bochum: Studienerlag Brockmeyer, 1983.

Walton, J. and Poole, R. The Lancashire Wakes in the Nineteenth Century. In R. Storch (ed.), *Popular Culture and Custom in Nineteenth Century England*, pp. 100–24. London: Croom Helm, 1982.

Walton, J. and Walvin, J. (eds) *Leisure in Britain.* Manchester: Manchester University Press, 1983.

Walvin, J. *Leisure and Society 1830–1950.* London: Longman, 1978.

Wayne Gordon, C. and Babchuk, N. A. Typology of Voluntary Associations. *American Sociological Review*, vol. 24 (1959), pp. 22–9.

Weber, E. Gymnastics and Sports in Fin-de-Siecle France: Opium of the Classes? *American Historical Review*, vol. 76 (1971), pp. 70–98.

Weber, E. *Peasants into Frenchmen.* London: Chatto & Windus, 1977.

Wehler, H-U. *Krisenherde des Kaiserreichs.* Göttingen: Vandenhoek & Ruprecht, 1969.

Weidenhaupt, H. *Kleine Geschichte der Stadt Düsseldorf.* Düsseldorf: Schwann, 1983.

Welch, D. Cinema and Society in Imperial Germany, 1905–1918. *German History*, vol. 8 (1990), pp. 28–45.

West, M. A. Spectrum of Spectators: Circus Audiences in Nineteenth Century America. *Journal of Social History*, vol. 15 (1981–2), pp. 265–70.

Wettstein-Adelt, M. *3½ Monate Fabrikarbeiterin.* Berlin: J. Leiser, 1893.

Wheeler, R. Organised Sport and Organised Labour: The Workers' Sport Movement. *Journal of Contemporary History*, vol. 13 (1978), pp. 191–210.

Wilensky, H. Work, Careers and Social Integration. *International Social Science Journal*, vol. 12 (1960), pp. 543–60.

Winkler, H. A. *Der Schein der Normalität, Arbeiter und Arbeiterbewegung in der Weimarer Republik 1924 bis 1930.* Berlin/Bonn: Dietz, 1985.

Woeltz, R. A. Sport, Culture and Society in late Imperial and Weimar Germany: Some Suggestions for Future Research. *British Journal of Sports History*, vol. 4 (1987), pp. 295–315.

Wunderer, H. Alkoholismus und Arbeiterschaft im 19. Jahrhundert. Kritische

Anmerkungen zu James S. Roberts: der Alkoholkonsum deutscher Arbeiter im 19. Jahrhundert. *Geschichte und Gesellschaft*, vol. 8 (1982), pp. 141–4.

Wyrwa, U. Der Alkoholgenuss der Hamburgischen Unterschichten. *Bochumer Archiv für die Geschichte des Widerstandes und der Arbeit*, vol. 6 (1984), pp. 45–75.

Wyrwa, U. *Branntwein und 'echtes' Bier. Die Trinkkultur der Hamburger Arbeiter im 19. Jahrhundert.* Hamburg: Junius, 1990.

Zeldin, T. *France 1848–1945, vol. 2: Intellect, Taste and Anxiety.* Oxford: Clarendon, 1977.

Zeller, B. (ed.) *Hätte Ich Das Kino.* Stuttgart: Sonderausstellungen des Schiller-Nationalmuseums, 1976.

Index

Aachen 37, 41, 42, 43, 49, 57
Absenteeism 39–41, 42, 56
Accidents 70, 71
Alcohol 6, 63–91
   alcohol abuse 41, 70–2, 78–80, 82–3, 158
   alcohol consumption 66, 69, 73–6
   alcohol-free beverages 71, 73–5
   Association for the Prevention of Alcohol
      Abuse 70, 74, 76, 142
   German Social Democratic Abstinent
      Workers' League 75, 82
Allotments 86, 123–4, 131, 134, 155
Alltagsgeschichte 4
Animals
   animal breeding associations 96, 122–3,
      129, 131, 134
   animal sports 65, 95–6, 178
   badger-baiting 95
   bear-baiting 95
   bull-baiting 95
   dog-fighting 95
   Society for the Prevention of Cruelty to
      Animals 122
Animierkneipen 65, 106
Anti-Socialist Law 19–20, 21, 53, 118–19,
   143, 145
Artisans' Chamber (Handwerkskammer) 19,
   45–7
Association for Social Policy 9, 140, 157
Associations 6, 81, 114–38, 160
   bourgeois 115–18
   confessional 124–7, 133
   membership 130–1
   Polish 127–8
   socialist 116–20, 133–4
   workers' 118–19, 121–4, 133–5

Barmen 39, 43, 149
Beer 64–5, 69, 72, 73, 83
   bottled beer 68, 70, 76
Bildungsbürgertum 94, 96–7, 140, 142, 160
Bismarck, Otto von 7, 52, 142, 193
Blacklegs (Arbeitswilliger) 41
Blauen Montag (Saint Monday) 40, 71

Bochum
   bourgeoisie 50
   Catholics 16–17
   housing 25–6
   industrialists 18
   industrialization 14
   migration 15–16
   Mittelstand 18–19, 50
   Poles 17
   population 14, 16, 170
   Protestants 16–17
   working class 18–19
Bochumer Verein 14, 16, 18, 25, 28, 69, 70,
   141
Böhmert, Viktor 143–4
Bourgeoisie 6, 18–19, 21, 52, 99, 106, 110,
   115–16, 117, 140, 157–8, 169, 190
Boxing (see pugilism)
Brunnenfeiern 34
Bücher, Karl 141, 143

Calendar 34–5
Carnival 19, 48–50, 190
Catholics 13, 16–17, 39, 52, 193
   catholic clergy 37, 38
   Centre Party 14, 19, 126, 133
Censorship 150, 174, 176–7
Central Association for Social Reform 143
Central Association for the Welfare of the
   Working Class (ZWAK) 143–4
Chamber of Commerce (Handelskammer) 18,
   40–1, 42, 44–6
Children 29, 51, 63, 76, 77, 98, 156–7, 158,
   174, 185
Christian Social Workers' Association 118,
   124–5, 126, 142
Christian trade-unions 39. 107, 142
Christmas 34
Church consecration 34, 35, 36
Cinema 6–7, 86, 169–70, 172–7, 182
   Association of German Cinema Owners
      174
   Universum Film Aktiengesellschaft (UFA)
      174

Circus 6, 29, 92, 97–9
Cologne 15, 40, 41, 49, 107
Colonies (workers') 25–7, 141, 155
Colporteur novels 146–7
Comedy 97, 183
Commercial entertainment 6, 30, 36, 42, 58, 92–113, 163, 181
Communists (KPD) 85, 182, 184, 194
Construction industry 15, 17, 70, 72, 75
Consumerism 184–5
Courtship 35, 105, 106, 175
Credit 78
Crew, David 18–19
Crime 5, 47, 76, 147, 175
Culture
　bourgeois 181, 183, 195
　labour movement culture
　　(*Arbeiterbewegungskultur*) 4–5, 8, 116–17, 120–1, 133–4, 192, 193, 195
　mass culture 177–85
　popular culture 93, 104, 173, 189–90, 193, 194
　workers' culture (*Arbeiterkultur*) 3, 4, 5, 8, 21, 30, 37, 38, 66, 84, 86, 100, 103, 109, 120, 133, 177, 183–4, 192, 194–5
Culture of poverty 5, 192
Cycling 101, 119, 172

Dancing 6, 36, 80, 103–8, 130, 190
Day trips 169–70
Diet 40, 77–8, 83, 107, 122–3
Dockworkers 5, 78
Domestic service 16
Domestic violence 79–80
Dortmund 53, 73, 101, 103, 125, 149
Drinking 5, 63–4, 68, 75
Drunkenness *see* Alcohol abuse
Duisburg 71, 78
Düsseldorf
　Catholics 16
　city council 44–7
　employment 17–18
　industrialisation 14–15
　industrialists 18, 41, 45
　migration 15–16
　Mittelstand 18–19, 47
　population 14-15, 170
　Protestants 16
　working class 17, 19, 47, 107

Easter 34, 36, 172
Education 4, 5, 125, 142, 144, 149, 181, 184, 192
Eight-hour day 22, 30, 54, 152, 170, 191
Elberfeld 15, 75, 101, 129, 149, 152
Embourgeoisement 120
Entertainment tax 101, 174

Essen 15, 43, 71, 72, 76, 83, 101, 125, 150, 173, 176

Factory system 13, 57
Family 7, 25–7, 63, 76–81, 130–2, 184
Fashion 170, 180, 185
Festivals (Fairs) 5–6, 30, 34–62
　harvest 34
　parish (*Kirmes*) 35–48, 53, 55, 56, 57–8
　shooting 53
　socialist 48, 53–6
　trade union 55–6
Fiction 150, 153
Films 173–4, 176, 179, 183, 184
Football 30, 158, 162, 170–2, 179–80, 184, 185, 191, 194
Funfairs 169–70

Gambling 35, 66, 139
Germanization 128, 181
Glassworks 15, 119, 141
Göhre, Paul 24–5, 105, 152
Good literature 147, 149–50, 153
Gramaphone 171
Grüttner, Michael 5
Guilds 35, 64
Gymnastics 117–18, 119, 130, 160

Hamborn 40, 47
Herne 36
Hickey, Stephen 21, 132–3, 134
Holidays 4, 22–3, 39
Household expenditure 29, 77
Housewives 77–8
Housing 16, 25–6, 79, 131, 141, 154, 181, 184

Illegitimacy 5
Industrialists 18, 45
Itinerant entertainment 36, 45, 66, 93–4

Jazz 181, 183

Kautsky, Karl 81–2
Kirmes (*see* parish fair)
Knappschaftsvereine 114, 118
Kocka, Jürgen 3, 4
Kostgänger (*see* lodgers)
Krefeld 15, 150
Krupp 24, 47, 55, 70, 141, 151
Kulturkampf 39, 193

Labour movement (*see* Social Democratic Party)
Lange, Mayor 26, 154–5
Langewiesche, Dieter 5, 23, 134
Leisure
　and family 7, 27, 131–2

and work 7, 22, 27, 40, 64, 80, 109, 123, 162
  commercial 135, 180–1, 194
  expenditure on 13, 27–30, 64, 69, 73, 77, 102, 104, 146, 152
  leisure industry 30, 108, 170, 194
  leisure time 13, 22, 25, 109, 131, 143, 170, 189
  pre-industrial 13, 57
Lent 34,48
Levenstein, Adolf 63, 75, 79–80
Lex Heinze 100, 106, 148
Libraries 29, 125, 145–53
  public 145, 148–50, 191
  socialist 150–1, 153, 183
Licensing
  public houses 67–9, 72–3
  street entertainment 93
Linden 38
Literacy 146, 148
Lodgers (*Kostgänger*) 16, 25–6
Lumpenproletariat 5, 21, 82

Maifest 19, 50–1
Märzfeier 48, 54
Mass entertainment 37, 169–72, 177
Mass media 170, 185, 194
Masurians 13, 127
May Day 48, 54–6, 57, 84
Menageries 36, 96–7
Metal industry 17, 42
  metal workers 17, 20, 28, 80, 152
Migration 15–16, 25, 39, 57, 193
Mineral water 70–1, 73, 74
Mining 17, 20, 22, 23, 24, 28, 71, 122–3, 190
Mittelstand 18–19, 46, 48–50, 151
Mönchengladbach 15, 104, 125, 155
Mülheim/Ruhr 76, 149, 175
Municipal councils 18, 21, 45–6, 141–2, 144, 155–6, 163, 169
Music hall 6, 100, 109–10, 191

Nationalism
  German 51–2, 147, 178, 180, 185
  Polish 127–8, 130
National Liberals 14, 19, 45, 125–6
National Socialists 85, 184, 185
Newspapers 65
Nolan, Mary 17, 21, 118
North-Rhine Westphalia 13

Olympic games 180
Organ grinders 93
Overtime 23, 24

Pamphlet fiction (*see* popular fiction)
Parks 154–60, 169, 191
Paternalism 129, 141, 161

Patron saints 34, 36
Pay day 71–2
Pigeon fancying 123, 129, 190
Pilgrimages 34, 37
Poles 13, 17, 127–8, 193
  Polish catholicism 128
  Polish Party 127
Police 9, 21, 46, 47, 71, 73, 74, 93, 103–4, 191
Polkakneipen 92, 99
Popular culture 93, 104, 173, 189–90, 193, 194
Popular fiction 146–8, 153, 172–3
Pornography 100–1, 147–8
Poverty 76, 79, 143
Promenades 154, 156
Prostitution 5, 36, 47, 65, 100, 105–6, 158–9
Protestants 13, 16–17
  clergy 39, 142
  Protestant Workers' Association 51, 118, 125–6
Public entertainment evenings 144–5
Public houses 22, 65–9, 70, 80, 81–2, 86, 129, 131–2, 143, 155, 173, 184
Public space 93–4, 154, 157–8
Publicans 21, 36, 43, 44–5, 66, 78, 82–3, 94, 105, 108, 129, 143, 178
Pugilism 95, 98, 172, 179, 181

Radio 170, 180, 183, 194
Rational recreation 139–68, 144, 155, 161, 169–70
Reading 9, 118, 146–8
Remscheid 40, 41
Ritter, Gerhard 4

Sabbath (*see* Sunday)
Saving 29, 40, 76, 140, 192
Schnapps 22, 64–5, 69, 71, 72, 73, 82, 83, 139, 158
  schnapps boycott 83–4
  schnapskasinos 72–3, 192
Secularization 37, 39, 125–6, 181
Sedan Day 48, 51–2, 57, 130, 178
Sexuality 35, 106, 108
Shooting associations (*Schützenvereine*) 46, 50–1
  shooting festivals 53
Shopkeepers 43, 45
Singing clubs 118–19, 127
Social control 7–8, 48, 126, 161–3, 170, 181
Social Democratic Party (SPD)
  and cinema 182–3
  and culture 53–4, 181–2, 184, 191–2
  and drink 81–5
  and women 84
  associations 4–5, 8, 114, 116–17, 119–21, 133–4

Bochum 19–20, 53
Düsseldorf 20–1
leadership 8, 83
membership 21, 81
Social harmony 140–3, 155, 161, 183
Social reform 86, 140, 143, 155, 161
Society for Social Reform 140
Society for the Spread of Public Education
142, 149
Sokolvereine 127
Solingen 15, 149, 176
Sport 86, 160, 169–70, 180, 183
Street entertainment 6, 30, 93–4
Strikes 24, 42

Tango 105, 139
Tavern (*see* public house)
Temperance 64, 74–5, 82, 84, 143, 160–1,
190
Textile workers 16, 41, 70, 80
Theatre 99, 101, 102
Tingel-Tangel 66, 92, 94, 99–101
Trade unions 122, 151
in Bochum 20
in Düsseldorf 21, 119
trade-union festivals 55–6
Transport 38, 170, 171–2, 179

Unemployment 40, 152, 194

Verbrecherkeller 65
Vereinsmeierei 114, 116
Voluntary association (*see* associations)

Wages 24, 27–8, 78, 170
Walking 9, 30, 157
Waltz 105
War veterans 51, 119
Weber, Adolf 141, 143
Weimar Republic 9, 85, 177, 181, 193
Whitsun 34, 38, 172
Wilhelm II 7, 24, 46
Winding-time 22
Women 9, 16, 28, 29, 41–2, 78–81, 84, 108,
125, 126, 132, 152, 174, 185
Woodworking 15, 152
Work
and leisure 7, 190
hours 22–4
workplace drinking 69–76
Working class
class consciousness 8, 54, 73, 82, 126,
192–3
respectable 5, 56, 162
rough 56, 162
skilled 5, 21, 28, 120, 151, 160–1, 162,
190–1
unskilled 28, 79, 82, 120, 151
World turned upside down 49
World War One 46, 106–8, 124, 163, 171,
176

Young people 27, 29, 104, 106, 109, 125,
173–6, 180, 185
Youth associations 180

Zoos 96–7, 169